HARPER'S ANTHOLOGY
OF 20TH CENTURY
NATIVE AMERICAN POETRY

HARPER'S
ANTHOLOGY
OF
20ᵀᴴ CENTURY
NATIVE
AMERICAN
POETRY

EDITED BY
DUANE NIATUM

1817

Harper & Row, Publishers, San Francisco
Cambridge, Hagerstown, New York, Philadelphia, Washington
London, Mexico City, São Paulo, Singapore, Sydney

Acknowledgments appear on pp. 375–377.

FIRST EDITION

Designed by Melanie Haage

Library of Congress Cataloging-in-Publication Data

Harper's anthology of 20th century Native American
    poetry.

    Bibliography: p.
    Includes indexes.
    1. American poetry—Indian authors.   2. American poetry—20th
Century.   3. Indians of North America—Poetry. I. Niatum, Duane,
1938–   . II. Title: Anthology of 20th century Native American
poetry.   III. Title: Harper's anthology of twentieth century Native
American poetry.
PS591.I55H37   1987   811'.5'080897   86-45023
ISBN 0-06-250666-8 (pbk.)
ISBN 0-06-250665-A (hardcover)

88 89 90 91 92 RRD 10 9 8 7 6 5 4 3 2 1

CONTENTS

"Human rebirth has no end."

Pablo Neruda

PREFACE

In 1975, *Carriers of the Dream Wheel* was published by
Harper & Row. In that anthology, I brought together the
work of sixteen Native American poets in an effort to offer
readers the poetry of a new generation and the spirit of an
age-old people. That work made clear that, even without a
uniformity of subject matter, metaphor, or style, Native
American poets carry with them the spirit of a common
cultural heritage, expressed in divergent and often stunning
ways, in their individual poetry. That spirit has not died.
On the contrary, it has grown and is growing.

In *Harper's Anthology of 20th Century Native American
Poetry,* the mature fruit of that earlier effort, I have brought
together the work of thirty-six poets who attest to the
health of both the Native American spirit and American lit-
erature. Within these pages you will find poems by several
of the most widely read and respected Native American
writers as well as a generous selection of poems by new and
young writers who are pushing American art and literature
in new directions. Together these poets constitute a power-
ful force in the American literary tradition—one far older,
given the oral tradition, than the present republic yet in
full-voiced, radiant bloom.

We simplify when we call the present volume the work
of modern Native American poets. According to Vine Delo-
ria Jr.'s count, there still remain three hundred and fifteen
tribes in the U.S. alone.[1] And more than thirty tribes are
represented by the poets here. They are Native Americans,
but these poets are also Miwok, Hopi, Cheyenne, Blackfeet,
Laguna Pueblo, Creek, Mohawk, Sioux, Athabaskan,
Yakima, Kiowa, Navajo, Tlingit and more. As Kenneth Lin-
coln explains in his essay in *Smoothing the Ground,* "each
tribe, whether an Alaskan Tlingit fishing village of forty

extended kin or the Navajo nation of one hundred and forty
thousand in Arizona, Utah, and New Mexico, can be tradi-
tionally defined through a native language, an inherited
place, and a set of traditions—a daily speech, a teaching
folklore, ceremony and religion, a heritage passed on genera-
tion to generation in songs, legends, jokes, morality plays,
healing rituals, event-histories, social-protocol, spiritual
rites of passage and vision journeys to the sacred world.
These cultural traditions evolved before the Old World dis-
covered the New World, and many have adapted to changing
circumstances and remain strong today."[2]

These cultural traditions do remain strong today. They
are deeply ingrained despite the fact that over half of the
Native American population lives off of the reservation. Na-
tive Americans have returned to the places of their ancestors
which have been given new names like New York, Los Ange-
les, Kansas, Chicago, and Seattle. Tribal peoples are distinct,
and to a large extent dispersed, but they have common con-
cerns: kinship, Nature, art as a part of tribal religion, and
cultural survival and rebirth. These concerns have been
shaped and reshaped in the culture for thousands of years.
Native Americans today have a further common tie: they are
witnesses to an act of dispossession forced on them as na-
tive "Indians." For the majority of poets here, the various
uniting Native concerns—the traditions, the myths and sto-
ries, the mutual sense of historical displacement—work to
create a growing together, a common space, in the face of
strong personal differences of viewpoint.

Written narrative, the common mode of expression in
poetry today, owes its existence to the stories and songs
from the oral tradition, on which Native American poets
base their explorations of both ancient and modern themes.
None of them may be more important than a sense of place,
of land and geography. Jarold Ramsey points out in *Reading
the Fire* that this reverence is not "like the vaguely guilty
and nostalgic sense of place and feeling for landscape that
we inherit from Romanticism; it is altogether sterner, more
pragmatic as to ecological necessities, and more caught up

in the narrative."[3] On this sterner ground Native Americans have stood for centuries. Every tribe or clan has at least one storyteller who chants the stories of the people for everyone in the community to hear. As Octavio Paz has said in *In Praise of Hands,* poets will often speak of "a mutually shared physical life that is firmly planted, not fallen from on high. So instead, it springs up from below."[4] It is precisely this sense of coming from the land and not to it that gives the Native American voice its clarity and range. It is this living heritage of place and tradition which provides Native American writers with vision and focus, thus giving them power to encounter and grapple with both contemporary issues—such as the legacy of the Vietnam War, the threat of nuclear annihilation, and the imbroglio of politics—and age-old questions of meaning and existence—the mystery of life and death, the tension between peace and war, the essence of art and creation, and the miraculous resiliency of the human spirit.

Because of the restrictions on space, there had to be the inevitable exclusions. I regret that I have not been able to include many other qualified poets. I also greatly regret my decision to limit the work to Native Americans north of the border with Mexico. But to have included writers from a broader geographical area would have created a different book. It is important to situate this anthology in the context of the contemporary North American literary scene. These poets are part of the American culture-at-large, and should be heard and celebrated by that larger culture. Finally, it is a long-held hope of mine that this anthology will help critics and scholars approach Native American literature, whether ancient song or legend or very modern poem, story, or novel, with the same rigor and recognition accorded to non-Native American work.

There are a few writers and scholars I would like to thank for offering to help in the selection of poets and in other matters relating to the book's production. All the members of the editorial board deserve special acknowledgment for excellent comments and suggestions. They are Gretchen Bataille, Joseph Bruchac III, Kenneth Lincoln, and Brian Swann. In regard to Canadian poets, I want to thank Marilyn Bowering, Tom King, and Bruce Meyer for very helpful suggestions. Wendy Rose and Maurice Kenny also made noteworthy suggestions. And it seems only right to thank Robert San Souci, Alan Hillesheim, and Yvonne Keller, all of Harper & Row, who on more than one occasion, remained patient and understanding under the most trying of circumstances during the book's long production.

Duane Niatum
Ann Arbor, Michigan
1987

INTRODUCTION:
ONLY THE BEGINNING

Discovering America

In four World's Fairs held between the Civil War and
World War I, writes Frederick E. Hoxie, white attitudes to-
ward Native Americans moved from the social evolutionists'
optimism in Philadelphia in 1876, with their belief in the
Indians' "progress" and future, to the opinion in San Fran-
cisco in 1915 that Indians were "an interesting but limited
people whose future was of only marginal concern to their
fellow Americans."[1] Indians didn't figure largely in the 1915
Panama-Pacific International Exposition in San Francisco,
but the most prominent presentation of native life was the
bronze statue by James Earle Fraser, "The End of the Trail":
an exhausted Indian slumped in the saddle of a broken-
down pony. This statue won a gold medal, and was one of
the Exposition's most popular attractions. Today, if the Indi-
ans are thought about at all, the general assumption is that
they have long since fallen from their ponies and vanished.
Today, despite something of a resurrection of interest in the
Indians in the 1960s and early 1970s, they are still likely to
be seen by most people as victims of inevitable progress,
their tribal names used to sell cars and trucks, the heads of
their heroes (such as Crazy Horse, who was murdered by
whites) used to decorate postage stamps.[2]

   D. H. Lawrence wrote that "the real American day"
would only dawn when Americans "at last discover America
and their wholeness."[3] But America still refuses to look at

---

Poems cited in the introduction without reference nota-
tions may be found in this anthology.

itself and its history. We still refuse to acknowledge the truth of William Carlos Williams' statement: "History! History! We fools, what do we know or care? History begins for us with murder and enslavement, not with discovery."[4] And today we remain ignorant of the plight of Indians living in cities (more than half of the Native American population) and of life on the reservations that, according to a recent article in the *New York Times* (December 11, 1986), are in terrible shape, with conditions "bad and worsening with no immediate help in sight." As Suzan Harjo, executive director of The National Congress of American Indians, says in the *Times* article: "The situation in Indian country is a national disgrace."[5]

Despite everything, however, the Indian has not disappeared. In fact, more and more Native Americans are now writing about their lives and experiences in fiction, nonfiction, poetry, drama, and autobiography than ever before. There is, indeed, a Native American renaissance in the arts, which we non-Indians ignore to our impoverishment, and even to our peril. If at this late date we still believe in "the real American day," then the writings of Native Americans are a good place to begin to "discover America."

Native American Literature: A Brief Survey

There are approximately two million Native American people in the United States, some one-half of one percent of the total population. In that figure are some of the most interesting poets and writers in the English language— poets and writers present in such numbers, given the tiny percentage, that one can only wonder at their determination, energy, and skill and the power of the tradition and culture that has nurtured them.

In fact, Indians have been writing in English for over two centuries. The earliest autobiographies were produced by Christianized Indians, the first in 1768 by the Reverend Samson Occum, a Mohegan (who also wrote *Choice Collections of Hymns and Spiritual Songs* in 1774), and the second by the Pequot William Apes whose *Son of the Forest* appeared in 1829. Then came books on various subjects by David Cusick (Tuscarora), the Sioux Ohiyesa (Dr. Charles Eastman), Luther Standing Bear (also Sioux), and John Joseph Mathews (Osage). The first fiction (a fictionalized conversion story) was written by the Cherokee Elias Boudinot in 1823, while the first "true" novel, entitled *The Life and Adventures of Joaquín Murieta,* was produced in 1854 by John Rollin Ridge, another Cherokee. The earliest known book of poems by an Indian is *The Ojibway Conquest* (1850) by the Ojibway George Copway (Kah-ge-ga-gah-bowh). Ridge's *Poems,* the second poetry book, appeared in 1868. Other nineteenth and twentieth century poets include the Creek Alex Posey (1873–1908), whose *Collected Poems* was posthumously published in 1910; the Mohawk E. Pauline Johnson (1862–1913), whose *Flint and Feather* came out posthumously in 1917; and the Wyandot Bertrand Walker.[6]

There are many others. Wendy Rose is preparing a multi-genre bibliography of book-length works by Native American and Eskimo authors. She has discovered nearly three hundred books from the 1950s to the present. Still, they are hardly household titles or household names, and they are seldom, if ever, found in standard histories of American literature. In fact, until about the last twenty years, what interest there was in Native American literature (though it wasn't called literature) was concentrated in the fields of anthropology, linguistics, and folklore and on certain poets and writers. These include Mary Austin, Hart Crane, William Carlos Williams, Charles Olsen, Frank Waters, and more recently Jerome Rothenberg and Gary Snyder—the full story is told in Michael Castro's *Interpreting the Indian: Twentieth Century Poets and the Native American* (1984).

The earliest collection of aboriginal poetry appeared in 1918 with George W. Cronyn's *The Path on the Rainbow: An*

Anthology of Songs and Chants. There followed Mary Austin's *The American Rhythm: Studies and Re-expressions of Amerindian Songs* (1932), Margot Astrov's *The Winged Serpent: An Anthology of American Indian Prose and Poetry* (1946), and A. Grove Day's *The Sky Clears: Poetry of the American Indians* (1951).[7] Native Americans were writing poetry, drama, and fiction during the years from 1918 to 1951, notably the Flathead D'Arcy McNickle and the Cherokee Lynn Riggs (one of whose plays was made into the musical "Oklahoma!").

But prior to the 1960s there was little interest in Native American poetry and prose, and it was difficult to find, since it was published mostly in small magazines with small circulations.[8] Then came John Milton's two collections of contemporary Native American poetry, prose, and art in *South Dakota Review* (vol. 7, no. 2, Summer 1969, and vol. 9, no. 2, Summer 1971). In the Summer 1969 issue, for the first time in one place, appeared the poetry of Simon Ortiz and James Welch; the Summer 1971 issue carried the poetry of Duane Niatum, Ray Young Bear, and others. All this took place about the time that N. Scott Momaday won the Pulitzer Prize in 1969 for *House Made of Dawn,* which went far in establishing the worth of Native American literature in the eyes of a mainstream literary audience.

In 1975 *Carriers of the Dream Wheel,* the predecessor of this anthology, made a distinguished appearance as "the first substantial collection of contemporary Native American poetry."[9] It was poetry of mingled roots, drawing on Faulkner, Winters, Vallejo, Hugo, Wright, Roethke, Neruda, and other sources available to late twentieth-century writers, as well as on the native oral tradition and individual vision. Since then, Native American literature has become one of the most lively developments on the American art scene. But it still fights for recognition and acceptance in the curricula of our schools and colleges, and it is still something of a secret.[10] Few large publishing houses have shown serious interest in the phenomenon, preferring to give the world *The Teachings of Don Juan, Rolling Thunder,* or *Hanta Yo.* So

Native American poets must still rely on the small presses and magazines as well as some university presses—Illinois, Purdue, Washington, and Massachusetts have recently published volumes by Native American poets. Moreover, in a consistent pattern of omission, contemporary poetry anthologies generally ignore Native American poets. *The Harvard Book of Contemporary American Poets* edited by Helen Vendler (1985), William Heyen's *The Generation of 2000* (1984), *New American Poets of the 80s* edited by John Meyers and Roger Weingarten (1984), and *The Norton Anthology of American Literature* edited by Nina Baym et al. (1985), contain not one Native American poet. Three anthologies contain one Native American poet each. They are Daniel Halpern's *The American Poetry Anthology* (1975) which contains five poems by James Welch, *The Norton Anthology of Poetry* (1983) edited by Alexander W. Allison et al., which contains three poems by Leslie Silko, and *The Morrow Anthology of Younger American Poets* (1985) edited by Dave Smith and David Bottoms, which has four poems by Simon Ortiz. So, while some poets say they don't like the idea of segregated anthologies, they still seem necessary until those who edit major anthologies and publish books of poems abandon their tokenism and parochialism.

What Distinguishes Native American Poetry?

Vine Deloria, Jr., has written that modern Indian poetry can "tell you more about the Indian's travels in historical experience than all the books written and lectures given."[11] Although a poem is an individual response to experience, Deloria's remark is illuminating. More than most poetry being written today, Native American poetry is the poetry of historic witness. It grows out of a past that is very much a present. Anglo-America, in the main, does not believe in history. Things simply turned out the way they did through a natural process, one of whose names is Manifest Destiny. History can be taken for granted, in the way of the conqueror, because things worked out the way they were supposed to. But the Native American poet *is* his or her history, with all its ambiguities and complications. Their history is not something external to be learned, molded, or ignored, though it may be something that has to be acknowledged and recovered. It is embodied and unavoidable because the weight and consequences of that history make up the continuum of the present. This fact gives an urgency to the utterance, a resonance to the art that carries it deeper than much of the poetry one finds today. The poets are still "singing for power."

So what distinguishes Native American poetry? Isn't it simply a sub-branch of Western regional literature, as the chief editor of a reputable publishing house once suggested to me? Or is it just poetry with a variety of themes and techniques that happens to be written by Native Americans? Some of the poets themselves are uneasy with the term. "There is no *genre* of 'Indian literature,' " writes Wendy Rose, "because we are all different. There is only literature written by people who are Indian and who, therefore, infuse their work with their own lives the same way that you do."[12] Duane Niatum, too, asks if there is an "Indian Aesthetic that is different from a non-Indian."[13] He answers that there is not. "Anyone who claims there is encourages a conventional response from both Indians and non-Indians, and as a result actually inhibits the reader's imagination."[14] Jim Barnes doesn't like terms such as "regional writer," "ethnic writer," or "Native American writer" because all are reductive. "The writer is first a writer, second a Native American, a Black, a Chicano."[15]

Of course these poets are right. Too often a classification can reduce attention to what is special; it can be used to pigeonhole and thereby deny full regard. But if we use a term such as "Native American poetry" appropriately, if we use it knowing that such a grouping is only a start, a convenience, an aid to understanding that leads to reinforcement and intensification of attention, then it is useful. It helps us to hold on to something new and distinct. The poets vary widely from each other in many ways, but they are also similar in many ways. One thing is certain: these poets can hold their own on the American literary scene today. They are an integral part of it.

The well-known Luiseño painter Fritz Scholder expands this question of classification to the visual arts. He too objects to arranging artists by race or sex. "Painting, like most of the visual arts, is an individual activity that is completely personal, and can only be developed through one's own unique frame of reference. If one is to make a statement in whatever medium, one must find out who one is and fully accept it."[16] There is a point to be made here, even if we ignore Yeats's dictum that it is out of the *quarrel* with ourselves that we make poetry. It is true that an artist or poet today must achieve an individual voice or vision. But to talk about an individual artistic activity that is "completely personal," capable of being developed through "one's own unique frame of reference" sounds more typically Anglo-American than Native American. The Native American poet seems to work from a sense of social responsibility to the group as much as from an intense individuality. In fact, a poet wrote to me recently, "I have heard Indian critics say, referring to poetry, that it is best if there are no I's in it. I grew up and continue to live among people who penalize you for talking about yourself and going on endlessly about your struggles."[17] And another poet wrote, "My attitude is that it is not my personal life that is important, but the work that comes through me somehow. It is something deeply ingrained and difficult to overcome."[18] The individual voice in Native American literature would seem to be at its strongest when it is not just "individual" (and it is all a matter of degree) but also "representative." Often the individual speaks for, is spoken through. We see this across the spectrum of Native American artists—from traditional singers to the contemporary poet Joy Harjo: "She learned to speak for the ground / the voice coming through her like

roots that / have long hungered for water" ("For Alva Ben-
son . . . "). Many Native American poets regard themselves
as both distinct individual voices and voices that speak for
whatever cannot speak, as in Linda Hogan's poem "Who
Will Speak," which desires to speak for the animals and the
earth.[19]

If I approach a definition of Native American poetry
obliquely and hesitantly it is not simply because of problems
such as the foregoing. If one says Native American poetry is
poetry written by Native Americans the difficulty might ap-
pear to be solved—more on that in a short while. The best
way might be to say I'm not really interested in defining
this poetry. Its full and generous presence in this volume
will *announce* what it is in its own terms, using its own
names—"we wonder / whether anyone will ever hear / our
own names for things / we do" (Gail Tremblay, "Indian Sing-
ing in 20th Century America").

I cannot define "Indian" or "Native American" with any
confidence. We whites, from our arrival on this earth on
turtle's back, have gotten it all wrong. (Even white insis-
tence on telling the Indians that they migrated over the Ber-
ing Strait is contradicted by Indian legend and tradition—
legend and tradition more culturally significant than any
archaeological proof.) The latest insult is to measure blood.
To be enrolled in a tribe, says the Bureau of Indian Affairs
(the BIA), one must possess one-quarter Indian blood.[20]
The best definition I can arrive at is this: Native Americans
are Native Americans if they say they are, if other Native
Americans say they are and accept them, and (possibly) if
the values that are held close and acted upon are values
upheld by the various native peoples who live in the Ameri-
cas. It would be presumptuous for me to define further.
Many questions such as whether a person is Native Ameri-
can if he or she has rejected tribal values and identity I
leave to others, for it does not concern us here. All the poets
in these pages come from a Native American background
and, as James Welch has said, "For the most part an Indian
knows who he is."[21] Elizabeth Cook-Lynn's words ring in

the ears: "Writing, for me . . . is an act of defiance born of the need to survive. I am me. I exist. I am a Dakotah. I write. It is the quintessential act of optimism born of frustration. It is an act of courage, I think. And, in the end, as Simon [Ortiz] says, it is an act which defies oppression."[22]

Climate of Change: Poetic Emergence

Why and how has Native American poetry achieved such distinction in so few years? One reason is that the intellectual climate changed during the 1960s. These years and their legacy brought about for many a rejection of the supremacy of Western civilization and a rejection of the Western idea of high art. The prevailing ideas of political and artistic hegemony were confronted and the established canon challenged. New beginnings were sought, and Native American writers responded. In addition, while, as we have noted, much remains to be done, channels for Native Americans have opened. Some have studied with famous authors who have encouraged and fostered their work and careers. My own interest in Native American poetry was sparked when I picked up a special supplement of *The American Poetry Review* in 1975 entitled "Young American Indian Poets: Roberta Hill, Ray A. Young Bear, Duane Niatum, James Welch." The supplement was edited by the distinguished poet Richard Hugo, who at the time was teaching at the University of Montana in the Master of Fine Arts Writing Program.

In his introduction, Hugo discusses what attracts him to Native American poetry. He finds it "both imaginative and highly individualistic."[23] He believes that the poets are mining the same seam as major twentieth-century poets such as Eliot and Yeats "who felt we inherited ruined worlds that, before they were ruined, gave man a sense of self-esteem, social unity, spiritual certainty and being at home on the earth."[24] This is due to the fact, Hugo suggests, that Indians come from "a recently destroyed civilization. No other minority group does"[25] (a qualifiable statement). For white poets, Hugo continues, no matter how true this theme of ruined worlds may be, it nevertheless results from "an idealization of a past they never knew."[26] But for the Indians this ruin is fact, a real, known fact. So, says Hugo, the Indian poet is an authentic paradigm of the modern condition. However, if individual isolation is the source of much lyric poetry today, in the Indian poet it is combined with a cultural tradition that is "still a living thing in the memory,"[27] and consists of "establishing personal identity through ritualistic discovery of kinship with objects and creatures of nature."[28] We may want to qualify such statements. The cultural tradition does not just exist in the memory. It exists in act, thought, speech; the "ritualistic discovery of kinship" sounds peculiarly mechanical and quaint. Nevertheless, Hugo renders us a service by directing us toward this new poetry and trying to help us enter its world, even though he discusses it on the whole, not in relationship to contemporary "mainstream" work, but to other "minority" poetry. In comparison with these unnamed other "minority" poets, he finds that Native American poetry "seems most to involve emotional possession of materials."[29] Since he claims that "no audience save the self is presumed,"[30] we may deduce that he sees Native American poetry in contradistinction to the poetry of social and political commitment, presumably mostly Black poetry, being written at the time. He praises Native American poetry "for creating interesting sounds with poetry,"[31] that is, for craft.

For Richard Hugo, then, Native American poetry is thoroughly modern, yet it reaches back to a cultural tradition substantially different from that available to other modern poets. Native American poetry is not overtly, militantly, or stridently political; it has depth of emotion and consciousness of form. Whatever the shortcomings of Hugo's essay (the political and "committed" element in Native American poetry is ignored, although most of it appeared after Hugo's essay), this presentation of younger Native American poets to the larger literary world via a magazine with large circulation and prestige by a well-known and respected poet represented a major advance.

Poetic Themes

What are some of the themes of Native American poetry? Reading this anthology, each of us can come up with answers. I will suggest a few. Both cultural traditions and Native American society itself are under stress. Suicide, alcoholism, unemployment abound. The situation is a national disgrace. The poets have responded to this crisis, and none more powerfully than James Welch in his novels and poems. His well-known poem "Harlem, Montana: Just Off the Reservation," with its place name linking one place of disaffection in Montana with another in New York, indicts a whole country. And yet the anger is never strident. It is dissolved in an irony that infuses all details, from the Indians drinking in the "best" taverns, to "money is free if you're poor enough." Words accrete ironic weight by juxtapositions: "runners" (smugglers of liquor onto reservations), "running for office." Indians are "planted" in the jail by the local farmer/constable. Everything is confused; there is no cultural authenticity for white or Indian. Welch's complex language keeps alive confusion as a series of possibilities; it draws us into the poem but keeps us off balance. How are we to regard the drunk who "bugs the plaster man / on the cross with snakes"? Christ is no savior. The man on the cross is plaster, and the Indian world of animal-human relationships is reduced to something like the DTs with serpents (the serpents also recall the biblical ancient enemy). "Bugs" suggests intense annoyance on the part of the plaster man. In the drunken state, are these imaginary snakes seen as spies (reading "bugs" in the context of surveillance)? What could they hope to learn? It is a world of delirium and paranoia, bits and pieces of meaning. The drunk himself has no identity, or at best a mixed-up one. He is an ex-Methodist who is now a "saint" in the Indian church. We can no longer be sure of point of view. In whose eyes is he a saint? The language shoots out in a number of directions. We catch it as we can. The paradox is that Welch writes with such energy about cultural decay. Yet there is a crazy, surreal energy about the whole town, Indian and white (and Turk) that fights against decay. It is as if the poet were saying this inchoate place still has possibilities; there is still life here. The poem ends with the young bucks inside the shot-up store yelling that they're rich. The Indians have been sucked into a world of perverted values; they identified the ruined store with wealth and have shot their way into plenty, trapping themselves. But their prayer, "Help us, oh God, we're rich," is not just easy, if sharp, irony. They still have the power of prayer, even if only in the form of an exclamation or idiom. The poem certainly does not exactly end on an up beat, but it is not altogether bleak nihilism.[32]

We can see a slightly stronger expression of faith in the tradition in the poetry of Louise Erdrich. The problem for the uprooted drunk Raymond Twobears (in "Family Reunion") is to get home again. The key image is the turtle—a real snapper and not just some useful symbolic entity. And yet the turtle is also cultural *nuomenon,* for this is, after all, the earth on turtle's back ("the old house caulked with mud / sails into the middle of Metagoshe"), and Ray's smell is the "rank beef of fierce turtle pulled dripping from Metagoshe." Ray is a lost soul, unaware of cultural values. He blows off the turtle's head with a cherry bomb, an act of cruel and practical indifference. But the animal is not that easily destroyed. After Ray had gone "to sleep his own head off," the next day, "headless and clenched in his armor," the turtle drags himself off. Even though Ray doesn't know it, he and the turtle are still connected, despite the wasteland in the poem. The headless turtle climbs a hill and aims for "a small stream that deepens into a marsh." It has been hauled from the lake, had its head blown off, and now, in a kind of rebirth, finds a stream that will presumably widen into a lake. The cyclic pattern is still there. Turtle is not destroyed. "Somehow we find our way back." The line reverberates. But to what? The submerged image of the turtle gives strength. Ray's body pulls him toward home; his hands become "gray fins," and his face has "the calm patience of a child who has always / let bad wounds alone." Ray is clearly in bad shape and, with his weak heart, may be dying. His bad wounds should have been cared for. Yet in the strange world of the poem, realistic yet subliminal, Ray somehow is the turtle. The turtle seems to return to another, deeper existence, as if to grow another head, and Ray has the look of a creature "that has lived / for a long time underwater." The poem weaves opposites together, and ends very oddly with "angels," creatures from another range of reference altogether, "lowering their slings and litters" as if they were divine Red Cross workers or refugees from "Swing Low, Sweet Chariot." Does Ray, a being between two worlds (as his name "Twobears" suggests), take refuge in some form of Christianity? The last stanza reads like a hallucination. The poem does not present a conclusion; it simply presents a situation. But the most powerful entity in the poem is the turtle.

Time and time again in Native American poetry we find a picture of raw existence side by side with a refusal to cave in, often with hints of renewal through connection with tradition. In Erdrich's "I Was Sleeping Where the Black Oaks Move," the relentless water that has been dammed (cause of much lost Indian land), uproots the trees with their nests of herons. ("Nests" is a loaded cultural word. We recall Black Elk: "Our tepees were round like the nests of birds, and they were always set in a circle, the nation's hoop, a nest of many nests, where the Great Spirit meant for us to hatch our children."[33]) The forest is pulled through the spillway, and trees surface singly. The scene is fully presented realistically, yet the tenor is almost allegorical. The nation's hoop is broken; we are "below the reservation," after "the long removal." ("Removal" is as loaded a word for Indians as "holocaust" is for Jews.) Grandpa explains: herons are ghosts of people unable to rest. But there is a way back, symbolized by the dream, with its full Native American implication of a creative source:

> Sometimes now, we dream our way back to the heron
>   dance.
> Their long wings are bending the air
> into circles through which they fall.
> They rise again in shifting wheels.
> How long must we live in the broken figures
> their necks make, narrowing the sky?

The fall is really part of the full wing-beat and they rise again. The process is cyclical, circular. The poem ends, not with a question but a statement, almost an exclamation. This part of the circle has to be endured; it is as if it is necessary to live in the broken figures for a time, in the narrowing. As Yeats said, only that which has been broken can be whole.

Voices of the Past: The Oral Tradition

The oral tradition of speech is vital to Native American poets. In the anthology and elsewhere, poets write of how they were *told* what to do and how to be—told stories and legends. Time and again in the anthology one feels the presence of living *voices,* the commitment to orality in the non-oral medium of print, a form "locked in space, inanimate."[34] To be sure, Native American poets are aware of the emphasis in the poetry of the 50s and 60s on "breath"—one recalls the Black Mountain School, and in particular Charles Olson's important essay "Projective Verse" (1960), as well as the Beat poets, Allen Ginsberg especially. But the human voice in these pages—insistent, animating, animated—I

like to think of as the direct descendant, or literary equiva-
lent, of the language of song and chant used to communi-
cate with (and largely derived from) the world of the spirit,
the language of the fullest life of being itself. In the oral
tradition this language *is* life. As David Guss notes of the
Yekuana, a people from the northern Amazon, "words are
not simply uttered or sung but infused with the actual spirit
of the chanter."[35] Native American poets attempt in their
insistent utterances to lessen the distance created by print,
to transform the "passive word of the written page" into an
"active immediacy."[36] The talking, the singing, the telling,
the writing pass on the voice to an anonymous audience and
attempt to make a community. The poems do not withdraw
into style, but project into life.

We should, then, listen to these poems as well as read
them. For, as N. Scott Momaday's Rev. J. B. B. Tosamah in
House Made of Dawn asserts, when you hold onto things
heard you come directly into the presence of mind and
spirit. The white man, he says, has taken words and litera-
ture for granted. He has "diluted and multiplied the word"
and is therefore "sated and insensitive."[37] This is not just
another book of poems. We must use the printed word, and
go beyond it, go back to its sources.[38]

Reverencing Tradition: Ancestors and Myth

Parents play a major part in Native American poetry, in
the passing on of tradition; Momaday has noted in *House
Made of Dawn,* the oral tradition is always but one genera-
tion from extinction.[39] None of the poets surpasses Simon
Ortiz in parent-reverence. We see his father in the poem "A
Story of How a Wall Stands," a poem about the oral tradi-
tion itself, and in his essay "Song, Poetry, and Language—
Expression and Perception," where he gives a full and loving
portrait of his father, the "thousand year old man," keeper of

ancient traditions.[40] Paula Gunn Allen has described how her mother constantly told her stories, "and in these stories she told me who I was, who I was supposed to be, whom I came from, and who would follow me."[41]

Grandparents play a large part, perhaps because they are felt to be closer to sources. Simon Ortiz was told by his grandfather, medicine man and elder of the kiva, "how we must sacredly concern ourselves with the people and the holy earth."[42] He remembers how his words "were about how we must regard ourselves and others with compassion and love."[43] This belief permeates Ortiz's work. "My grandfather represented for me a link to the past that is important for me to hold in my memory because it is not only memory but knowledge that substantiates my present existence,"[44] Ortiz writes. "He and the grandmothers and grandfathers before him thought about us as they lived, confirmed in their belief of a continuing life, and they brought our present beings into existence by the beliefs they held. The consciousness of that belief is what informs my present concerns with language, poetry and fiction."[45] Such a statement holds true for many Native American writers. Meaningful and continuous contact with the past is a source of great strength in the present and for the future; it "release[s] the energy of the impulse to help my people,"[46] as Ortiz phrases it. Such contact, he continues, constitutes the strength of "the oral tradition of speech, social and religious ritual, elders' counsel and advice, countless and endless stories, everyday event."[47]

Likewise the editor of this volume has written of the spiritual connection he has maintained with the Klallam land, and the promise he made with his grandfather never to lose touch with his Coast Salish traditions, "never to abandon our cedar roots, never to forget any creature that shares this world, and never to allow or participate in a rape of the earth or the sea."[48] Elizabeth Cook-Lynn, in her poem "Grandfather at the Indian Health Clinic," depicts the old man as having great nobility; he is "averse to / an unceremonious world." In her "Journey," grandmothers are "old partisans of faith" and pass on their wisdom to their daughters. The old ones "go bail" for the present generation. Because of cultural genocide, all the survivors are ironically "sacristans." Yet the faith of the grandparents lives on in ceremonies and prevents total alienation or acculturation, despite the fact that "migration makes / new citizens of Rome."

Time and time again in Native American poetry one senses that grandparents are keepers of the faith, inspirational, powerful beings, symbols of rooted continuity, as in Mary TallMountain's "Matmiya," Gail Tremblay's "To Grandmother on Her Going," and "Night Gives Old Woman the Word" (where she is the Earth itself). They are there again in Robert E. Davis's "At the Door of the Native Studies Director," Wendy Rose's "Loo-wit" (where the old woman is a mountain), in Earle Thompson's "Mythology" (Thompson has said in his earlier biographical note for this volume that "obviously my roots lie in the oral tradition which I learned from listening to my grandfather telling legends"), in Lance Henson's "Grandfather" and "near twelve mile point," in Barney Bush's "The Memory Sire," and so on. This reverence, this presence, stands in stark contrast to non-Indian society with its headlong rush to jettison the past and its largely disjunct and separate generations.[49]

If grandparents are physical links to the past, myth is the eternal contact. In white culture, "myths are simply lies" (Roberta Hill Whiteman, "For Heather, Entering Kindergarten"). But for the Native American artist, myths and traditions are "a shield / against the social and spiritual plague of twentieth century consumer culture."[50] Non-Indians have largely given up on myth, or else have created their own from various sources, something that has been happening since at least the Romantic period. Contemporary poets find Jung cogenial because he directs them to archetypes that transcend any culture-specific origin. But the Native American poet has a rich variety of native myth to live in and draw on. He or she can draw upon specific characters, such as Raven, Mink, or Coyote—Coyote is rapidly becoming, in art and literature, a pan-Indian character. Or the poet can refer obliquely, relying on a certain shorthand connection to those in the know. And if, as readers, we are not in the know, we can make the same effort we would have to make if we were reading Greek or Russian literature. We may not need to know stories and myths of people turning into deer, myths of reciprocal obligation, trust, and love (as in "The Man Who Married a Deer Woman" in Leonard Bloomfield's *Menomini Texts*).[51] But such knowledge adds a timeless dimension to Louise Erdrich's timely "feminist" poem "Jacklight." This poem is a story of the need for the violent male principle to be inducted into the deep female woods. (I am not suggesting that Erdrich knew this Menomini version of the myth, though versions are widespread.)

Myth is vital if we are to retain a sense of "the orchestration and recognition of life energies,"[52] Frederick Turner has written. Myths are celebrations in which even dark tides of existence "lend the richness and tone of reality itself."[53] Thus, Turner continues, "living myths must include and speak of the interlocking cycles of animate and vegetable life, of water, sun, and even the stones, which have their own stories. It must embrace without distinction the phenomenal and the numinous. In such ways these vital fictions turn us toward the unchanged realities we must live amidst. They may yet prove to be our most successful response to life on this earth."[54] Native American poetry uses myth vitally, revitalizing it, feeding it from the source. Thus, in Leslie Silko's "Toe'osh: A Laguna Pueblo Coyote Story," the ancient mythic Coyote figure becomes a contemporary resident of Laguna, and in the last stanza is transformed into an Indian poet scattering "white people / out of bars all over Wisconsin."[55] And one of the most visionary, mystic poets today is Ray Young Bear, who creates from the deep base of the native tradition of the dream and from the surrealist alchemy of the unconscious—the "merveilleaux."[56]

Balancing Life: A Journey Toward Wholeness

What is striking about Native American poetry is not
the bitterness or anger, though they are there. Nor is it the
sense of loss, of living divided in two worlds, or alienation,
though they are there too. What is impressive is the courage
to continue, to write poetry that uses all the resources of
the English language, a language clearly loved for its
"beauty and poetic power."[57] There is energy and joy in exis-
tence; there is song and dance. Scott Momaday sings in his
"The Delight Song of Tsoai-Talee," "You see, I am alive, I
am alive,"[58] and Joy Harjo reaches way beyond psychic dual-
ism in "She Had Some Horses."[59] She releases her fear in "I
Give You Back," and transforms hatred in "Transformations."
There is humor and comedy from Louise Erdrich's "Old Man
Potchikoo" to Leslie Silko's "Toe'osh." And laughter is
needed, because "who would believe / the fantastic and terri-
ble story of all of our survival / those who were never
meant / to survive?" (Joy Harjo, "Anchorage"). The poems in
this collection reach for balance, for sanity in a mad world,
in the face of antagonism, past and present. One sees a
desire for wholeness—for balance, reconciliation, and heal-
ing—within the individual, the tribe, the community, the
nation; one sees an *insistence* on these things, on growth,
on rich survival. Gail Tremblay writes: "Change moves re-
lentlessly, / the pattern unfolding despite their planning. /
We're always there—singing round dance / songs, remem-
bering what supports / our life—impossible to ignore," ("In-
dian Singing in 20th Century America"). Coyote may often
appear to be dead, but he always seems to survive—part of
continuing metamorphosis and energetic change, a cosmic
force including everything. As Paula Gunn Allen's mother
told her: "Life is a circle, and everything has its place in
it."[60] "And there is always one more story."[61] The great seas
underground "have journeyed through the graveyards / of
our loved ones, / turning in their graves / to carry the stories
of life to air" (Linda Hogan, "To Light").

If contemporary "mainline" American poetry must have

"rubber, coal, uranium, moons, poems"[62] to fuel its voracious engines; and if, "like a shark, it contains a shoe,"[63] and must swim "through the desert / Uttering cries that are almost human,"[64] then Native American poetry is something different. Clearly, it can absorb and digest, though the preferred metaphor is different: "like the spider / we weave new beds around us / when old ones are swept away" (Linda Hogan, "To Light"). It is thoroughly modern. But it is not predatory, self-absorbed. And it is not a shark in the desert; it is not "almost human," but *human*. Its whole thrust is toward completeness of life, even in the desert. As Simon Ortiz writes:

> You see, son, the eagle is a person
> the way it lives; it means it has to do
> with paying attention to where it is, not
> the center of the earth especially, but part
> of it, one part among all parts, and that's
> only the beginning.[65]

Brian Swann
New York, New York
1987

FRANK PREWETT

(1893–1962)

The Red-Man

From wilderness remote he breaks
With stealthy springing tread,
And in the town a vision makes
Of time and manners dead.

He scorns to see the things we own,
And steadfast stares beyond,
Alone, impassive, cold, unknown;
With us he feels no bond.

The townsfolk nudging line the street
To see a red-man pass;
They feel ashamed of toil and heat,
and dream of springs and grass.

They see a breathless dusty town
They had not known before;
The red-man in his robes is gone,
The townsfolk toil once more.

And whence he came, and whither fled,
And why, is all unknown;
His ways are strange, his skin is red,
Our ways and skins our own.

The Pack

I lay dear treasure for you,
I have no treasure that I bear on my back,
Yet I lay riches in your view
Do not doubt me by the smallness of my pack.

All that I have I, delighted, bestow.
I lay it down, I spread it with care
At your feet: approve my show
It is the all of all love that lies there.

I Shall Take You in Rough Weather

I shall take you in rough weather
Where veering wind knows not to cease or settle,
Where December pine on blue and white tosses his feather.
Once you are out of doors the tang is good mettle.

When storms rage and filter under door,
Without you when the house rocks I am afraid.
Infinitude of enmity and cold and unbearable more
The loneliness within walls than in the glade.

We shall warm each other in the lee of trees
Where gale is hushed, where no obstinate wall
Angers the gale, where elemental enmities
For small creatures and lovers are musical.

If I Love You

If I love you, do I prize
What is your mind?
Am I dazzled by your eyes,
Which are grey and kind?

If I love you, do I know
That I doubt your breed,
That alone is best to go,
That your loving is your greed?

But better live than die
Until potency is dead:
Best at your feet to lie
Nor live whence life has fled.

Plea for Peace

A steep valley overhung by trees
And a ditch ripple, noiseless, nosing its way
Where dwell all seasons quiet and at ease,
Nor bird nor shine but comforting peace all day.

Let the plain be bare, wide and lone
That hides the valley, the noiseless rill:
Brack be the water, slippery the stone
So there be peace, peace and quiet still.

———— 🝫 ————

LOUIS (LITTLE COON) OLIVER

(1904–)

Empty Kettle

I do not waste what is wild
I only take what my cup
    can hold.
When the black kettle gapes
    empty
and children eat roasted acorns
    only,
it is time to rise-up early
    take no drink—eat no food
    sing the song of the hunter.
I see the Buck—I chant
I chant the deer chant:
    "He-hebah-Ah-kay-kee-no!"
My arrow, no woman has ever touched,
    finds its mark.
I open the way for the blood to pour
    back to Mother Earth
      the debt I owe.
My soul rises—rapturous
    and I sing a different song,
      I sing,
      I sing.

Wagon Full of Thunder

Now—wagon full of thunder—
    wheels of great whisperings
   striking flint boulders—spitting
        white—blinding cold fire.
In the moon of great white winter
  the Horned Owl prophesied:
When Buffalo hump sizzles
  on the pole—dropping
  oily tears on coals sputtering
     then
prepare for Thla-fo-thlako, the great winter.

Blackberry Bird told me then, too,
    speak the mystery words from
    great conch shell—sing the songs
of the wind, the Turtle and the Gar
      that never die.
Burn cedar and white sage
  whose fragrance turn
  body inside out to free
    Spirit of wisdom.

Deer told me—get down low, low
  form circle of warrior friends,
  eat not the gizzards of fowls
  that you not die of thirst
    in battle,
  but savor the raw meat of us
    for he-man vigor.

I breathe on these wheels turning
    —things scratched on rocks
   so wind and bird may carry
to the ends of Odee, earth
words off Indian tongue
    —from mind shell.

The Horned Snake

The snake snatched
   its single horn clipped
      for strong medicine,
to be used on a warrior
      or a chief who,
facing a volley of death
      from bullets
would be brave, unflinching
      —untouched.

When moon looked the other way,
      eclipsed,
and stillness—stark-naked
         stillness
      made ears ring,
the snake bobbed up from
      the wildest of wild springs
      —gave its horn
         to the medicine
            man.

GEORGE CLUTESI

(1905–   )

West Coast Indian

In the beginning he merely marked
Then he incised on rock.
Later he carved on wood to paint and color with rock and
    roe.
He believed in a God; he aspired to a generous heart.
Asked for strength of arm, a true aim for his bow,
To provide and share with his fellow man.

He did his work at summertime.
He waxed strong; his possessions increased with his toil.
With the thunderdrum he sang at wintertime,
Great feasts he gave because his heart was full,
He sang of deeds and glories won by his house and his clan.
He was at peace with his God; his life indeed was full.

He chose the timber wolf for his symbol,
The killer whale was lord of the salt-chuck,
The thunderbird meant power and might
Like the wind, rain and the thunder.
The lightning snake was its ally.
Mah-uk, leviathan of the sea, represented abundance.

Inspired thus, on great cedar planks he drew
The symbols of his tribe.
Earth and rock, the root and bark, the salmon roe,
Lent their colors, bold and true;
Indeed great men from far off lands marvelled to see
Art forms, shown nowhere else but here.

Allied to the Nootkas, the Tse-shahts
Belonged to the clan of the wolf.
With all the powers at hand,
A great potlatch he would now command.
To bid you: "Come, enter and share with me."
A rich cultural inheritance is his indeed.

Ko-Ishin-Mit Goes Fishing

Cloosmit the herring, hosts in the night.
The flash of silver, the flame of your gold,
With the grey of the dawn you are gone.
Cloosmit the herring, the shoal of the sea,
Come! Dance upon the waters in a sea of spray.
Come! Feed the children of the land with your spawn.

Cloosmit the herring, hosts in the night.
The flash of silver, the flame of your gold.
Come! Make thunder upon the waters in the bay.
With your hosts make thunder in a sea of spray.
Come! Dance upon the waters with the dawn.
Come! Feed the children of the land with your spawn.

The Beast in Man

From out of the waters it came with a moan.
Was it an animal? Was it a man?
Alone it came for no other would condescend
To be its foe and not a friend.

You saw it gnash a dog in twain,
You saw the gore spill down the chin
While it the water trod.
You saw a grisly sight driven deep within the mind.

In the black waters of our lore
You saw a savage, a savage to the core.
The evil that you saw in the mist of the morn—
It was the beast in man.

A Song of the Yellow Cedar Face

A tale is told of long ago:
All things, it is said, must come and go,
All things, it is said, have a spirit,
The moss, the bracken, the tree with a bole.
To your lodge, with no warning, it will come.
Shun him not but make room for his welcome.

A howling clamorous rogue from the wood,
Over all braves he towers with manhood.
His arms are long like the limb of the cedar;
His legs are strong and full of power;
His feet are big, his weight to sustain;
His hands, enormous for might and main.

It is said, he a mission must maintain
For men of our clan and also your own,
When still they are young and growing with strength.
For a vessel he seeks that he must unearth.
No man with pride and dignity true
Inside a house, this vessel should use.

Should the vessel he seeks, it is said
Be kept in a lodge or in a shed,
A visit from him will be made forthright
With a voice that is skookum with might.
No pillars, no doors, will stay his wrath
Till the kiss-duh he seeks he does unearth.

Make room, it is said and anger him not
He will to the clootchmen stay coy
Make room for him, for rare is the chance
To witness him, for the children dance.
He is big, he is strong without a doubt
But he is kind, big-hearted to a fault.

Yea, his back is strong like the cedar tall
But his mind is slow feeble and dull.
The sense of his smell is keen—acute
But bleary the eye and weak is the sight.
Strong and skookum is the howl.
A spirit with a mask of a cedar bole.

Skookum–powerful
Kiss-duh–chamber pot
Clootchmen–wives

MARY TALLMOUNTAIN

(1918–   )

The Women in Old Parkas

snapping gunshot cold
blue stubborn lips clapped shut
the women in old parkas
loosen snares   intent and slow

they handle muskrat   Yukon way
appease his spirit *yeega'*
bare purple hands
stiffen   must set lines again

        .   .   .

night drops quick black
in winterhouse   round shadows
cook fresh meat soup steam floats
thin bellies grumble

they pick up skinwork   squint
turn lamp-wick down   kerosene
almost gone   sew anyway

Oh! This winter is the worst
everything running out not much furs
they make soft woman hum . . .

but hey! How about those new parkas
we hung up for Stick Dance!
How the people sing!
How crazy shadows dip and stamp
on dancehouse walls! Remembering,
they raise their arms like birdwings

.   .   .

At morning they look into the sky
laugh at little lines of rain
finger their old parkas
think: spring comes soon

There Is No Word for Goodbye

Sokoya, I said, looking through
        the net of wrinkles into
        wise black pools
        of her eyes.

What do you say in Athabaskan
        when you leave each other?
        What is the word
        for goodbye?

A shade of feeling rippled
        the wind-tanned skin.
        Ah, nothing, she said,
        watching the river flash.

She looked at me close.
> We just say, Tlaa. That means,
> See you.
> We never leave each other.
> When does your mouth
> say goodbye to your heart?

She touched me light
> as a bluebell.
> You forget when you leave us;
> you're so small then.
> We don't use that word.

We always think you're coming back,
> but if you don't,
> we'll see you someplace else.
> You understand.
> There is no word for goodbye.

_____

Sokoya–aunt (mother's sister)

Matmiya

for my grandmother

I see you sitting
Implanted by roots
Coiled deep from your thighs.
Roots, flesh red, centuries pale.
Hairsprings wound tight
Through fertile earthscapes
Where each layer feeds the next
Into depths immutable.

Though you must rise, must
Move large and slow
When it is time, O my
Gnarled mother-vine, ancient
As vanished ages,
Your spirit remains
Nourished,
Nourishing me.

I see your figure wrapped in skins
Curved into a mound of earth
Holding your rich dark roots.
Matmiya,
I see you sitting.

Peeling Pippins

I sit down beside my brass lamp
To peel a pan of pippins.
How the spry sap springs, how
Quickly white flesh turns rust.
I muse on a green-skinned quarter.
The brass mirrors my fingers,
A brown cup holding a curve of green.
Pippin, created round: from pips
To plump dimples; inward to
Faint outline of its heart.
Taut little skins curl. The core
Falls abandoned to my sharp knife.
Saluting pippin's hardihood
I slice blizzard, thunder, deluge.

There will be jars of sauce.
Pippin shall feed bone and marrow;
Cells shall transmute,
Emerald be crimson; sap be blood
In pippin's winter odyssey:
Profusions of life, linked
In the continuum.

NORA DAUENHAUER

(1927–   )

Voices

We sound like crying bullheads
when we sing
our songs.

Granddaughters dancing,
blossoms
swaying in the wind.

Kelp

Ribbons of iodine
unrolled by the hands
of the waves.

Skiing on Russian Christmas

Southeast at low tide:
how the frosted trees
are heavy with herring eggs.

Branches in water:
how the birds fly to them
spawning their roe.

Frosted alders:
shapes of coral
clawing outward.

How to Make Good Baked Salmon from the River

for Simon Ortiz
and for all our friends and relatives
who love it

It's best made in dry-fish camp on a beach by a
fish stream on sticks over an open fire, or during
fishing, or during cannery season.

In this case, we'll make it in the city baked in
an electric oven on a black fry pan.

INGREDIENTS
Barbecue sticks of alder wood.
In this case, the oven will do.
Salmon: River salmon, current supermarket cost
$4.99 a pound.
In this case, salmon poached from river.
Seal oil or olachen oil.
In this case, butter or Wesson oil, if available.

DIRECTIONS
To butcher, split head up the jaw. Cut through,
remove gills. Split from throat down the belly.
Gut, but make sure you toss all to the seagulls and
the ravens because they're your kin, and make sure
you speak to them while you're feeding them.
Then split down along the back bone and through
the skin. Enjoy how nice it looks when it's split.

Push stake through flesh and skin like pushing
a needle through cloth, so that it hangs on stakes
while cooking over fire made from alder wood.

Then sit around and watch the slime on the salmon
begin to dry out. Notice how red the flesh is,
and how silvery the skin looks. Watch and listen
to the grease crackle, and smell its delicious
aroma drifting around on a breeze.

Mash some fresh berries to go along for dessert.
Pour seal oil in with a little water. Set aside.

In this case, put the poached salmon in a fry pan.
Smell how good it smells while it's cooking,
because it's soooooooo important.

Cut up an onion. Put in a small dish. Notice how
nice this smells too and how good it will taste.
Cook a pot of rice to go along with salmon. Find
some soy sauce to put on rice, maybe borrow some.

In this case, think about how nice the berries would
have been after the salmon, but open a can of fruit
cocktail instead.

Then go out by the cool stream and get some skunk
cabbage, because it's biodegradable, to serve the
salmon from. Before you take back the skunk cabbage
you can make a cup out of one to drink from the
cool stream.

In this case, plastic forks paper plates and cups will do, and
drink cool water from the faucet.

TO SERVE

After smelling smoke and fish and watching the
cooking, smelling the skunk cabbage and the berries
mixed with seal oil, when the salmon is done, put
the salmon on stakes on the skunk cabbage and pour
some seal oil over it and watch the oil run into
the nice cooked flakey flesh which has now turned
pink.

Shoo mosquitos off the salmon, and shoo the ravens
away, but don't insult them because the mosquitoes
are known to be the ashes of the cannibal giant,
and Raven is known to take off with just about
anything.

In this case, dish out on paper plates from fry pan.
Serve to all relatives and friends you have invited
to the barbecue and those who love it.

And think how good it is that we have good spirits
that still bring salmon and oil.

TO EAT

Everyone knows that you can eat just about every
part of the salmon, so I don't have to tell you
that you start with the head because it's everyone's
favorite. You take it apart bone by bone, but make
sure you don't miss the eyes, the cheeks, the nose,
and the very best part—the jawbone.

You start on the mandible with a glottalized
alveolar fricative action as expressed in the Tlingit
verb als'oss'.

Chew on the tasty, crispy skins before you start
on the bones. Eeeeeeeeeeeee!!!! How delicious.

Then you start on the body by sucking on the fins
with the same action. Include crispy skins, then
the meat with grease dripping all over it.

Have some cool water from the stream with the salmon.

In this case, water from the faucet will do.
Enjoy how the water tastes sweeter with salmon.

When done, toss the bones to the ravens and
seagulls and mosquitoes, but don't throw them in
the salmon stream because the salmon have spirits
and don't like to see the remains of their kin
among them in the stream.

In this case, put bones in plastic bag to put
in dumpster.

Now settle back to a story telling session, while
someone feeds the fire.

In this case, small talk and jokes with friends
will do while you drink beer. If you shouldn't
drink beer, tea or coffee will do nicely.

Gunalchéesh for coming to my barbecue.

MAURICE KENNY

(1929–   )

First Rule

stones must form a circle first not a wall
open so that it may expand
to take in new grass and hills
tall pines and a river
expand as sun on weeds, an elm, robins;
the prime importance is to circle stones
where footsteps are erased by winds
assured old men and wolves sleep
where children play games
catch snow flakes if they wish;
words cannot be spoken first

as summer turns spring
caterpillars into butterflies
new stones will be found for the circle;
it will ripple out a pool
grown from the touch
of a water-spider's wing;
words cannot be spoken first

that is the way to start
with stones forming a wide circle
marsh marigolds in bloom
hawks hunting mice
boys climbing hills
to sit under the sun to dream
of eagle wings and antelope;
words cannot be spoken first

Sweetgrass

for Jerome and Diane Rothenberg

Seeded in the mud on turtle's back
Greened in the breath of the west wind
Fingered by the children of the dawn
Arrowed to the morning sun
Blessed by the hawk and sparrow
Plucked by the many hands in the laughter
    of young girls and the art of old women

You hold the moments of the frost and the thaw
You hold the light of the star and the moon
You hold the darkness of the moist night
    and the music of the river and the drum
You are the antler of the deer
You are the watery fire of the trout
You are the dance of the morning
You are the grunts and the groans
    the whimpers and whistles of the forest

You are the blood of the feet
    and the balm for the wound
You are the flint and the spark
You are the child of the loins
    and the twin of the armpit
You are the rock of the field
    and the great pine of the mountain
You are the river that passes in the burnt afternoon
You are the light on the beak and the stump
    and the one-legged heron in the marsh
You are the elk in the snow
You are the groundhog and the bear
You are the claw of the muskrat

You are the ache in the spine
    yet the scent of summer

You are the plum and the squash and the gooseberry
   the flower of the bean
You are the bark of the house

You are the rainbow
   and the parched corn in your woven basket
You are the seed of my flesh
   and I am the flesh of your seed

Legacy

my face is grass
             color of April rain;
arms, legs are the limbs
             of birch, cedar;
my thoughts are winds
             which blow;
pictures in my mind
             are the climb up hill
             to dream in the sun;
             hawk feathers, and quills
             of porcupine running
             the edge of the stream
             which reflects stories
             of my many mornings
             and the dark faces of night
             mingled with victories
             of dawn and tomorrow;
corn of the fields and squash . . .
             the daughters of my mother
             who collect honey
             and all the fruits;

meadow and sky are the end of my day,
         the stretch of my night
         yet the birth of my dust;
my wind is the breath of a fawn
         the cry of the cub
         the trot of the wolf
         whose print covers
         the tracks of my feet;
my word, my word,
         loaned
legacy, the obligation I hand
         to the blood of my flesh
         the sinew of the loins
to hold to the sun
         and the moon
which direct the river
         that carries my song
         and the beat of the drum
to the fires of the village
         which endures.

Strawberrying

morning
broods
     in the wide river
Mama bends
     light
     bleeds
     always
     in her days of
     picking
(our fields are stained)

the moon, bats
     tell us
     to go
in the scent of
     berries

fox
   awaken
       in stars

They Tell Me I Am Lost

for Lance Henson

my feet are elms, roots in the earth
my heart is the hawk
my thought the arrow that rides
   the wind across the valley
my spirit eats with eagles on the mountain crag
   and clashes with the thunder
my grass is the breath of my flesh
   and the deer is the bone of my child
my toes dance on the drum
   in the light of the eyes of the old turtle

my chant is the wind
my chant is the muskrat
my chant is the seed
my chant is the tadpole
my chant is the grandfather
   and his many grandchildren
   sired in the frost of March
   and the summer noon of brown August

my chant is the field that turns with the sun
   and feeds the mice
   and the bear red berries and honey
my chant is the river
   that quenches the thirst of the sun
my chant is the woman who bore me
   and my blood and my flesh of tomorrow
my chant is the herb that heals
   and the moon that moves the tide
   and the wind that cleans the earth
    of old bones singing in the morning dust
my chant is the rabbit, skunk, heron
my chant is the red willow, the clay
   and the great pine that bulges the woods
   and the axe that fells the birch
   and the hand that breaks the corn from the stalk
   and waters the squash and catches stars
my chant is a blessing to the trout, beaver
   and a blessing to the young pheasant
    that warms my winter
my chant is the wolf in the dark
my chant is the crow flying against the sun
my chant is the sun
   sleeping on the back of the grass
    in marriage
my chant is the sun
   while there is sun I cannot be lost
my chant is the quaking of the earth
   angry and bold

although I hide in the thick forest
   or the deep pool of the slow river
   though I hide in a shack, a prison
   though I hide in a word, a law

though I hide in a glass of beer
   or high on steel girders over the city
   or in the slums of that city
though I hide in a mallard feather
   or the petals of the milkwort
   or a story told by my father

though there are eyes that do not see me
   and ears that do not hear my drum
   or hands that do not feel my wind
   and tongues which do not taste my blood
I am the shadow on the field
   the rain on the rock
   the snow on the limb
   the footprint on the water
   the vetch on the grave
I am the sweat on the boy
   the smile on the woman
   the paint on the man
I am the singer of songs
   and the hunter of fox
I am the glare on the sun
   the frost on the fruit
   the notch on the cedar
I am the foot on the golden snake
I am the foot on the silver snake
I am the tongue of the wind
   and the nourishment of grubs
I am the claw and the hoof and the shell
I am the stalk and the bloom and the pollen
I am the boulder on the rim of the hill
I am the sun and the moon
   the light and the dark
I am the shadow on the field

I am the string, the bow and the arrow

O Wendy, Arthur

One more night my blood
keeps sleep from the hard pillow.
Sula purrs at the foot of the bed
trying to sing me into dreams.
It doesn't work anymore
than warm milk, valium, or exhaustion.
I sit here attempting poems
and fantasizing tours around the world,
wanting to feel your words,
desperate to talk, to tell
how spring climbed up with dawn
and iris bloomed the ridge of my arm,
and we three walked blackberry brambles
balancing on railroad tracks
through blue meadows. Could it be
that sleep defies some drift of happiness
that I can't measure, pin, explicate,
nor file away for the days when that sun
doesn't rise with wild flowers on my cheek.

This particular case of insomnia almost
feels good especially knowing you'll be here Wednesday.

Wolf 'Aunt'

for Rochelle Ratner

They came to the lodge door
and called him by name.
Blackrobe, they called.
Blackrobe, come out.

Foolish and determined.
Obstinate, adamant.
Oh! He'll save these children
all right, but from the throne of his god.

I tried to persuade him
to return to the Hurons, his friends.
I told him not to carry that cross
when he walked alone in the village . . .

holding it, flaunting it in the faces
of both the chiefs and clan mothers.
I told him to stop mumbling
over the sick children,

that the duties of curing
belonged to our doctors
who have centuries of service
and the herbs to heal.

Would he listen! No!
At hearing of an illness
he would drop his bowl of food
and rush out into a blizzard

that cross before him, those beads
clanking on the wind.
I gave him a warm place to sleep,
and deer meat my brother killed.

With my own hands I sewed him moccasins.
I thought he would learn our ways.
All he learned was our language
so he could "speak to the people."

I threatened him
and told him the false-faces
would come when walking
in the woods, they would

bite his flesh and suck
out his spirit. Did he
listen! No, of course not.
Instead he made signs

over me, always smiling what others
thought a smirk, a leer, but he was
smiling. He was too dumb to smirk.
No, not dumb, but foolish.

I was positive that one day the Bear
would grow tired of his posturing,
that some doctor or other would become
jealous, fearful of his powers,

that a clan mother would envy his
living within my lodge,
that some boy would resent his stares,
and that a child would hear his

mumblings and scream out to his
uncle for help. I told him this
every morning of his life
and every night that predicted his death.

And finally they came to the door,
called him by name.
Blackrobe, they called.
Blackrobe, come out!

The moon was very beautiful that night.
Full and yellow. The shadows cast
were long, ominous.
The air was bright, sky blue.

He barely placed his foot on the earth
outside the lodge
when I heard a thump and I knew
his body crumpled under the club.

I will be searching
his bones for years . . .
bone by bone.

December

Set up the drum.
Winter's on the creek.

Dark men sit in dark kitchens.
Words move in the air.
A neighbor is sick.
Needs prayer.

Women thaw frozen
strawberries.

In the dark . . . a drum.

> Kids hang out
> eating burgers
> at McDonalds.
> The Williams boy
> is drunk.

Set up the drum.

Berries thaw,
are crushed,
fingers stained, and tongues.

Set up the drum
A neighbor is sick.
Say a prayer.
Dark men sit in dark kitchens.

Wind rattles the moon.

Reverberation

A north wind heard is heard always.
Drums reverberate like circles of a disturbed pool
into an incomprehensible time;
the banging of the drum does not stop
once thumped in the ceremony of life.

How can I explain optical illusion?
Can I cut her heart muscle into tiny pieces,
her brain, and set these pieces down on paper,
or in the palm of my hand? Memory weeds chaff.
Attempting to re-create the woman she was
through jottings of conversations, hand movements,
facial expressions, thought pattern, she
becomes a quirk of the imagination.
There remains a strong need in the blood,
strong in the verb orphaned in aloneness,
roots pulled out by the hair. Are lips
still too close to nipple and breath?
Will she also come and sit at midnight?

I'll chatter with shadows filtering rooms,
watch the rocking chair rock, smell an apple pie
bubbling in a cold oven, hear a tea cup smash
on the floor of a vacant kitchen, or hear whispers
in the parlor where there are no voices.

They stay where they are wanted . . .

Wild Strawberry

for Helene

And I rode the Greyhound down to Brooklyn
where I sit now eating woody strawberries
grown on the backs of Mexican farmers
imported from the fields of their hands,
juices without color or sweetness

      my wild blood berries of spring meadows
      sucked by June bees and protected by hawks
      have stained my face and honeyed
      my tongue . . . healed the sorrow in my flesh

      vines crawl across the grassy floor
      of the north, scatter to the world
      seeking the light of the sun and innocent
      tap of the rain to feed the roots
      and bud small white flowers that in June
      will burst fruit and announce spring
      when wolf will drop winter fur
      and wrens will break the egg

my blood, blood berries that brought laughter
and the ache in the stooped back that vied
with dandelions for the plucking,
and the wines nourished our youth and heralded
iris, corn and summer melon

we fought bluebirds for the seeds
armed against garter snakes, field mice;
won the battle with the burning sun
which blinded our eyes and froze our hands
to the vines and the earth where knees knelt
and we laughed in the morning dew like worms
and grubs; we scented age and wisdom

my mother wrapped the wounds of the world
with a sassafras poultice and we ate
wild berries with their juices running
down the roots of our mouths and our joy

I sit here in Brooklyn eating Mexican
berries which I did not pick, nor do
I know the hands which did, nor their stories . . .
January snow falls, listen . . .

ELIZABETH COOK-LYNN

(1930–   )

Grandfather at the Indian Health Clinic

It's cold at last and cautious winds creep
softly into coves along the riverbank. At my insistence
he wears his denim cowboy coat high on his neck; averse to
an unceremonious world, he follows me through
hallways pushing down the easy rage he always has
with me, a youngest child, and smiles.
This morning the lodge is closed to the dance
and he reminds me these are not the men who
raise the bag above the painted marks; for the young
intern from New Jersey he bares his chest
but keeps a scarf tied on his steel-gray braids
and thinks of days that have no turning: he wore
yellow chaps and went as far as Canada to ride
Mad Dog and then came home to drive the Greenwood
    Woman's
cattle to his brother's place,
two hundred miles
along the timber line
the trees were bright
he turned his hat brim down in summer rain.

Now winter's here, he says, in this white lighted place
where lives are sometimes saved by
throwing blankets over spaces where the leaves are brushed
    away
and giving brilliant gourd-shell rattles
to everyone who comes.

My Grandmother's Burial Ground:

Paul Wahukezatininkeya, July 12, 1892

> *"Words are coins*
> *thrown on a table to settle a debt, a sign*
> *that nothing's settled."*
>   James J. McAuley, *An Irish Bull*

I walked beside the stone
that bore your name and date
and felt the threat of history
give rise to sudden chill, like wind
from unseen creek. Ancestral bones
lie in anonymity in this New World
except that History called you Christian
and your name
kill-in-war-with-spear
vouched for you.

Grave Paul,
Your name as pale as northern Tamarack
in fall, and names of all born then or since
are played like coins
in games of chance. I stand, alone,
and cast a shadow on the sunken mounds: mute metaphors,
I think, for carelessness of Memory
not then or now for sale or trade.

Never mind, the coins invaders played
which made you play your hand against your will
won't pay the debt. History,
that counterfeit absurdity
is no match for Buffalo bones
and dried skins of crows.

Journey

I.

Dream

                                    Wet, sickly
smells of cattle yard silage fill the prairie air
far beyond the timber; the nightmare only just
begun, a blackened cloud moves past the sun
to dim the river's glare, a malady of modern times.
                                    We prayed
to the giver of prayers and traveled to the spirit
mounds we thought were forever; awake, we feared that
hollow trees no longer hid the venerable ones we were
   taught
to believe in.

II.

Memory

Dancers with cane whistles,
the prairie's wise and knowing kinsmen.
They trimmed their deer skins
in red down feathers,
made drum sticks from the gray grouse,
metaphorically speaking, and knocked on doors
which faced the East.
Dancers with cane whistles,
born under the sign of hollow stems,
after earth and air and fire and water
you conjure faith to clear the day.
Stunningly, blessedly you pierce the sky
with sound so clear each winged creature soars.

In my mind Grandmothers, those old partisans of faith
who long for shrill and glowing rituals of the past,
recall the times they went on long communal
buffalo hunts; because of this they tell the
lithe and lissome daughters:
> look for men who know the sacred ways
> look for men who wear the white-striped quill
> look for dancers with cane whistles
> and seek the house of relatives to stay the night.

III.

Sacristans

This journey through another world, beyond bad dreams
beyond the memories of a murdered generation,
cartographed in captivity by bare survivors
makes sacristans of us all.

The old ones go our bail, we oblate preachers of our tribes.
Be careful, they say, don't hock the beads of
kinship agonies; The moire-effect of unfamiliar hymns
upon our own, a change in pitch or shrillness of the voice
transforms the waves of song to words of poetry or prose
and makes distinctions
no one recognizes.
Surrounded and absorbed, we treat like Etruscans
on the edge of useless law; we pray
to the giver of prayers, we give the cane whistle
in ceremony, we swing the heavy silver chain
of incense burners. Migration makes
new citizens of Rome.

CARTER REVARD

(1931–   )

Driving in Oklahoma

On humming rubber along this white concrete
    lighthearted between the gravities
of source and destination like a man
        halfway to the moon
    in this bubble of tuneless whistling
at seventy miles an hour from the windvents
            over prairie swells rising
    and falling, over the quick offramp
that drops to its underpass and the truck
            thundering beneath as I cross
with the country music twanging out my windows,
        I'm grooving down this highway feeling
technology is freedom's other name when
        —a meadowlark
        comes sailing across my windshield
            with breast shining yellow
        and five notes pierce
            the windroar like a flash
            of nectar on mind
gone as the country music swells up and
        drops me wheeling down
    my notch of cement-bottomed sky
        between home and away
            and wanting
to move again through country that a bird
    has defined wholly with song
            and maybe next time see how
he flies so easy, when he sings.

In Kansas

The '49 dawn set me high on a roaring yellow tractor,
slipping the clutch or gunning a twenty-foot combine
to spurt that red-gold wheat into Ceres' mechanical womb:
I'd set her on course and roll for a straight two miles
before turning left, and that got monotonous as hell,
at first all the roar and dust and the jiggling stems
                    collapsing
to whisk up that scything platform and be stripped of
                    their seed,
then even the boiling from under of rats and rabbits
                    scrambling
to hide again in their shrinking island of tawny grain
as the hawks hung waiting their harvest of torn fur
                    and blood.
So I'd play little god with sunflowers drooping
                    their yellow heads;
see a clump coming and spin the wheel left, right,
                    straight.
The shuddering combine swiveled on its balljoint hitch
first right, then left, its great chatter of blades
                    swinging
so the tip barely brushed those flowers and left
                    their clump standing
like a small green nipple out from the golden breastline
            and next time past
reversing wheel-spins cut free a sinuous lozenge left
            for the bumblebees
with butter-and-black-velvet tops limp-nodding over
                    wilted leaves.
But sunflowers weren't enough. I left on the slick stubble
            islets
of blue-flowered chicory, scarlet poppies, and just
            for the hell of it cockleburrs:
"From now on, kid, you run that sumbitch straight,"
                    the farmer said.

Hell's bells, out on that high prairie I bet goldfinches,
bobwhites, and pheasants still are feasting
        in that farmer's fields
on the flower seeds I left out, summer, fall, and
            winter harvests
that make the bread I eat taste better
        by not being ground up with it,
          then or now.

Looking Before and After

     Under the new pond-dam
        a trickle
          like a spring fills
      old pools among
        the button-bushes where you
       step between rusting bedsprings
              blackberry vines
persimmon trees & wild grape tangles and
   where the matted grass gives
 way to shining there is
         footdeep water so clear that over
     its brown silt bottom haloes dazzle round the
     shadows trailed by water-striders in
       their spindly-crooked dimpling across its
        springy surface so
  each bright-edged darkness glides up to
  and over brown crawdads bulldozing through
       the mud-dust
           and see, one shadow-cluster is
  a gliding skull whose two
      great eyes stare above its
           nose and three black teeth,
          it wanders,

lunges, glides,
                        spins upside down and turns
        to butterfly! that stops precisely underneath
            an image of white larkspur nodding upon
                the water's surface so it seems
        that dimly there
                among cruising crawdads a
            butterfly of shadows tastes
                    sweet light again.

And Don't Be Deaf to the Singing Beyond

You never could tell what my deaf Uncle Arthur heard.
That Sunday when the black storm-cloud came at us
He sat there churning butter in a bedroom window.
We saw this strange cloud way off west on the hills,
A little dark funnel with specks dancing round.
"It's only a big whirlwind," he said with a smile.
Well, pretty soon we saw the specks were trees
And heard this rumble like freight trains on a trestle,
But Uncle Arthur was deaf and wouldn't believe us.
We ran like hell to the car and drove off east;
When hail and rain came blasting after to blind us.
He still sat up in his window, churning away.
Of course the storm passed before we got to the school
And ran down steps to stand in its flooded cellar;
So, after fifteen minutes, we drove back home.
When we got in, he had two pounds of butter
All worked, salted, and molded onto dishes.
The funnel had passed a half-mile north and west—
Its swath, a quarter-mile wide of levelled blackjacks,
Went up and over the valley's northern rim.
We drove up north to find out who'd been killed,
But in the dirt yard of the paintless two-room house
Our Holy Roller friends were standing unharmed.
"We knelt and prayed; God turned his wrath aside,"
                        they said.

Which tasted sweeter'd be hard to say, by now,
That Jersey butter from Uncle Arthur's churn
Or the name of God in Mrs. Parks' mouth.
I still get peeved, thinking of what missed them
So close they saw the lightning up in its blackness,
And what we missed, down in our scorpion-filled cellar.
Well, when my Uncle Arthur died years later
He was way the hell out in California
And Aunt Jewel, my Uncle Woody's wife,
Saw him collapse there with his coronary
And when she ran up he lay there on his back
Turned his eyes to her, smiled, closed them, was dead.
"He was so deaf," she said, "and he saw my mouth
Just calling and calling, and seemed to think it was funny."

My Right Hand Don't Leave Me No More

When you were drunk you could always whip Joe Louis—
Lucky he never stopped by Bartlesville
On a Saturday night in the Green Lantern Saloon,
Or he'd have been forced to let you knock him out.
I think he'd have done it; not even the local bullies
Would take advantage when you were fighting drunk.
And sober, you were so goddamned meek and truthful
You once outfaced the big fat deputy star
Who came to take our bootlegging uncle away.
My uncle was holding his breath up in our attic.
The sheriff believed he'd been around our place
But thought he'd hid out back somewhere in the hills.
The laws all knew that you never told a lie,
So when they'd searched, this one came out and asked,
"Now Alex, is your boy anywheres around here?"
"Wellsir," you said, straightfaced, "He *was* around."

One time though, I didn't think you'd make it.
Out in the chipstrewn yard beside my window
I saw you face the drunk with his butcher knife:
He raised it over your deprecating hands
And weary eyes that held its point with meekness—
I saw him halt and scowl, then stumble close:
"Old man, your time has come, you hear old man?"
One thing you did kept his knife from slashing;
You did not meet his eyes. I saw him turn
Bewildered eyes to me; you took the knife
From his passive hands, heard drunken apologies,
Then brought him into the house and had a drink with
    him.
You dealt with time that way, and better ways:
You fixed the broken farm. Your hands once drove
A shining nail, squeaking under the hammer, into
The massive gatepost's new-peeled oaken bulk;
I marvelled how those huge things yielded to you
Under scrapegong blows of the hammer's bluesteel arc
In the grip of your hands—
I thought your hands that held off shame and poverty
From all of us could keep off death from you,
My grandfather, but I was gone when he came
And did not help. You died bringing in wood for the fire.

JIM BARNES

(1933–   )

An ex-Deputy Sheriff Remembers the Eastern Oklahoma Murderers

i. Summerfield

They took a tire tool to his head,
this gentle stranger from Wyoming.
Oh, we caught them over
at Talihina drinking beer
at Lester's Place, calling
the myna bird bad names
and shooting shuffleboard.
I'm telling you
they were meek in the muzzle
of our guns. They claimed innocence
and: why, they went fishing
with the Cowboy just the other day.
We said we knew, knew too
the way they stole him blind
that night. We spoke of blood,
the way the dogs had lapped his face.

The youngest of the three bad brothers,
barely thirteen, began to cry:
"He told us everything was all right
and we hit him till he died."
And that is how it was,
a simple thing, like breathing,
they hit him until he died,
until he bled Wyoming dry
there on the road
in that part of Oklahoma
no stranger has ever owned.

ii. Red Oak

We shot the Choctaw way back in '94,
last legal execution by firing squad.
He didn't die, through the heart, square
and he didn't die.
The high sheriff, my old boss,
stuffed his own shirt down
the Choctaw's neck
to stop the rattle in his throat.
You couldn't shoot a downed man
no matter what and he had to die.
Damned good Choctaw, I'll say that.
Red Oak had no jail and it was too
blasted cruel to execute him
before his crop was in. The judge
scheduled it for the fall, first Saturday
after the corn was in the Choctaw's crib.

That damned fool Choctaw gathered
his corn like any other dirt farmer,
dressed clean, and kept his word.
"I'm ready" is all he said that day.
You got to admire a man like that,
Indian or not, murderer or just plain fool.
He'd shot three men for sleeping
in his barn and taking the milk bucket
away from his little girl, though she
wasn't harmed at all, and he showed up
just like he'd said he would.

                    There
was a picnic in the shade after we choked
the Choctaw to death and took the rifle home.
First time I'd ever seen a camera,
big damned black thing on legs,
smelled like seven kinds of sin every time
it popped. Had fresh hominy and chicken and the last
of some damned fine late sweet red watermelons.

iii. LeFlore

Goddamnest thing I ever saw
was when old Mac ran down that poor old LeFlore boy.
Old Mac was drunk as thunder
when we chained him to the tree
he'd just pissed on back of his house.
Said he'd wanted to see what it was like
to bounce a man off the hood
of the truck he hauled pulpwood on.
No other reason than just that.
Hell of a note, but I've heard worse.
They all have got some sort of song and dance.
Old Mac's kids were screaming louder
than the crows and threatening us with garden hoes.

We shooed them off with fake fast draws.
That poor old LeFlore boy was as deaf as stone,
a condition they say came with the color of his skin,
though as mild in his ways as the first fall winds.
Old Mac had hit him from behind. Coming
down the gravel road, lord, he must have been
doing sixty and with a full two-cord load.
Hit him dead on. Center. Cracked his
back in half all the way through. That poor
old LeFlore boy's rubber boots were left
standing exactly where he last had stood.
How can you account for that, those silly
rubber boots standing bolt upright
dead in the middle of the goddamned road?

iv. Wister

What made him think he could get away with it
is beyond me. Hell, he'd lived over at Glendale
all his life. Everybody knew he had a stiff
little finger on his right hand. The mask hid
nothing, not even the fear and tobacco juice
he always drooled out the corners of his mouth.
He shot the teller right between the eyes and
made the others strip. Don't ask why. Cleaned
out the vault of a thousand dollars, mostly
fives, and made it fifty yards down the Frisco
tracks before Mathes, the bank's owner, naked
as a jaybird and pissing a blue streak, blew
his left shoulder off with a 30.06. I've got
the cartridge shell to this day. Was going to
have one of them little lighters, size of your
finger, made out of it. But I decided to quit.

Autobiography, Chapter XLII:
Three Days in Louisville

> *Everything is the cause of itself.*
> Ralph Waldo Emerson

i.

Coming down into an air brown as whiskey, the plane
    drops onto the strip like a practiced crow ready
    for another's kill, talons wild for dead game.

This fierce town will hold you three days running:
    the nervous prance that cracks your bones tells
    you plain there's nothing sure about sure things.

You count your chances for survival slim; this is no
    town for poets: the weather is never right, the
    air a constant sour mash and scream.

The city sprawls like a gutted horse, and the taxi
    you take can't even offer tours, the hotel so
    cold it smells of juniper and gin.

In East St. Louis this morning a stable burned;
    the horses screaming in their stalls, a total
    loss; and now you burn, wild mares beating in
    your brain, but you're no hero, barely sane.

You will read your poems to whoever is there or to
    the night; you will read something with hoofs
    in it, something with hands, something in the
    saddle to ride mankind.

ii.

You eat Italian with your friends, who have driven a
     thousand
          miles, weathered well through the gangstered middle of
               this
          land, are green for poetry and bourbon on the rocks.

The horses in your head are pulling at the reins, anxious for
     the race they cannot run; a heavy smell of char stings
     your eyes, the sight of steak singed and bloody turns
     you cold.

There is no muse to pull a poem out of this pot; your fat
     friend across your plate plays Petrarchian with his
          words,
     the bad sonnet falling from his mouth like sauce.

When you were young, the horses in the meadows danced
     and the grooming wind greened their eyes and the sun
     filled their hoofs with fire.

Now the horses die, die, and the violent sky cracks with
     the thunder of stampede, gods gone crazy in the
     whiskey dark.

Hands above your head to keep your vision clear, you rush
     the car, stagger in mid-air: half buried in the rainy
     pavement at your feet is a spent cartridge of a Smith
     and Wesson .45.

iii.

The muraled walls are big with horses' heads; paddocks
     and colonels are cornering at every turn you make.

You enter the Poetry Room at half-lope, late, your bones
     popping like pistols at the track. Three days in
     Louisville and your brain ferments a race you swore
     you'd never see: you dream pasterns broken, nostrils
     flared, a bullet between the eyes.

You loose your poems and the words run out, but you can't
     loose the horses in your head: in Tennessee, or
          somewhere
     down from here, they wrap the pasterns tight in wire
     and the Walking Horse learns his name dancing three-
     quarter time.

You've come to dread the afterwards, the taking stock that
     follows poems that's supposed to help you tighten up
     the pace. You know it's hard to drop a line or life.
     Always too much at stake.

The bourbon you finally allow yourself in bed is pure flame.
     You take it like you take the lie of sunny weather on
     TV. Agape. On the nightstand a phonebook and a
          Gideon
     lie neck to neck.

Return to La Plata, Missouri

The warping bandstand reminds you of the hard rage
you felt in the heart of the town the day you said goodbye
to the park, silver jet, and cicadas dead in the sage.

The town is basic red, although it browns. A cry
of murder, rape, or wrong will always bend the night
hard into the broken grass. You listen close for sighs

of lovers on the ground. The darkness gathers light
and throws it down: something glows that you cannot name,
something fierce, abstract, given time and space you might

on a journey leave behind, a stone to carve your fame
on, or a simple word like *love*. The sun is down
or always going down in La Plata, the same

sun. Same too the child's cry that turns the mother's frown
brittle as chalk or the town's face against the moon.
Same too the moan of dog and diesel circling the town

in an air so heavy with cloud that there is little room
for breath or moon. Strange: in a town so country, so
foreign, you never hear a song nor see a loom

pattern dark threads into a history you would know
   and would not know. You think you see one silver star.
   But the town offers only itself, and you must go.

Tracking the Siuslaw Man

for Lethe Easterling

Ice honed by wind
is sharp with messages from the north.
Firs split under silver blades,
and tracks are fossils under glass.

You read the rigid trail
under a sun dead as amber,
tell yourself the cold you feel
can't touch the fear

in the marrow of your bones.
Siuslaw passed this way is what you know
from footprints hairy with frost
and shadows in the wood that will not freeze.

The trail always ends
on solid stone mute with glyphs
that send you back centuries
or into a dream you never want to have.

You hack the last print
from the glazed ground, feel it shatter
in your hand while somewhere
a dark Siuslaw raven calls

and snow men bend to the task of mountains.

Autobiography, Chapter XVII: Floating the Big Piney

How the river cools your blood is something you can't
   explain: you search the bottom stones for words
   unscientific, words fleshed with the sound of sense,
   maybe a chant laid upon the water the time
   words were all and fathers sang their sons ways
   to be and the river flowed sure of its pace.

You lie back in the canoe. Your own child points the bow
   now into the blue breath of sky: trees course
   overhead, and your eyes bend with pillars
   of air, the cornering birds; you lie back into
   the dream you know you'll have just once, a token
   from a far time, a river you can't explain.

All words are lost and you want to sing the meaning
    and origin of things, to make an appositive
    of light, something solid as a stone to hand
    this man-child. But all you have to offer is
    pause, the silence of water and the small
    knowledge that the river takes you over all.

La Plata, Missouri: Clear November Night

Last night in La Plata an avalanche of stars
buried the town in constant light the way the red
coalburners on the Santa Fe used to send fires

climbing night and falling back again, burning sheds,
hay, carriages, whatever was set along the track.
An avalanche of stars, last night the Leonids

fired every farm with ancient light, curdled milk
in Amish churns, and sent dogs howling through field
and tangled wood. Never was there such a night like

this. Lovers sprang from one another's arms, reeled
away from lurching cars and thoughts into a state
of starry wonder no human act could have revealed.

As if by common will, house lights went out. The late
work left, families settled out into the snow
unaware of cold, unaware of all except that state

which held us all for those long moments. We saw
and saw again the falling stars course Bear and Swan,
take field and farm, take all, and give it back as though

a gift given was given once again. Our lawn
on earth was full of promise in the snowing light.
Earthbound, we knew our engine on a rare November run.

Four Things Choctaw

1.
Nashoba. This my father taught
me how to sing: Wolf, I look long
for you—you know to hide your scrawn-
y hide behind the darkest wind.

2.
Isuba. Horse: not one less than
twenty hands and all fast as hounds
with foxes in their eyes and off.
Chahta isuba cheli. Once
Choctaws bred horses not many
winds could catch. Listen: isuba
still races winter's darkest wind.

3.
Baii. Notice the oak, the high
white bark, the heavy leaves, how they
fall. Winters are long in mountains:
springs freeze at the source and wind bows baii.

4.
Abukbo. The feather that all
my life I sought beyond the sun.
I have fashioned a sacred shaft,
smoothed it red with wet clay and poke.
The feather will guide its arc down
skies where grandfathers walk the woods
quick with game, heavy with the wind's wild mint.

A Sunday Dreamer's Guide to Yarrow, Missouri

for Brian and Sharon Bedard

The town is tilted toward the stream,
oblique as shadows toward twilight.
But only the stream is on the move.
No wind to shake the rusty leaves
off trees that have never known a spring.

Standing on the bridge, you think the town
a creeper, some gray vine, thirsting
after a force to drive it home
into the hill.

                   And on the hill
all the houses are asleep, or dead.
Rainbow Bread is basic metal now,
and Stamper Feeds has only ghosts
of gears. You want a flight of birds.

Yarrow was once a flowered town:
you think of mint. There is no one
to ask, no one to tell you now
where forebears lie.
                  There are echoes
you are afraid to hear. You look
hard into the water and put a leaf
lightly against an eyelid to see
who is in your thoughts. A vision
dances on the skin: it is you,
the dancer and the dance.

                   On the hill
a last fresh grave blooms prismatic
in its finality.

A Season of Loss

We left the horses in the draw
and climbed the painted ledge to see
the blue and distance home but saw
an autumn sun set fire to trees

on ridges we had yet to pass:
gnarled trees that burned and stood
more than a shifting phoenix, cast
in colors other than mild moods.

Our blood was now too thin to know
the half-moon brother, our skin too pale;
yet we, hands out, tried again to sow
our spirit in the stars. A frail

effort: our fathers' blood pulsed slow.
At our back a glyph grew perfect:
hard in stone a hand drew back to throw,
a sun stood still, a moon arced, sticks

grew into bones. Only human,
we touched thoughts, hands, eyes,
assured ourselves of the moment,
and leaned together hard against the sky.

Heartland

The houses die, and will not die.
The force of walls remains. Take
the family portrait hanging oval
on the wall and, underneath it
on the chifforobe, a dish of mints.

There are houses that fall, but their
shadows stay, lightly against a summer's
dusk. And there are photographs that
show ghosts of mothers walking halls,
of fathers fiddling in moonlight.

Even in disrepair, there's a life
to the houses. The rush of wind stirs
a soul: footfalls on wood and stone,
the creak of kitchen door, the last
words of a son gone away to war.

The houses die, and do not die.
There is something that will not let
a space be given solely to grass.
The aura holds, the center will
not fold, forever framed against
the graying sky, the coming night.

N. SCOTT MOMADAY

(1934–   )

The Bear

What ruse of vision,
escarping the wall of leaves,
rending incision
into countless surfaces,

would cull and color
his somnolence, whose old age
has outworn valor,
all but the fact of courage?

Seen, he does not come,
move, but seems forever there,
dimensionless, dumb,
in the windless noon's hot glare.

More scarred than others
these years since the trap maimed him,
pain slants his withers,
drawing up the crooked limb.

Then he is gone, whole,
without urgency, from sight,
as buzzards control,
imperceptibly, their flight.

Pit Viper

The cordate head meanders through himself:
Metamorphosis. Slowly the new thing,
Kindled to flares along his length, curves out.
From the evergreen shade where he has lain,
Through inland seas and catacombs he moves.
Blurred eyes that ever see have seen him waste,
Acquire, and undiminished: have seen death—
Or simile—come nigh and overcome.
Alone among his kind, old, almost wise,
Mere hunger cannot urge him from this drowse.

Earth and I Gave You Turquoise

Earth and I gave you turquoise
        when you walked singing
We lived laughing in my house
        and told old stories
You grew ill when the owl cried
We will meet on Black Mountain

I will bring corn for planting
        and we will make fire
Children will come to your breast
        You will heal my heart
I speak your name many times
The wild cane remembers you

My young brother's house is filled
        I go there to sing
We have not spoken of you
        but our songs are sad
When Moon Woman goes to you
I will follow her white way

Tonight they dance near Chinle
    by the seven elms
There your loom whispered beauty
    They will eat mutton
and drink coffee till morning
You and I will not be there

I saw a crow by Red Rock
    standing on one leg
It was the black of your hair
    The years are heavy
I will ride the swiftest horse
You will hear the drumming hooves

Four Notions of Love and Marriage

for Judith and Richardson Morse, their wedding

1.

Formerly I thought of you twice,
as it were.
Presently I think of you once
and for all.

2.

I wish you well:
that you are the runners of a wild vine,
that you are the roan and russet of dusk,
that you are a hawk and the hawk's shadow,
that you are grown old in love and delight,
I wish you well.

3.

Be still, lovers.
When the moon falls away westward,
there is your story in the stars.

4.

In my regalia,
in moccasins,
with gourd and eagle-feather fan,
in my regalia
imagine me;
imagine that I sing
and dance at your wedding.

The Story of a Well-Made Shield

    Now in the dawn before it dies, the eagle swings
low and wide in a great arc, curving downward
to the place of origin. There is no wind, but there
is a long roaring on the air. It is like the wind—
nor is it quite like the wind—but more powerful.

Rainy Mountain Cemetery

Most is your name the name of this dark stone.
Deranged in death, the mind to be inheres
Forever in the nominal unknown,
The wake of nothing audible he hears
Who listens here and now to hear your name.

The early sun, red as a hunter's moon,
Runs in the plain. The mountain burns and shines;
And silence is the long approach of noon
Upon the shadow that your name defines—
and death this cold, black density of stone.

Angle of Geese

How shall we adorn
Recognition with our speech?—
Now the dead firstborn
Will lag in the wake of words.

Custom intervenes;
We are civil, something more:
More than language means,
The mute presence mulls and marks.

Almost of a mind,
We take measure of the loss;
I am slow to find
The mere margin of repose.

And one November
It was longer in the watch,
As if forever,
Of the huge ancestral goose.

So much symmetry!—
Like the pale angle of time
And eternity.
The great shape labored and fell.

North Dakota, North Light

The cold comes about
among the sheer, lucent planes.

Rabbits rest in the foreground;
the sky is clenched upon them.

A glassy wind glances
from the ball of bone in my wrist
even as I brace myself,
and I cannot conceive
of summer;

and another man in me
stands for it,
wills even to remain,

figurative, fixed,

among the hard, hunchbacked rabbits,
among the sheer, shining planes.

To a Child Running
with Outstretched Arms
in Canyon de Chelly

You are small and intense
In your excitement, whole,
Embodied in delight.
The backdrop is immense;

The sand banks break and roll
Through cleavages of light
And shadow. You embrace
The spirit of this place.

The Burning

In the numb, numberless days
There were disasters in the distance,
Strange upheavals. No one understood them.
At night the sky was scored with light,
For the far planes of the planet buckled and burned.
In the dawns were intervals of darkness
On the scorched sky, clusters of clouds and eclipse,
And cinders descending.
Nearer in the noons
The air lay low and ominous and inert.
And eventually at evening, or morning, or midday,
At the sheer wall of the wood,
Were shapes in the shadows approaching,
Always, and always alien and alike.
And in the foreground the fields were fixed in fire,
And the flames flowered in our flesh.

GERALD VIZENOR

(1934–   )

White Earth

Images and Agonies

late october sun
breaks over the cottonwoods

tricksters
roam the rearview mirrors
government sloughs

colonial remembrance cards
capture trees
cultures close for the season

beaded crucifixion
double over in the reeds

shamans at the centerfolds
pave the roads
publish their poems

fiscal storms
close the last survival school

animals at the treelines
send back the hats and rusted traps

touchwood at bad medicine

March in North Dakota

the whole moon
burns behind jamestown

seven wings of geese
light the thin ice

asian sun
bleeds on the interstate

pressed flowers
tremble in the prairie stubble

paced on the mirror
my fingerprints blot the past

Shaman Breaks

1

colonists
unearth their wealth
and tease
the old stone man
over the breaks

moths batter
the cold windows
their light
is not our day

leaves abide the seasons
the last crows
smarten the poplars

2

tourists
discover their ruins
and mimic
the old stone woman
over the breaks

nasturtiums
dress the barbed wire
fences down
down to the wild sea

magnolias
bloom under a whole moon
words fall apart

3

soldiers
bleach the landscapes
hound the shamans

wild stories
break from the stones

Surrendered Names

late that summer
we concluded our longest war
behind the hand cream

outback at the dock
we promised the world to assassins
but no one ever died

the earth moved
we surrendered our names
carved on bricks

later we touch the wounds
hold our prisoners to the last season
change their names

Seasons in Santa Fe

Four Haiku:

mountain snow
warblers search the apricots
no apologies

the poplars chatter
our words come close to winter
hail on the lawn chairs

catalpa blossoms
spread over a new black car
catch our breath

social bees
wheel inside a paper cup
children at the park

PETER BLUE CLOUD

(1935–   )

To-ta Ti-om

for an aunt

my aunt was an herb doctor, one-eyed with crooked yellow
    teeth
       the Christians called her pagan witch
       and their children taunted her
       or ran in fear of their bible lives
          at her approach,
her house of barn lumber leaned into the wind as if toppling
       in winter it grew squat with snow
       and bright sparks from the wood stove
       hissed the snowflakes into steam
          icing the roof,
"when my body dies it will be in winter just in time to see
       the spring"
       she told this while rolling leaves
       to powder between her boney hands
       for her duty as a medicine person
          was to cure,
in early summer grandfather and i would begin planting
       the corn and beans and squash
       just behind my aunt's house
       and she'd hobble over to help
          plant the tobacco,
as the first green shoots emerged into sunlight
       she would sit on the steps
       grating dried roots into a bowl
       stopping every so often to gaze
          at the garden,

when the time of tobacco curing came she'd be there
    feeling and smelling and tasting
    and every season she would approve
    then later sit by the woodstove
        smoking her pipe,
"Come," she would say to me, "the time for onanoron is
        here,"
    and she would walk to the pond
    and she would point out strong plants
    for me to wade to and slowly pull
        those medicine roots,
we strung the roots of twisted brown above the woodstove
    to preserve their sacred power
    to be released as needed
    by those who had need
        of such strength,
tiny bundles were made of the roots with bits of string
    then she named the persons
    i was to take onanoron to
    and tied all in a blue bandana
        and said, "go,"
this is for Kaienwaktatse and this for Kaerine
    Lives Close to Town
    and She Bends the Boughs
    a penny or two and bread and jam
        I shyly ate,
the pennies slowly filled the glass jar on the table
    until my aunt went to the store
    a block of salt pork one finger square
    a nutmeg, salt and four candies
        just for me,
sitting there by the woodstove I would steal a glance
    at her tired wrinkled face
    and I'd want to shout loud
    feeling a tightening in my throat
        and maybe cry,

"she was sitting at her table with a bowl in her lap
　　and it was just turning Spring,"
　　my grandfather wrote this to me
　　and i went somewhere to be alone
　　　　and just sat,
it's planting time again and all done except tobacco
　　grandfather's leaning on the hoe
　　and looking at my aunt's house
　　then he smiles and I smile back
　　　　lonely, like crying.

Ochre Iron

Falling forever
with over and under
falling forever from
pink to purple bridgeways
my father's floating, falling,
decays many schemes
in youth's web-footed anger
　　of balance.

I wonder how many, if any,
boyhoods my father portrayed
upon my reservation's
　　starving soil,
or how many puppies yapped his heels
as over and over he fell,
or which of the mothers
cast shy eyes at fleeing feet,
　　and was it this
same lonesome loon
keening his sunset fears.

Falling forever
among wheeling stars
transfixed upon a canvas
        of universes,
my boot's sad dust
in vain retracing
a highway's straight
and naked hostility,
as over and under
        falling forever
I scream his outrage
to echoing hills and
vibrating steel bridges.
        I scream
                falling,
as cities collapse to my cry
and layer upon layer of lies
of twisted iron beams and braces
cut limbs tearing searing pains.

I wonder forever how many
if any, stole of rest within
the rich hayloft world
of another's dreaming,
and how many now deserted
campfires cast a warmth
in a taste of winter
found in hidden springs
        along that lonely highway.

Bent and twisted he sat
fashioning handles of hickory
with eyes always centered within
to stare down the pain,
so young to be an ancient
too tired to want anything,
smiling, at last, crookedly,
when death offered its dark robe.

And grandfather's bones stirred
once in mute grief, and made room
for the son he barely knew
and the pain was passed on
    and on
not only to another son,
but to a tribe.

And falling forever
with over and under,
I clutch at naked sky
to stand on firm earth,
    father,
I live you moment by moment.

Crazy Horse Monument

Hailstones falling like sharp blue sky chips
howling winds the brown grass bends, while
buffalo paw and stamp and blow billowing steam,
and prairie wolves chorus the moon in morning.

The spotted snake of a village on the move
a silent file of horses rounding hills,
in a robe of grey, the sky chief clutches thunder
and winter seeks to find the strongest men.

    Crazy Horse rides the circle of his people's sleep,
      from Little Big Horn to Wounded Knee,
    Black Hills, their shadows are his only robe
      dark breast feathers of a future storm.

Those of broken bodies piled in death,
of frozen blood upon the white of snow,
yours is now the sky chant of spirit making,
pacing the rhythm of Crazy Horse's mount.

And he would cry in anger of a single death,
and dare the guns of mounted soldiers blue,
for his was the blood and pulse of rivers,
and mountains and plains taken in sacred trust.

> Crazy Horse rides the circle of his people's sleep,
> from Little Big Horn to Wounded Knee,
> Black Hills, their shadows are his only robe
> dark breast feathers of a future storm.

And what would he think of the cold steel chisel,
and of dynamite blasting a mountain's face,
what value the crumbled glories of Greece and Rome,
to a people made cold and hungry?

To capture in stone the essence of a man's spirit,
to portray the love and respect of children and elders,
fashion instead the point of a hunting arrow sharp,
and leave to the elements the wearing-down of time.

> Crazy Horse rides the circle of his people's sleep,
> from Little Big Horn to Wounded Knee,
> Black Hills, their shadows are his only robe
> dark breast feathers of a future storm.

Yellowjacket

for Coyote

He rode into town upon a wild-eyed mountain horse
his hat pulled low and down his back and shoulders
swaying and blowing in wind, long black and grey hair,
and no one saw the eyes, but even the soldiers felt
themselves being studied, maybe as coldly as the wind
    blowing downriver,
man and horse, passing through town in silent watching
stirring along small puffs of dust and leaving behind
the strong odors of buckskin and cedar smoke,
"he carries a pistol besides that rifle," someone said,
and a young and respectful voice said, "a real bad one, too,
    I hear."
an old man, a healer who still dared perform the rituals
of curing, but in hiding from the eyes of soldier and
    missionary
hummed and muttered an old mountain song under his
    breath
and whispered, "a spirit rides with him, and he carries
a whole tribe; he is what remains of a tribe, and we, the
    ghosts."
"yes," said the sergeant, "another goddam fence has been
ripped down and dragged until tangled and useless. we give
the heathens a whole valley to live in, but it ain't good
enough for them, should round them up and shoot the lot,
like he was doing before; or at least the real bad ones,
    especially Yellowjacket."
with a half a butchered steer tied to his horse
he approached his sister's tiny shack at the edge of town,
"the deer are moved to the high mountains like me, don't
    like
the smell of oiled leather and iron stoves. here is meat
of a kind best left for the buzzards, but meat at least to eat."

another fence was torn down and three head of cattle
slaughtered, and the meat left at the edge of town, as a dare
to the hungry to take, and to eat and to live a while longer,
and a soldier, too, found with slit throat, a quick and
clean kill and no signs of cruelty or anger, a hunter killed
    by the hunted.
and mounted, the soldiers rode through town
and the people watched and knew a longing,
a feeling for a something lost, just out of reach,
but not a one of them mounted a horse or reached for a
    rifle,
but merely watched and waited, ashamed to raise their eyes
    to one another.
and they saw him, hatless and riding slowly, so slowly
into town, and the clean upriver mountain air wildly
blew his hair about, and as he passed he stared into
the eyes of each with no reproach, and each of them saw
the holes and streaming blood as he rode through their
    midst.
and was never seen again, and the talking, too, stopped
when his sister said to a crowd of them, "don't speak
of him again, you don't deserve his name." and they
watched her saddle up and take her child
and turn her back upon her husband and home and never
    look back.
and on that same evening, a few youngsters, too, saddled
up and for the first time in many seasons, openly
showed their rifles, and some old people joined them
and they rode upriver, up toward the clean air and
naked stone, and the soldiers saw them pass, and dared not
    interfere.

Turtle

The winds are dark passages among the stars,   ·
leading to whirling void pockets
encircled by seeds of thought,
life force of the Creation.
     I am turtle,
and slowly, my great flippers move
propelling my body through space,
and starflowers scatter crystals
which fall as mist upon my lidded eyes.
     I am turtle,
and the ocean of my life swim
is a single chant in the Creation,
as I pass others of my kind,
     my own, unborn, and those,
the holy ancients of my childhood.

My swim is steady and untiring
for great is the burden given me,
the praise and privilege of my eternity
rests upon my back as a single seed
to which I am guardian and giver.
     I am turtle,
and my tribes forever remain countless,
from the day I first raised my head
to gaze back upon the horn of my body,
     and my head was a sun,
     and Creation breathed life upon the seed
     and four times, and again four times,
     I wept for joy the birthing of my tribes,
     and chanted Creation the glory
of all these wondrous days.

The wrinkles and cracks upon this ancient shell
are the natural contours created
by the feel and request of burdened rock
and soil, blood and sustenance to
clans within clans,

I am turtle,
and the earth I carry is but
a particle in the greater Creation,
my mountains, plains and oceans,
mere reflections in a vaster sea.
Turtle, I am called,
and breathe clouds of rain,
and turn slowly my body to seasons
in cycle with my grandchild, Eagle,
whose wings enfold thunder pulses,
back to back, and
seldom meeting in time.

Patience was given me by Creation,
ancient song on tomorrow's wind,
this chant that was taught my tribes
is now unsung by many clans
of a single tribe,
and truly
such pains that exist for this moment,
which slay so many of the innocent
cannot but end in pain repeated
as all are reflected twins to self.
I am turtle,
and await the council of my tribes
clan into clan, the merging thought
that evil was never the star path, and
then the chant to the four directions,
I am turtle,
and death is not yet my robe,
for drums still throb the many
centers of my tribes, and a young
child smiles me of tomorrow,
"and grandparent,"
another child whispers, "please,
tell again my clan's beginning."

Bear:
A Totem Dance As Seen by Raven

for Ranoies

The black bear does a strange and shuffling dance
foot to foot slowly, head back, eyes closed
          like that of a man.
Beneath a loosely falling robe,
mouth sewn shut upon protruding tongue
          of red-stained cedar shreddings.
Foot to foot slowly in lumbering
                              shadow dance
within the fog and rain of high, thick ferns,
beneath a dripping, tapping spruce,
          echo of raven
morning cry of night visions unwanted.

A heavy, leaning snag it seems at first
the sound of crashing fall
               suspended
          between ground and lowered sky.
then swirl of fog unveils
               a huge head
carved atop the pole, a silver-grey of cedar.

Gnashing of angry teeth at driftwood shore
and killer whale spews up
               a wreckage
          of pock-infested sailors.

Foot to foot slowly, the totem dance continues,
sky to earth the leaning weight
                    of pole
          and people and bear
          and now the drum,
rectangular and fringed with clacking claws.

A chant begins of deep-voiced rumbling,
of the black slate carved
                into bowls now broken
with fragments scattered in despair
        of a death not prophesied.

Great cedar poles in moist earth,
these dwellings speak with dark passages,
        (the rib of a tribe is a brittle section
                        of a dugout
        or what is left
                of a stolen house post,
        vast heritage dragged
            into strange museums)

and still, and forever, foot to foot slowly
the strange and shuffling dance continues.
And day after day the mourning chants
and keening voices silence all else
                as dugouts
        with quiet paddles
convey the dead to sacred islands
        in endless procession.

And soil seeps thru roof cracks to fill
the huge and silent dwellings.
And totems lean from which
                great eyes
gaze either up to sky or down to earth,
And the death of a village is a great sorrow,
and the pain of the survivors
        is a great anguish
                never to heal.

Slowly and gently
        foot to foot balanced
and awkward in beauty
           the child dances.
And grandfather taps,
        delicately taps
the drum and his voice is very, very low,
    and the song is a promise
    given a people
in the ancient days of tomorrow.

And grandmother's stiff
        and swollen fingers
weave cedar and fern and spruce,
    and occasionally
    in a far away closeness
her eyes seek the dancing child.

The bear pauses in his quest for food
    to stand and sniff the air
then in a dream like a fasting
          he begins
    to shuffle
    foot to foot slowly
as the dance continues.

Wolf

burrowing deep into earth until the grave is complete,
hiding in daytime shadows, panting,
        sweat,
    dry matted blood
    and stump of a leg,
wolf, his growls into whimpers of pain unending.

she-wolf keening the stiffened, frozen cubs,
licking the frosted muzzles cyanide tracings, sweet
      the steaming meat
      she gently places
as an offering, through she knows they are dead.

run down to earth the snow with bursting heart
down to the bright red hammering pulse, and further
                down
      one by one
      the rifle shot
echo resounding a terrible, alien blood lust.

protruding, blackened tongues, no more the night chant,
blanket of sound, the earth her moaning,
             futile,
      her emptied womb,
      and the seed
dried and rustling among forgotten leaves.

a wind of running leaves across the prairie,
a scent of pine in frozen north the muskeg
      lakes
        lent footprints
      cast in sandstone
grains rubbing time the desert's constant edge.

softly contoured voices moaning night,
the wolves in circle council the moon
      shadows
        bent starlight
      of fingered sleet
rattles the gourd of earth down feathered roots.

beyond beginnings the earth her many tribes
and clans their life songs merge into one
     chant
       welcome dance
     to the unborn
awaiting birth in the sun-fingered dawn.

and to each creation the heartline trail
is etched in delicate memory pattern
     webs
       so intricate
     in a unity
of day into night the seasons follow.

the moaning low of wolves to ears of men
first wisdom gained by another's quiet
     song
       of meditation
     circle of council
bound together by their basic power.

and the quiet way of learning was the food
and spark the hearth of compassion warm
     enfolding
       all others
     born of earth
in the harmony of mutual need.

in thanks the minds of curious men
sought further wisdom from the brother
     wolf
       his clan
     a social order
of strength through lasting kinship.

and recognized the she-wolf's place
in balance with that of the male leader
        heads
                of family
        to be obeyed
because their first law was survival.

and studied the pattern of the hunt
where each had a particular role
        defined
                by need
        and acted upon
without the slightest hesitation.

and moaning low the wolf song,
head bent the drummer and voice to sky
        singer
                in thanks
        to brother wolf,
now your song will sing in our voices.

again the rifle shot and snapping jaws
of steel traps and poisoned bait,
the bounty hunter and fur trapper
        predators
        of greed
whose minds create vast lies.

and moaning low in death chant
the one remaining wolf staggers
        and falls
        to death
as winds carry his voice into tomorrow.

and the voice is an accusation howling
within the brain heart pulling sinews
        harshly
        you, too
I hang my death about your neck in circle.

mourn the buffalo and the beaver,
keen the fox and mountain cat,
        shout
        the grizzly
antelope elk moose caribou and many

more gone into death the prime breeders
to fashion garments of vanity,
        Indian,
        brother,
cleanse the blood lust from your naked spirit

and fast and pray your spirit's new growth
and be reborn into childhood innocence
        purity
        our maker
awaits your ancient promise.

the wolf in dream has petitioned
for his voice to be heard in council
        now
        in this place
        let us open our minds.

scattered and lost the people fall,
orphaned, the child feels hunger,
        where is tomorrow,
        where does it hide?
there are four voices coming
from four directions
        the center is harmony
        the center is beginning

scouts and messengers called back,
the council is the mind
            it is merging thought
            the nation's birth.
now when warriors feast,
they eat of embers
            of fire's heat
            stored energy.
the warrior society
is the wolf society
            is the clan family
            heart of tribe.
anger seeking wisdom,
council after meditation
            there is a vision
            held in sacred trust.

I dance upon my three remaining legs,
                              look,
the memory of the fourth keeps my balance,
                                    see,
my wispy white and cyanide fog-breath,
                              hah!
taut sinews vibrate the sky's held thunder,
                                huh!
steel traps I weave a necklace of your making,
                                  hah!
puffs of dust I quick-stomp with paw feet,
                              huh!
I am becoming you dancing for them,
                          hah!
I jump upon your back a heavy robe,
                          huh!
my shadow will nip your pumping ankle,
                              huh!
you will think you me in the full moon night,
                                  huh!

I crush your long bones sucking marrow,
nose your severed head before me the trail,
tear strips of flesh the ribbons weave a net,
chew hair and fingernails into mash
I slap upon my festered stump your human glue,

                                        hah!

now you are dancing,
                    brother
                                now you are dancing.

Within the Seasons

winter solstice

When darkness settles itself
upon a blanket of crystal snow
and stars are like piercing thoughts
of reason in the mind of Creation,
     we bank the hearth's fire, that
morning finds the children warm.

We taste last summer's gifts
of corn and beans and squash.
At winter's table we give thanks
and praise Creation in quiet song,
     then we too settle beneath robes
to dream the promise of tomorrow.

On a morning so brilliant that
load stirs the children to noisy play,
the maples call to us in rising sap
and a whole nation responds.
     Nothing else quite so festive as
the all night fires of a sugar camp.

spring equinox

Now day and night sit balanced.
From a silence that seemed forever,
the first booming crash of break-up
thunders from the river. Smiling,
        an elder oils the handle of a hoe
and listens for that great, warm wind.

Creation is a song, a trickling become
a gurgling, chuckling water voice.
Winds which bend the snows to melting
carry clouds of rain storms on shoulder.
        Green islands appear on turtle's back
grasses long asleep beneath the snow.

Dawn of a glorious season, flowers
in merging, undulating waves of color
The taste of strawberries, anticipate
in their blossoms, the rich and fertile
        smells of soil we bend to,
breaking the ground for summer's corn.

summer solstice

Come, bring the children. Let them
feel for a moment the rhythm
of the hoe. Let them experience
the wonder of green shoots emerging
        from earth, earth given us
in guardianship from the Creation.

Body, mind, and spirit full to bursting
with ripe, sweet berries, the first
tender green beans, and corn. We give
thanks, and thanks again. The twin
      concepts of Reason and Peace are
seen in each kernel of an ear of corn.

Perhaps we repair our lodges
as do the beavers living close by.
Our children swim like river otters
and as their laughter reaches us,
      we join them for a while
in these hottest of summer days.

autumn equinox

Again, day and night sit balanced
and the black bear begins to put on fat.
We begin harvesting mature crops
to store for winter. Our elders
      choose and carefully store away
the seeds to be planted in tomorrow.

That sacred song of departure,
dry cornstalks rustling in wind.
At their feet huge, fat pumpkins.
Above us, the sky darkens with
      a great passage of birds.
Again, we pause to give thanks.

Wood piled high close to lodges,
we walk upon crackling, brown,
frozen grasses. Evening calls to us,
softly, in gentle song. And soon
      the first large flakes of snow
call us to rest beneath winter's robe.

The Old Man's Lazy,

I heard the Indian Agent say,
has no pride, no get up
and go. Well, he came out
here and walked around my
place, that agent. Steps
all thru the milkweed and
curing wormwood; tells me
my place is overgrown
and should be made use
of.

The old split cedar
fence stands at many
angles, and much of it
lies on the ground like
a curving sentence of
stick writing. An old
language, too, black with
age, with different
shades of green of moss
and lichen.
      He always
says he understands us
Indians,
      and why don't
I fix the fence at least;
so I took some fine
hawk feathers fixed
to a miniature woven
shield
      and hung this
from an upright post
near the house.

He
came by last week
and looked all around
again, eyed the feathers
for a long time.
He didn't
say anything, and he didn't
smile even, or look within
himself for the hawk.

Maybe sometime I'll
tell him that the fence
isn't mine to begin with,
but was put up by
the white guy who used
to live next door.
It was
years ago. He built a cabin,
then put up the fence. He
only looked at me once,
after his fence was up,
he nodded at me as if
to show that he knew I
was here, I guess.
It was
a pretty fence, enclosing
that guy, and I felt lucky
to be on the outside
of it.
Well, that guy
dug holes all over his
place, looking for gold,
and I guess
he never
found any. I watched
him grow old for over
twenty years, and bitter,
I could feel his anger
all over the place.

        And
that's when I took to
leaving my place to do
a lot of visiting.
        Then
one time I came home
and knew he was gone
for good.

My children would
always ask me why I
didn't move to town
and be closer to them.

Now, they
tell me I'm lucky to be
living way out here.
        And
they bring their children
and come out and visit me,
and I can feel that they
want to live out here
too, but can't
for some reason, do it.

Each day
a different story is
told me by the fence,
the rain and wind and snow,
the sun and moon shadows,
this wonderful earth,
        this Creation.
I tell my grandchildren
many of these stories,
        perhaps
this too is one of them.

Rattle

When a new world is born, the old
turns itself inside out, to cleanse
and prepare for a new beginning.
                        It is
told by some that the stars are
small holes piercing the great
intestine
of a sleeping creature. The earth is
a hollow gourd and earthquakes are
gas rumblings and restless dreaming
of the sleeping creature.
                        What
sleeping plant sings the seed
shaken in the globe of a rattle,
the quick breath of the singer warms
and awakens the seed to life.

    The old man rolled fibres of
milkweed across his thigh, softly
speaking to grandchildren, slowly
saying
the thanksgiving to a sacred plant.

His left hand coiled the string as it
grew, thin and very strong; as he
explained the strength of a unity
of threads combined.
                        He took his
small basket of cocoons and poured
grains of coarse sand, poured from
his hand the coarse sand like a
funnel

Let us shake
the rattle
to call back
a rattlesnake
to dream back
the dancers.

When the wind
sweeps earth
there is fullness
of sound,
we are given
a beat
to dance by
and drum
now joins us

and flutes
are like gentle
birds and

crickets on
    branches,
swaying trees.
The fan of
winged hawks
brush clouds like
streaks of
white clay upon
a field
of blue sky

of wind, a cone between hand and
cocoon.

     Then, seven by seven, he bound
these nests to a stick with the
string,
and took the sap of white blood
of the plant, and with a finger,
rubbed
the encircling string.
          And waited, holding
the rattle to the sun for drying. And
when
he shook the first sound, the
children
sucked in their breaths and felt
strange
stirrings in their minds and
stomachs.
And when he sang the first song of
many,
the leaves of the cottonwood joined
in,
and desert winds shifted sand.
          And the
children closed their eyes, the better
  to hear tomorrow.

What sleeping plant sings the seed
in the gourd of night within the
hollow moon, the ladder going down,
down into the core of this good earth
leads to stars and wheeling suns
and
planets beyond count.
          What sound
is that in the moist womb of the sea;
the softly swaying motion in a

water base.
The seeds in

the pod
of a plant

are children
of the sun

of earth
that we sing
we are

a rainfall voice

a plumed

and sacred bird

we are

shadows come back

to protect
the tiny seedlings
we are
a memory in

single dance
which is all
dancing forever.
We are eyes
looking about

for the children
do they
run and play
our echos

multitude of sleeping seeds.
                    Maybe it
is rattlesnake, the medicine singer.
                    And
it is gourd, cocoon, seed pod, hollow
horn,
shell of snapping turtle, bark of
birch,
hollowed cedar, intestines of
creatures,
    rattle
is an endless element in sound and
vibration, singing the joys of
awakening,
shushing like the dry stalks of corn
in wind, the cradle songs of night.
    Hail-heavy wind bending upon
a roof of elm bark,
                    the howling song
of a midwinter blizzard heard by
a people sitting in circle close to
the fire. The fire is the sun, is the
burning core of Creation's seed,
sputtering
and seeking the womb of life.

    When someone asked Coyote, why
is there loneliness, and what is the
reason and meaning of loneliness:
Coyote
took an empty gourd and began
shaking
it, and he shook it for a long time.
                    Then
he took a single pebble and put it
into the gourd, and again began to
shake the gourd for many days, and
the pebble was indeed loneliness.

our former joys
in today?
Let us shake
the rattle
for the ancients

who dwell

upon this land

whose spirits
joined to ours
guide us

and direct us
that we
may ever walk
a harmony
that our songs
be clear.
Let us shake
the rattle
for the fliers

and swimmers

for the trees
and mushrooms
for tall grasses

blessed by

a snake's passage
for insects
keeping the balance,
and winds
which bring rain
and rivers

        Again
Coyote paused to put a handful of
pebbles into the gourd.
        And the sound
now had a wholeness and a meaning
beyond questioning.

going to sea
and all
things of Creation.
Let us
shake the rattle
    always, forever.

DUANE NIATUM

(1938–   )

Lines for Roethke Twenty Years after His Death

I

You asked us to hear the softest vocable of wind,
whether slow or swift, rising or falling to earth;
its fragments will drop in to place in the end.
You said, believe, endure, the ironies of birth!
If we succeeded in sleeping like thorns on a rose,
the nerves awake to the pulse, folklore of the sun,
the interior drifts may loosen, the nights freeze,
the passions whirl, not ramble until undone.
And no one colors the years black, but crow,
retouches the ruins, fakes the moon, pocks the beach.
Laugh right back, you sang, let it take hold,
it'll grow bored, forget whoever may be in reach.
Let your hand trace the riddle on the wave,
rejoice in the tale that leaves the ear a cave.

II

To give each death its light reflects the maze,
the promise bacteria also favor green.
You secretly burned your tracks to fan the blaze,
and warned the world'll tell us what to dream.
This is why you spoke in tongues to the vine,
wren, snail, bear, sloth, and swamp air.
You almost found an island without decline,

where roots kept your soul exposed to every layer.
You suggested we see the spirit's gift in the eye,
but the eye in the gut, the slug in the mossy field.
Taught us ghosts can love as well as mortify,
yet the heart's the actor; we must bow and yield.
When your body's a wheat impulse, nothing's stale;
even thunder's crack is music to the whale.

III

The mind follows currents deeper than any fish,
gropes with otter and duck for food in the river,
it knows water tumbling over rocks restores the flesh,
awaits the moon in the poplars, its first cover—
to meet extremes face to face, seed to seed,
be anonymous as a fly's grave at dark.
Fill solitude with creatures other than your need;
let the wolf take your shade, teach you to bark.
How to breathe with form? Proceed like the worm;
help desire cross the bridge of the brain;
it relieves paralysis, the wrong turn.
Kiss the petals before and after rain.
Climb out of yourself; edge in close to fate;
smell mortality like the lily on the lake.

IV

You scolded, we can't spin the wheel that spins night,
can't shed the scars from birth like old skin.
Better drift in your bones than with the kite;
better croak with bluejay, picking at the limb.
And imagination swims for the Muse on her shell,
while her tribe tickles our inner ear.
Don't mistake; her cymbals taunt the devil;

as she dances, he shreds like pulp all year
so we dream, barter seasons with the dead,
if we accept when they embrace, they cling.
All's headless as love, you sighed, all shapes you wed,
your senses burnt-orange, bold stranger to nothing
but yourself, your lips as white as Michigan snow.
Show us again how to reap the fire and glow.

Pieces

I

Her refusal to accept a room of solitude
in their house is why he pulls
the curtain on their comedy in black.

II

Since their song was erased the day she left,
he vows never to close the door
on a stranger. He will offer each new friend
what remains of her clay sculptures;
what the wounds have not yet dragged
deep into the forest's marsh.

III

Who appeared to answer the riddle they
confused with their dying cells?
Was it the wind come to whirl
more snow round his feet?

IV

The nerves snap even with the dead;
release the rainbirds with abuse;
name the animal stealing the dark from his blood
willowed to the window. What can he say
to the singers carrying his broken chain?

V

He told her there were days he felt
snared in a nightmare like a sparrow
in the eye of an owl. He also wondered if tied
to a boat mast, on violent water, would
he ask for a rest?

VI

The moment he saw himself asleep in another
bed between two yellow sheets,
he no longer wove a labyrinth
in and around his graves.

VII

Those pine roots exposed to wind and ice
are what prove the childhood hurdles
he made on the run, not his blood
at cross-currents, nor scars in revolt.

VIII

A man shatters all but the heartbeats.
He knows when his shoes touch pavement
the street will be the guide.

IX

A woman who struts in her beauty,
without holding a little earth in her hand
as the sun warms her cheeks,
may miss the moon when it powders
the mirror's stick figures.

X

His father abandoned the house when
he was six. The thought that he
is his father's shadow creates a macabre
phantom that pulls in the walls.

XI

The stars are the companions that endure us.

XII

He takes nightly walks to accommodate the spirit,
since the day mocks the minor suicides.

XIII

Drunk at the end of the night's film,
he laughs at the face on the wall because
the face in the moon is not laughing.

XIV

He stares into the teacup out of awe,
rarely vanity. The eyes grow raven,
and the flight of wings are his.

XV

The women he loved and lost before she
took grief for a permanent ride
are never far away. Like her, they carved
into his spirit the gift
to make the same mistake.

XVI

He did give her fair warning
that each abyss is servant to a scar,
even the songs relinquished to the sea.

XVII

He admitted his sufferings are small
and occasional; they will find new pieces
in the junkyard of the age.
They know better than to complain of the burden.

XVIII

This story is a tribute to her art
and a stone at the bottom of the river,
but a stone that shares the rapids with you.

First Spring

Drifting off the wheel of a past
looking like a redskin American gothic,
staring through forty-one years
of rain-pelted windows, I bear
with modest grace, diminished nerves,
narrowing light, half-formed figures:
the memories floating in purgatory.

Renting a small house, the first
in fifteen years, I admire each hour
the diffidence of the elders walking by,
their snow-cave eyes, their hands
dancing like puppets. When a lost love
calls, having abandoned another,
I say,—*sorry, sorry, I'm too*

busy with the friends still left.
I'll call you. The lie of copper on my tongue.
Why tell her they're the birds at the feeder,
bees in the lilacs, roses, and plum trees,
books on the shelves and everywhere,
paintings on the walls, wind at the door
and on the roof?

　　It is called giving your body
　　a river to jump into,
　　it is called giving your brain cells
　　a field to get planted in.
　　It is called standing on your head
　　before the women you lost,
　　sleeping in the embers of your name.

The Reality of Autumn

In my season as red as the red-breasted
woodpecker, I am the parts I fall from;
the urban accidents climbing from the ditch,
the years in reverse before eclipse;
the voices cracking like pods,
too weary to break the glass wheels
of the mirror, dance with the cubistic
caravan, the teeter-totter benefactors.

As the incurables in the photographs fade
with the sun, the day withdraws, takes
the fire, what I built from scars,
the earth, the mythology of dream.
What does it matter that I am
the animal whose one pliant structure
dies a song? So I look for the birth
of myself once more in the eyes of a woman
whose seesaw gift is joy and pain.
To mold the dark to the dark.

Maggie

She skips on to the day's next blue radius,
a tulip weaving down the summer hill.

She circles with the sun on a wind beat,
her dress, the color of its equinox.

She inhales the impossible, light's fragrances.
When she blows a kiss to the Monarch,

death loses the laughter, the wheel rolling
back, the air. Just nine, cruelty hasn't

flipped her spine like a penny, chance
mined her dream with its arbitrary surprise.

Even the lilacs in her hair haven't heard
the earth call with its tuning fork of bees.

And when she swirls round her home on a dare,
even the rain begins to fall yellow.

The Traveler

He still believes by middle-age
that freedom is a bread
to break every day. He wants
to go on resisting the narrow,
search for what form of rose will grow
from a plane, a train,
a candle-lit café.

He thinks to be another stranger
in the night is perfect;
night figures are seldom wasted.
He welcomes the accidental,
the unknown woman he might meet.
To the hour, he stumbles
with the blind for sight.

He walks in the country when the sky
clears. In the town
of Kinderdijk, windmills
hint of the tenth century.
Far from his red earth,
he mourns what the Dutch have lost,
seeing the world is out
of balance even there.

The days spent in museums make
him weary but the Brueghels,
Goyas, Rubens, mark their worth.
From Amsterdam to Paris
to Copenhagen, his spirit seeks to mix
his life like the colors on their palettes,
while his body sips its sherry.

To enjoy the people, the speech,
the cadence of train and bus
and boat, he empties his mind
of the global pollution,
the bottles and cans and stench
of each consumer institution,
all obsessions, why
his family calls him odd.

His woman-friend says the storms
could be worse, he should
explore the wind-funneled sand hills,
the force, face the sea,
let mind and body divorce and remarry,
navigate the winter course.

Though fond of her and the Netherlands,
he mentions the inverted scenes,
the salmon self that smells
nuclear rain, nuclear thunder, our blue
labyrinth of pain, the iceberg
he slept on through recent dreams.

Who hasn't thought these clouds might
ignite the globe, their
ominous showers penetrate our flesh,
soak us in their radial,
atmospheric mesh?
Who hasn't heard his own blood
dry at the bone?

But perhaps one morning he'll awake
to find it has been
merely an outhouse joke of Raven.
Now a stone mask, there is the chance
his will is getting even,
found the path to being a sand grain.

Snowy Owl near Ocean Shores

Snowy Owl, storm cast from the arctic tundra,
sits on a stump in an abandoned farmer's
field. Beyond the dunes cattails dance as steady
as the surf, rushing and crashing down the jetty.

From two-hundred feet away he seems to spot
a meal crawl from mud hole to grass-patch.
When half an hour passes and nothing darts,
a North Pole creature shows us how to last.

The wind ruffles his feathers from crown to claws
while he continues gazing at the salt-slick rain.
So when a double-rainbow arced the sky
before us, we left him to his white refrain.

Apology

> *But a man cannot learn heroism from*
> *another,*
> *he owes the world some death of his own*
> *invention.*
>> William Meredith
>> *Dying Away*

Great Uncle Joe,
can you hear me keen?
Now that my temples are as salt and pepper as yours
I am a weed in the wind
on the path to your house.

I still awake in the night
to the moment you said, *don't, don't stare at him,*
when my eyes rolled and snagged.
You knew I had no choice but to follow
my mind pulling me so close to the elder man
in the next bed that my breath was his,
and his mine. Trapped in confusion's tide
I fought for the courage that would stop
my knees from knocking against your bed,
my head from spinning out the door.
To keep me steady you told of how your own
youth snapped nerve by nerve.

On the next visit you admitted
your neighbor had died by morning.
No, you did not shake your head in loathing.
Instead, you spoke in the way of our ancestors,
the Klallams, Swinomish, and Snohomish,
that it was good I had turned from him
whose owl had torn a hole in the window.

Great Uncle Joe,
can you see my hand reaching for yours?
I am a weed in the field of your totem,

the hawk, because your face was free of scorn;
a weed rooted to this shame for more than
two decades after your death, yet loyal
to your path, my grandfather's, and your sister's
who gave me your father's name,
why, I don't know, and sense she too is dead,
will never know. Cedar man,
I bury my youth on your land; its red earth
shields my song woven into the years for you
and the body of rock on Old Patsy's mound,
for mine, chanting to be near yours,
when I am the elder in the next bed.

Drawings of the Song Animals

I

Treefrog winks without springing
from its elderberry hideaway.
Before the day is buried in dusk
I will trust the crumbling earth.

II

Foghorns, the bleached absence
of the Cascade and Olympic mountains.
The bay sleeps in a shell of haze.
Anchorless as the night,
the blue-winged teal dredges for the moon.

III

Thistle plumed,
a raccoon pillages my garbage.
When did we plug its nose with concrete?
Whose eyes lie embedded in chemicals?

IV

Dams abridge the Columbia Basin.
On the rim of a rotting barrel,
a crow. The imperishable remains
of a cedar man's salmon trap.

V

Deer crossing the freeway—
don't graze near us, don't trust our signs.
We hold your ears in our teeth,
your hoofs on our dashboards.

VI

Shells, gravel musings from the deep,
dwellings from the labyrinth of worms.
Crabs crawl sideways into another layer of dark.

VII

Bumblebee,
a husk of winter and the wind.
I will dance in your field
if the void is in bloom.

VIII

A lizard appears, startled by my basket
of blackberries. In the white
of the afternoon we are lost to the stream.
Forty years to unmask the soul!

The Art of Clay

The years in the blood keep us naked to the bone.
So many hours of darkness we fail to sublimate.
Light breaks down the days to printless stone.

I sing what I sang before, it's the dream alone.
We fall like the sun when the moon's our fate.
The years in the blood keep us naked to the bone.

I wouldn't reach your hand, if I feared the dark alone;
My heart's a river, but is not chilled with hate.
Light breaks down the days to printless stone.

We dance for memory because it's here on loan.
And as the music stops, nothing's lost but the date.
The years in the blood keep us naked to the bone.

How round the sky, how the planets drink the unknown.
I gently touch; your eyes show it isn't late.
Light breaks down the days to printless stone.

What figures in this clay; gives a sharper hone?
What turns the spirit white? Wanting to abbreviate?
The years in the blood keep us naked to the bone.
Light breaks down the days to printless stone.

PAULA GUNN ALLEN

(1939–   )

Taku Skanskan

that history is an event
that life is
that I am event
ually to go do something
the metaphor for god.
eventuality.
activity.

what happens   *to be.*
what happens   *to me.*
god. history. action.
the Lakota word for it is:
whatmovesmoves.
they don't call god
"what moves something,"
not "prime mover"
"first mover" or
"who moves everything or nothing;"
not "action." "lights." "movement."
not "where" or "what" or "how"
but
event.   GOD
is what happens, is:
movesmoves.

riding a mare.
eventuality.
out of the corral into morning
taking her saddled and bridled
air thick with breath movesmoves
horsebreath, mybreath, earthbreath
skybreathing air. ing.
breathesbreathes movesmoves
in the cold. winterspringfall.
corral. ing. horse and breath.
air. through the gate moveswe.
lift we the wooden crossbar
movesmoves unlocks movesbreathes
lifebreath of winter soul
swings wide sweet corral gate
happens to be frozenstiff in place
happens to be cold. so I and mare
wear clothes that move in event
of frozen. shaggy hair dressers for the air
breathes breathe we: flows: movesmoves:
god it's cold.
no other place but movesmoves
horse me gate hinge air bright frost lungs
swing gate out far morning winter rides
movesmovingmoves Lakota words: god.
what we do.

Dear World

Mother has lupus.
She says it's a disease
of self-attack.
It's like a mugger broke into your home
and you called the police
and when they came they beat up on you
instead of on your attackers,
she says.

I say that makes sense.
It's in the blood,
in the dynamic.
A half-breed woman
can hardly do anything else
but attack herself,
her blood attacks itself.
There are historical reasons
for this.

I know you can't make peace
being Indian and white.
They cancel each other out.
Leaving no one in the place.
And somebody's gotta be there,
to take care of the house,
to provide the food.
And that's gotta be the mother.
But if she's gone to war.
If she's beaten and robbed.
If she's attacked by everyone.
Conquered, occupied, destroyed
by her own blood's diverse strains,
its conflicting stains?

Well, world. What's to be done?
We just wait and see
what will happen next
The old ways go,
tormented in the fires of disease.
My mother's eyes burn,
they tear themselves apart.
Her skin darkens in her fire's heat,
her joints swell to the point
of explosion, eruption.
And oh, the ache: her lungs
don't want to take in more air,
refuse further oxygenation:
in such circumstances,
when volatile substances are intertwined,
when irreconcilable opposites meet,
the crucible and its contents vaporize.

Meditations on the Moon

1. What the Moon Said

The moon lives in all the alone places
all alone. "There are things
I work out for myself," she says.
"You don't have to be depressed about them.
These are my places, and walking through them
is my right. You don't need to care
when I'm down.

"Or if I'm mad at myself, don't believe
I'm mad at you. If I glare it is not
your face I am staring at but my own.
If I weep, it is not your tears that flow.

"And if I glow with the brush of twilight wings
if I rise round and warm above your bed,
if I sail through the irridescent autumn spaces
heavy with promise, with red and fruity light,
and leave your breath tangled in the tossing tops
of trees as I arise,
as I speed away into the far distance,
disappearing as you gaze, turning silver, turning white,
it is not your glory I reflect.
It is not your love that makes me pink,
copper, gold. It is mine."

The moon moves along the sky by her own willing.
It is her nature to shed some light, sometimes
to be full and close, heavy with unborn thought
on rising. It is her nature sometimes
to wander in some distant place, hidden, absent, gone.

Soundings

I

On such a day as this
something unknown, familiar stirs—
is it a thought? A breeze? A voice gotten through
the great sweep of space between there and here?
There, see just ahead that rise?
The turn in the path, just beneath those boughs
heavy with green, ground piled with needles,
mounds of old leaves, variegated moss,
sky deep with clouds, a-splatter with rain,
its soft sound?

Teeming, tangled growth of sun, riotous, congruent,
like life's unthinking scatterings of deeds, thoughts, wants,
loves, rages, delights, imaginings, and griefs
fallen soft through years onto shadowed,
iron-rich decay, earth spent
in the multitudes of unions, her vital force
shattered, splintering in the air.

How have I come here? Is this a time long told
in English tales about the journey some green knight
takes to find something that gleams with unearthly light,
to find it in some unearthly place?
Is the life-giving girdle something I must penetrate?

And do I now or just recently face
a new rise that when climbed
looks on another country far below
where beings other than the human ones we know
walk, singing spells, calling, eluding sight?

What stirs? A slender branch, heavy with fragrance,
hung with leaf and bud, whose petals
touched by wind, blown and swayed,
ring softly in my ear? Is it leaflight, sunlife,
undone from sky, falling into leaves,
transforming into sullen wood and brooding seed,
falling again into darkening shade, running down
as through successive lives,
to finally come to roost, exhausted, in the soil
to serve at last as mulch and mineral for the trees?
(Can light take root in clay unaided, unalloyed?)

Alone and long among the towering trees
safe in shadow, watching flickering brightness filter
through the narrow ridge of sight among the leaves,
I walk a path that faintly mars the ground,
deer walk, raccoon road, mouse path, snake slither slide,
so faint the track I pick my way along
half by belief, half by fear and rage.

I find a way however tangled, shadowy, brambled,
   overgrown,
seeking as much with fingertip as sight
as much with inward hearing as with outer ear.
I listen to soundings familiar from some other time
water falling, rippling, spray whispering, rising spume:
not a moan, not a sigh, not a sound I can describe
except to say it's the sound of petal fall,
along that line, or swift spray of inward wind
that rises and surrounds,
as though the air had voice to give its thought a form,
and craft to make and fire neurons to its call,
to shape living clay thrown and fired in tune
with another world of needs and tastes, other worldly
   minds.

Listen. Hear it?

It's not exactly water's fall, though it sounds as sweet;
it's not breath of fawn, not murmur of twilight bird
settling her feathers around her for the night;
it's not the sharp goldspray of dawn
presaging full daylight
on earthen place, on mortal lakes or streams.

The sound of which I speak
is not the rustle, soft, of tender new spring's leaves.
It's the voice of something gone forever,
of something over and over returned;
something like the sound of love, enspelling,
runic, tantric, budding, encanting, decanted, spilling,
a certain sound, fallen from another place,
some traveler's tale brought from dreamlike space,
not surreal, not like that sort of case,
but spilled perfume,
taste-of-honey when shimmering in the hive,
sound almost remembered, almost lost, ever alive.

On such a day as this
in a familiar fluster of fresh-sprung air
from somewhere other than here,
I hear the sound again
and stop,
hold my breath close within my chest
like a mother holds a child still
so she might hear some whisper she can't quite hear
and listens, teary-eyed, wonder-filled. So I
awaken once again to something recognized this morning
something at other times forgot.

Is it this that stirs like petals rippling in soft wind,
something neither air nor thought
that sprung from shadow and thick with grace
comes into view, momentarily sharp and dear,
elusive as memory, clear as crystal space,
a radiance exhaled by teeming plenitude,
a half caught vision of a half remembered place,
like yet unlike this where I sit and contemplate
what is so sweet as lightly it emanates
a familiar fragrance that falls,
soft as mist upon my every life,
caught brief for a tangled moment
in a certain kind of light.

Kopis'taya, A Gathering of Spirits

Because we live in the browning season
the heavy air blocking our breath,
and in this time when living
is only survival, we doubt the voices
that come shadowed on the air,

that weave within our brains
certain thoughts, a motion that is soft,
imperceptible, a twilight rain,
soft feather's fall, a small body dropping
into its nest, rustling, murmuring, settling
in for the night.

Because we live in the hardedged season,
where plastic brittle and gleaming shine,
and in this space that is cornered and angled,
we do not notice wet, moist, the significant
drops falling in perfect spheres
that are the certain measures of our minds;
almost invisible, those tears,
soft as dew, fragile, that cling to leaves,
petals, roots, gentle and sure,
every morning.

We are the women of the daylight, of clocks
and steel foundries, of drugstores
and streetlights, of superhighways
that slice our days in two. Wrapped around
in plastic and steel we ride our lives;
behind dark glasses we hide our eyes;
our thoughts, shaded, seem obscure.
Smoke fills our minds, whisky husks our songs
polyester cuts our bodies from our breath,
our feet from the welcoming stones of earth.
Our dreams are pale memories of themselves
and nagging doubt is the false measure
of our days.

Even so, the spirit voices are singing,
their thoughts are dancing in the dirty air.
Their feet touch the cement, the asphalt
delighting, still they weave dreams upon our
shadowed skulls, if we could listen.
If we could hear.

Let's go then. Let's find them.
Let's listen for the water, the careful
gleaming drops that glisten on the leaves,
the flowers. Let's ride
the midnight, the early dawn.
Feel the wind striding through our hair.
Let's dance the dance of feathers,
the dance of birds.

JIMMIE DURHAM

(1940–   )

Columbus Day

In school I was taught the names
Columbus, Cortez, and Pizzaro and
A dozen other filthy murderers.
A bloodline all the way to General Miles,
Daniel Boone and General Eisenhower.

No one mentioned the names
Of even a few of the victims.
But don't you remember Chaske, whose spine
Was crushed so quickly by Mr. Pizzaro's boot?
What words did he cry into the dust?

What was the familiar name
Of that young girl who danced so gracefully
That everyone in the village sang with her—
Before Cortez' sword hacked off her arms
As she protested the burning of her sweetheart?

That young man's name was Many Deeds,
And he had been a leader of a band of fighters
Called the Redstick Hummingbirds, who slowed
The march of Cortez' army with only a few
Spears and stones which now lay still
In the mountains and remember.

Greenrock Woman was the name
Of that old lady who walked right up
And spat in Columbus' face. We
Must remember that, and remember
Laughing Otter the Taino, who tried to stop
Columbus and who was taken away as a slave.
We never saw him again.

In school I learned of heroic discoveries
Made by liars and crooks. The courage
Of millions of sweet and true people
Was not commemorated.

Let us then declare a holiday
For ourselves, and make a parade that begins
With Columbus' victims and continues
Even to our grandchildren who will be named
In their honor.
Because isn't it true that even the summer
Grass here in this land whispers those names,
And every creek has accepted the responsibility
Of singing those names? And nothing can stop
The wind from howling those names around
The corners of the school.

Why else would the birds sing
So much sweeter here than in other lands?

A Woman Gave Me a Red Star to Wear on My Headband

We say that a loon, most graceful and dark
Of all water birds, sings a song
That makes stars fall onto its back,
And that is why a loon has those white spots.

The people sing for changes.

In the history of my people it is found,
"In 1833 stars fell," in a list of great events
Such as, "In 1814 we won a battle against
The soldiers."

The people remember changes.

It is known that we collected the iron
Of meteors and made of it knives like birds,
And impressed into the red hot knife blades
Patterns of stars. Star knives from that time
Are displayed in museums of the Americas, but
The Americans know nothing about patterns.

The people search for changes.

The Comanche chief Quanah followed the cult
Of Waterbird Dreamers, and in his old age painted
Stars on his roof. A Comanche friend of mine
Goes all over the hemisphere
Collecting what he calls "indigenous red stars."
Woven into blankets, painted on leather, spoken of
In stories, thought of—

The people prepare for changes.

Middle

In the middle of our times
There were so many battles
So many kinds of fights
Friends and brothers dropped
Before they knew what hit them.

Children went away as they made their first war cries
At the unfocused enemy.

We sang for our children
As we swatted hornets
In the cattle stampede.

Much passed by us,
And friends lost the use of their hands.
But in dances come from anguish
Expressible only by bodies
We held council with the universe.

The stars, eagles, loons and coyotes
Sang, "Time is with you."
"History is on your side."
Trees gave seeds.
And rocks encouraged.

Justiniano Lamé Has Been Killed

Justiniano Lamé has been killed.
It doesn't matter what year—
This year. During this long season
Of Indians being killed.

Jimmy Little has also been killed.
Anna Mae Aquash has also been killed.
Byron De Sersa has been killed.
Buddy Lamont has been killed.
Frank Clearwater has been killed.
Wes Bad Heart Bull has been killed.
Osceola has been killed.
Sitting Bull has been killed.
Red Bird Smith has been killed.

In Nicaragua Somoza bombs Indian villages.
In Paraguay the ranchers hunt Indians.
In Uruguay the last Indian was displayed in a cage,
And in Brazil Indians are caged in parks.

Before Justiniano Lamé was killed
He used to say,
Viva la unidad de todos los explotados.

After he was killed
the people said,
La mejor manera de recordar los compañeros caídos
En la lucha, es fortaleciendo nuestra organización,
Para enfrentar la represión, conquistar nuestras tierras
Y todos nuestros derechos.
The best way to honor our comrades who have fallen
In the struggle is to strengthen our organization,
To confront repression, regain our land and all
Our rights.

Justiniano Lamé has been killed,
But many have not.
I have not been killed,
And you have not been killed.

Justiniano Lamé was a Jaguar,
And there are Pumas, Cougars, Ocelots,
Panthers, and Mountain Lions.

We are the brothers and sisters
Who can bring a new season
For Justiniano Lamé.

JAMES WELCH

(1940–   )

Surviving

The day-long cold hard rain drove
like sun through all the cedar sky
we had that late fall. We huddled
close as cows before the bellied stove.
Told stories. Blackbird cleared his mind,
thought of things he'd left behind, spoke:

"Oftentimes, when sun was easy in my bones,
I dreamed of ways to make this land."
We envied eagles easy in their range.
"That thin girl, old cook's kid, stripped naked
for a coke or two and cooked her special stew
round back of the mess tent Sundays."
Sparrows skittered through the black brush.

That night the moon slipped a notch, hung
black for just a second, just long enough
for wet black things to sneak away our cache
of meat. To stay alive this way, it's hard. . . .

Harlem, Montana: Just Off the Reservation

We need no runners here. Booze is law
and all the Indians drink in the best tavern.
Money is free if you're poor enough.

Disgusted, busted whites are running
for office in this town. The constable,
a local farmer, plants the jail with wild
raven-haired stiffs who beg just one more drink.
One drunk, a former Methodist, becomes a saint
in the Indian church, bugs the plaster man
on the cross with snakes. If his knuckles broke,
he'd see those women wail the graves goodbye.

Goodbye, goodbye, Harlem on the rocks,
so bigoted, you forget the latest joke,
so lonely you'd welcome a battalion of Turks
to rule your women. What you don't know,
what you will never know or want to learn—
Turks aren't white. Turks are olive, unwelcome
alive in any town. Turks would use
your one dingy park to declare a need for loot.
Turks say bring it, step quickly, lay down and dead.

Here we are when men were nice. This photo, hung
in the New England Hotel lobby, shows them nicer
than pie, agreeable to the warring bands of redskins
who demanded protection money for the price of food.
Now, only Hutterites out north are nice. We hate
them. They are tough and their crops are always good.
We accuse them of idiocy and believe their belief all wrong.

Harlem, your hotel is overnamed, your children
are raggedy-assed but you go on, survive
the bad food from the two cafes and peddle
your hate for the wild who bring you money.
When you die, if you die, will you remember
the three young bucks who shot the grocery up,
locked themselves in and cried for days, we're rich,
help us, oh God, we're rich.

The Man from Washington

The end came easy for most of us.
Packed away in our crude beginnings
in some far corner of a flat world,
we didn't expect much more
than firewood and buffalo robes
to keep us warm. The man came down
a slouching dwarf with rainwater eyes,
and spoke to us. He promised
that life would go on as usual,
that treaties would be signed, and everyone—
man, woman, and child—would be inoculated
against a world in which we had no part,
a world of money, promise and disease.

Snow Country Weavers

A time to tell you things are well.
Birds flew south a year ago.
One returned, a blue-wing teal
wild with news of his mother's love.

Mention me to friends. Say
wolves are dying at my door,
the winter drives them from their meat.
Say this: say in my mind

I saw your spiders weaving threads
to bandage up the day. And more,
those webs were filled with words
that tumbled meaning into wind.

Magic Fox

They shook the green leaves down,
those men that rattled
in their sleep. Truth became
a nightmare to their fox.
He turned their horses into fish,
or was it horses strung
like fish, or fish like fish
hung naked in the wind?

Stars fell upon their catch.
A girl, not yet twenty-four
but blonde as morning birds, began
a dance that drew the men in
green around her skirts.
In dust her music jangled memories
of dawn, till fox and grief
turned nightmare in their sleep.

And this: fish not fish but stars
that fell into their dreams.

SIMON J. ORTIZ

(1941–   )

Dry Root in a Wash

The sand is a fine grit
and warm to the touch.
An old juniper root
lies by the cutbank of sand;
it lingers, waiting
for the next month of rain.

I feel like saying,
It will rain, but you know
better than I these centuries
don't mean much
for anyone to be waiting.

Upstream, towards the mountains,
the Shiwana work for rain.

They know we're waiting.

Underneath the fine sand
it is cool
with crystalline moisture,
the forming rain.

A Story of How a Wall Stands

At Acu, there is a wall almost 400 years old
which supports hundreds of tons of dirt and
bones—it's a graveyard built on a steep in-
cline—and it looks like it's about to fall
down the incline but will not for a long
time.

My father, who works with stone,
says, "That's just the part you see,
the stones which seem to be
just packed in on the outside,"
and with his hands puts the stone and mud
in place. "Underneath
what looks like loose stone,
there is stone woven together."
He ties one hand over the other,
fitting like the bones of his hands
and fingers. "That's what is
holding it together."

"It is built that carefully,"
he says, "the mud mixed
to a certain texture," patiently
"with the fingers," worked
in the palm of his hand. "So that
placed between the stones, they hold
together for a long, long time."

He tells me those things,
the story of them worked
with his fingers, in the palm
of his hands, working the stone
and the mud until they become
the wall that stands a long, long time.

Spreading Wings on Wind

a plane ride from Rough Rock to Phoenix
Winter Indian 1969

I must remember
that I am only one part
among many parts,
not a singular eagle
or one mountain. I am
a transparent breathing.

Below are dark lines of stone,
fluff of trees, mountains
and the Earth's People—all of it,
the Feather in a prayer.

Faint, misty clouds,
a sudden turbulence,
and steady, the solid earth.

"It looks like a good road,"
from Piñon to Low Mountain.
It branches off to First Mesa
and then Second and Third Mesa.

The Hopi humanity
which is theirs and ours.

Three of the Navajo Mountains
in our vision, "Those mountains
over there, see their darkness
and strength, full of legends,
heroes, trees, the wind, sun."

East, West, North, and South.
Those Directions and Mountains.
Mountain Taylor, San Francisco Peak,
Navajo Mountain, Dibentsaa.
The Navajo mind must have been
an eagle that time.

Breathe like this on the feather
and cornfood like this, this way.

Sometime before there were billboards
advertising Meteor Crater,
there must have been one hell of a jolt,
flame and then silence.
After many years, flowers and squirrels,
snow streaking down inside the cone.

Over Winslow is the question,
"Who the hell was Winslow, some cowboy?"
A miner? Surveyor? Missionary?
The forests are neatly trimmed hedges;
mines are feeble clawings at the earth.

What the hell are you doing to this land?
My grandfather hunted here, prayed,
dreamt; one day there was a big jolt,
flame, and then silence,
just the clouds forming.

Bend in the River

Flicker flies by.
His ochre wing
is tied to prayer sticks.
Pray for mountains,
the cold strong shelter.

Sun helps me to see
where Arkansas River
ripples over pebbles.
Glacial stone moves slowly;
it will take a while.

A sandbank cuts sharply
down to a poplar log
buried in damp sand.
Shadow lengths tell me
it is afternoon.

There are tracks
at river's edge, raccoon,
coyote, deer, crow,
and now my own.

My sight follows
the river upstream
until it bends.
Beyond the bend
is more river
and, soon, the mountains.
We shall arrive,
to see, soon.

Watching You

for Joy

I watch you
from the gentle slope
where it is warm
by your shoulder.
My eyes are closed.
I can feel the tap
of your blood
against my cheek.
Inside my mind,
I see the gentle move
ment of your valleys,
the undulations
of slow turnings.
Opening my eyes,
there is a soft dark
and beautiful butte
moving up and then down
as you breathe.
There are fine
and very tiny ferns
growing, and I can
make them move
by breathing.
I watch you with my skin
moving upon yours,
and I have known you well.

Wind and Glacier Voices

Laguna man said,
I only heard that glacier scraping
once, thirty thousand years ago.
My daughter was born then.
                              —a storytelling, continuing
                                 voice—

West of Yuma, a brown man murmurs
the motion of the solar wind.
                              —a harsh, searing
                                 voice—

Please don't tell me
how to live;
I've always lived this way.
                              —a protesting
                                 voice—

the last time I was in Fargo
I thought I heard the echo
of a glacier scraping.
                              —a remembering,
                                 beckoning
                                 voice—

And the wind, solar,
the big wind will come.
Solar, it will come.
It will pass by and through
and with everything.
                              —a longing, whispering,
                                 prophetic
                                 voice—

Returned from California

At the park
yesterday afternoon,
I found a dead crow
by the roots of a cottonwood.

Death is a bundle
of black feathers,
leather-lined dry holes
for eyes,
withered yellow feet.

Other crows
hollered from branches
above a scatter
of human garbage.
They forget easy enough.

Right now, I'm too tired
to scheme things,
but that will return
soon enough.
Dreams gather quickly
like Spring crows,
and they scatter.

My Father's Song

Wanting to say things,
I miss my father tonight.
His voice, the slight catch,
the depth from his thin chest,
the tremble of emotion
in something he has just said
to his son, his song:

We planted corn one spring at Acu—
we planted several times
but this one particular time
I remember the soft damp sand
in my hand.

My father had stopped at one point
to show me an overturned furrow;
the plowshare had unearthed
the burrow nest of a mouse
in the soft moist sand.

Very gently, he scooped tiny pink animals
into the palm of his hand
and told me to touch them.
We took them to the edge
of the field and put them in the shade
of a sand moist clod.

I remember the very softness
of cool and warm sand and tiny alive mice
and my father saying things.

The Creation, According to Coyote

"First of all, it's all true."
Coyote, he says this, this way,
humble yourself, motioning and meaning
what he says.

You were born when you came
from that body, the earth;
your black head burst from granite,
the ashes cooling,

until it began to rain.
It turned muddy then,
and then green and brown things
came without legs.

They looked strange.
Everything was strange.
There was nothing to know then,

until later, Coyote told me this,
and he was b.s.-ing probably,
two sons were born,
Uyuyayeh and Masaweh.

They were young then,
and then later on they were older.

And then the people were wondering
what was above.
They had heard rumors.

But, you know, Coyote,
he was mainly bragging
when he said (I think),
"My brothers, the Twins then said,
'Let's lead these poor creatures
and save them.' "

And later on, they came to light
after many exciting and colorful
and tragic things of adventure;
and this is the life, all these, all these.

My uncle told me all this, that time.
Coyote told me too, but you know
how he is, always talking to the gods,
the mountains, the stone all around.

And you know, I believe him.

Four Bird Songs

First Song

Is a little wind
fledgling
nestled
in mountain's crooked finger,

is a river
into a secret place
that shows everything,
little song.

In your breath,
hold this seed
only a while
and seek with it.

One single universe,
I
am
only a little.

Second Song

The sound
in wood,
a morning hollowness
of a cave on the flank of a small hill

startles
with its moan,
yearning,
a twitch of skin.

In the distant place,
a wind starts
coming here,
a waiting sound.

It is here now.
Shiver.
You are rewarded
for waiting.

Third Song

By breathing he started
into the space
before him
and around him,

cleared his throat,
said this song
maybe tomorrow
is for rain.

Lightly
hummed
a tight leathersound
and then heavily.

It rained
the next day,
and he sang
another song for that.

Fourth Song

An old stone
was an old blue,
spotted,
the egg's shell,

only moments before
under the sun
that had beome new
against old sand.

A tear falling,
stirring into space
filling it completely,
making new space.

When he touched it,
and it moved,
it was still warm
with that life.

EMMA LEE WARRIOR

(1941–   )

How I Came to Have a Man's Name

It's a good thing Dad deserted Mom
and all us kids for a cousin's wiles,
cause then we learned from Grampa
how to pray to the Sun, the Moon and Stars.

Before a January dawn, under a moondog sky,
Yellow Dust hitched up a team to a strawfilled sleigh.
Snow squeaked against the runners
in reply to the crisp crackling cottonwoods.
They bundled up bravely in buffalo robes,
their figures pronounced by the white of night;
the still distance of the Wolf Trail greeted them,
and Ipisowahs, the boy child of Natosi,
and Kokomiikiisom watched their hurry.
My momma's body was bent with pain.
Otohkostskaksin sensed the Morning Star's
presence and so he beseeched him:

"Aayo, Ipisowahs, you see us now,
pitiful creatures.
We are thankful there is no wind.
We are thankful for your light.
Guide us safely to our destination.
May my daughter give birth in a warm place.
May her baby be a boy; may he have your name.
May he be fortunate because of your name.
May he live long and be happy.
Bestow your name upon him, Ipisowahs.
His name will be Ipisowahs.
Aayo, help us, we are pitiful."

And Ipisowahs led them that icy night
through the Old Man River Valley
and out onto the frozen prairie.
They rushed to the hospital
where my mother pushed me into this world
and nobody bothered to change my name.

Wolf Trail–Milky Way
Ipisowahs–Blackfoot for the morning star
Natosi–Blackfoot for the sun
Kokomiikiisom–Blackfoot for the moon
Otohkostskaksin–Yellow Dust

Reginald Pugh, The Man Who Came from the Army

I lay in the Holy Cross
bandaged to the knee.
It was time to go home;

my skinny social worker,
a sniveling civil servant,
refused to find me a place.
He had a pig's skin;
I don't think he had a heart.

Transferred from
the Army Department
to Indian Affairs
he gave out orders
instead of solutions;
became the problem
of all Indians
sentenced to his files.
He berated us
for being Indians
but his harangues
were as useless
as my curses.

Once a Peigan woman
living with a Blackfoot man
was told she couldn't get
her welfare check
until her husband left.
She grabbed Mr. Pugh
and shook him the way
a dog shakes a weasel.

Sometimes I'll lie and dream
I throttled him
until his blue eyes slowly
popped from their sockets,
the spittle from his purple
lips dribbled; I'd make
sure he couldn't spit,
then stuff his head
into the garbage can under my bed.

The little two-faced bugger,
I saw him the other day.
He wanted to know when I
intended to return the rental
dole from last year.
I told him I would
let him wait forever, amen.

The Enemy's Eyes

My eyes are the enemy's eyes,
stigma of the spoiler,
invader of lands, bodies
who left behind his eyes.

Chameleonlike, their shades
mock my Indian pride:

"Don't play with cat eyes!
Go away, blue eyes!"
Those taunts forged my hate
for the tainter gone home to hell.

I must pay for that wretch's sins;
my eyes are his; his eyes are mine.

New Indian Medicine

You can become a shaman,
it's easy, ask that guy,
what's his name,
the one by Spokane.

He charges $350,
payable in advance, of course.

There're other cult leaders
who also want your treasures
for a dose of Indian medicine.
They pretend to cure you
or put a hex on an enemy.
Again, it'll cost;
if you don't have the bread,
your car will do
or a favorite horse,
maybe some artifacts.
Allegiance alone
isn't quite enough.

They mix a bit of Sioux,
a little Northwest Coast,
a dab of Southwest,
and just for good measure
a pinch of Plateau
sprinkled all over with Plains.

Crazy Horse's pipe,
how they got it's a mystery,
Sitting Bull sweats with them
every now and then.

Indian medicine, Hollywood style,
visions and visitations
bought with a welfare check.
Guardian spirits, Indian names,
plucked out of the air
like cottonwood in June.

Shamanism is lucrative,
a trip to New York,
Europe, around the world,
a book on the market,
a guest on a talk show,
awe, respect, fame,
paid for by the weak
grasping at straws,
seeking identity at any price;

government grants
for survival camps,
medicine people,
Indian Sun Myung Moons.

GLADYS CARDIFF

(1942–   )

Where Fire Burns

I.

Where fire burns in the hollow sycamore,
    smoke like a vague feather lifting
    up from the island,
    and the world is cold,
    where all the animals wait
    on the river's edge
    while Water Spider weaves
    a *tusti* bowl, and steals
    across the waves,
    where in the little crucible
    she carries on her back
    an orange piece of the Thunder's gift,
    there all the fires
    of hearth and harvest,
    the conflagrations to come,
    the everlasting fire of the sacred mounds,
    leap into being.

II.

Where fire burns in the Carolinas
    sweeping up the hillsides
    in a red and gold combustion
    of blossoming azaleas,
    and blue smoke rises above
    immovable mountains,
    and it is 1898,
    sixty years after Going Snake
    heard peal after peal of thunder
    on a cloudless day of departure,
    you Suate, implacable, a Chosen One,
    will speak to Sundays's congregation
    of Wasi and God's voice
    in a burning bush,
    and tell stories
    while the man from Washington
    writes in his book
    "The rabbit was the leader of them all
    in mischief."

III.

Where the fires of generation have brought me here
    to the opposite end of the land,
    to work late at night
    while my husband and children sleep,
    where out from the yellow pages
    the tongues of fire ignite
    and wily rabbit dances
    into the broom-grass
    tricking the wolf again,
    it is like gathering nuts
    after the leaf-burning, stirring and sifting
    through ashes and husks,
    cracking the vowels and consonants
    of a language I need to know,
    trying to get the taste of them.

Because of our son
with hair blacker than soot,
and eyes that become darker every year
and more impenetrable,
for our daughter with hair as orange
as fire on the hill,
her eyes the color of smoke,
I gather the names and places,
these nutmeats sweetened
with the char of fire,
that they may hold
wherever they go
inextinguishable seeds,
words that say
tsita'ga, "I am standing,"
da nita'ga, "They are standing
together as one."

Tsa'lagi Council Tree

This is a story my father told to me
when I was a girl.

Hilahi', long ago,
before the whites,
hilahi'yu, long, long ago
in buckskin days,
the old men and women of the people
met at the place of the Principal Wood.
The elders held council,
some sitting in the branches
of this *u'tanu ata'ya.*

They smoked the old tobacco
in a whitestone pipe.
The pipe had seven bores, one for each.
They spoke of many mysteries
and matters of law
words that were pleasing to all
who heard them.
Here, trails from every direction met.
Tsa' nadiska, they say
the rustling leaves sang green enchantments,
red and yellow songs,
reminding always to honor *ela e'ladi,*
the earth below, the place of roots.

Now we burn the wood of oak trees,
and do not believe that bugle weed
will necessarily make our children
eloquent. But this is what the old man
said to him when he was a boy,
hilahi', hilahi'yu, long ago.

Making Lists

The lists became shorter
and shorter
get up
wash hair
make dinner
even the science
of looking to the past
was a destroyer of lists
a ladder
of crossing out
not this
not this

. . .

I stopped making lists
yet the falling down in the afternoon
continued. Someone stood outside the door knocking,
or rustled through leaves below the window
jingling coins in his pocket.
But I was too slow in rising
and found only the cat
wrapped like a package on the doorsill,
or a shake of small black birds
falling through trees
like pepper.
I couldn't get enough sleep.

. . .

She wore an American Beauty rose
pinned to her dress
of such five-petaled elegance
roses became my obsession.
With a chisel
she showed me how to rough-cut facets
until I could see the stone inside,
and inside the stone, plane after plane of brilliance.
This is a rose-cut, she said, and this gem is loss.
Windows and doors lost their corners
and became rose windows.
Secretly, privately, sub-rosa,
I learned to float in place
with the specific radiance of thirty-two points,
like a mariner's compass rose.
The days have become beads on a rosary,
there is a thread running through.
Everyday my lists get longer,
rising out of abundance.

Candelaria and the Sea Turtle:

"The god approached dissolves in air"
—William Empson

This is a story Jung would understand
about secretly ordered events
when time and space are freed by God
in a surreal accident.
A lady in distress, a creature from
the depths, a dream
journey, all play their parts as I
am playing mine in the telling. . . .

The story begins:

The ferry Aloha
leaving Zamboanga del Norte
heads south along the Sulu Arch.
From here on the broken horizon,
she is a blow dart
pointing to Sabah,
cutting through the broad swells
of the Sulu sea,
her wake ruffing out
like thistledown.
Being June, the equatorial sun
leans a great weight,
and Candelaria, dressed
in loose cotton, rests
salty arms on the railing
and lifts her face
to the sweltering southwind.
The captain too looks skyward
as a cloud slides over the sun
erasing the colors from the sea.

He steers unaware
toward the irrevocable shadow
rising in the water,
a reef or log, something as sure
as the splintering hull, and the squeal
of propellers yanked like piglets
from their mother, and Holy Mother of God
Candelaria is flying and falling,
and Virgilio sitting in Pasonance Park
with his home-made cage between his feet
waiting with Jefe until time for the cockfight
not knowing, and the cold
becoming less as she rises to the surface
her sandals bobbing along beside her.

Chelonia mydas the green turtle speaks;

More years than are numbered ago
I forsook the land.
When the flood tide
and full moon call my name,
only then a drudging impulse drives me
toward the jagged horizon
of Casuarina trees and cocoanut palms
to cross the rock belittered sand.
Then my shell is my prison.
The gulls flock around me,
terns and frigate birds
squabble in the rivers of my track.

I am the opposite black planet
to the sun.
My underside is light
so that the shark looking up
thinks he sees the sun or moon
through the water.
I was caught once
while sleeping under a coral shelf.

He cut a harbor in my shell.
When I lived on land
my shell was broken
in many pieces,
but I threw myself
into a river and
sewed myself up.
But I've lost the trick
to that.

Rafts of sargassum
bring me food and a place
to rest where the golden sea snake
weaves like a ripple of sun.
She is riding on my back.
I am an island for her
and feel no need to escape.
I am content to float here.
When I lived on land
time was separated into happenings,
but here, all is the same to me,
the circle of night and day, the currents spiral,
I am a living calendar of endurance.

The dream

I am afraid
     of this gift.
          We are one shadow
   cast adrift on a living mirror,
a gold mirror, a blue mirror, a mirror of expectation.
My foot against the jagged edge of shell
fits like a tongue on a broken tooth,
          there is no pain,
      only the steady heartbeat
    and great thrust of its body.
  As we move I hear the sound of cogon grass
when the wind blows through.

Last night,
      did we fly through water
or swim through air?
Whose dream did I enter
                riding
    on four slow wings
through moon and stars?
I cannot separate what is real
from what is real.
Liquid fires flared in our wake.
Waking into dream,
we saw Zamboanga fishing villages on stilts
bowed like exposed ribs along the southern coast.
We hovered above a woman with a remote look
as she cooked her dinner in a can. We became
the buzz of flies in a dank field
where carabao, tilted like abandoned cars,
each with one flat tire, were sleeping.
Cebu, Leyte, Samar, moments of menace
and mercy, absences vast and redolent
with dirt, diesel, ripening fruit unrolled below us.
We circled the bloodstained rubble of Intramuro,
the admonishing spires of Saint Augustine,
palaces bursting with the false fireworks of lighted
   fountains.
We saw men gathering in the hills,
their shirts bulging
with knives and guns.
We swam the whole length from Mindanao to Luzon,
and I knew it was possible to read them like rocks
spilled from a bag
for their prophecy.

There is rain
            like breath on a mirror,
      and I am me again
drinking the tears of this turtle,
from eyes as big as teacups,
I press my cheek against the humid scent of barnacles.
                        Motes
                  dance before my eyes.
            The priest,
my mother, even Virgilio
could not believe
a journey such as this.

The Captain speaks:

Lt. Cesario F. Mana here
of the vessel Kalantia.
I would not have believed it
if I had merely heard it.
She was clinging to what appeared
to be a huge oil drum.
When we threw her the lift ring
the drum sank.
We started hauling her up,
and then it rose again,
and we realized it was a giant
sea turtle. The creature
even circled twice before disappearing
into the depths of the sea,
as if to reassure itself.
Mrs. Villanueva herself
kept quiet on the episode,
giving some the impression
she did not believe
it ever happened at all.

And though "The god approached
dissolves in air,"
He knows not change.
Time is our synchrony.
Is it not a matter for wonder
to know
that somewhere in the great confluence
a spirit of compassion dwells?

This story is taken from a true event that was reported
in the Seattle Times newspaper in 1975.

Hunting the Dugong

Here, watching T.V.
I came close
while the small man on the screen,
miniaturized,
but living, really, life-sized
in New Guinea, prepares to hunt
the dugong.
                  He is painting two eyes,
two eyes that see into deep holes
in the sea. As he paints, he whispers
"My magic is at home,
I have it here,
I have it here."
Great shapes turn in the sea,
swim toward lighter water.

Memory, hearing the call of magic,
leaps as it will
backward
to when our son was three,
sleepwalking in green pajamas.
We laugh, side by side in the dark,
watching him under the sink light
as he drinks from the gold-edged oval
mirror.
      He lifts it like a round of melon,
again, and again to his lips
in a ritual drinking
until his thirst is quenched.
Is it his own reflection that he drinks,
or does that dish of light open
into the deep lake of joy?

In the Highlands of New Guinea
men wear photos of the Pope
and advertisements
stuck between the feathers
of their headdresses.
They are forgetting who they are.
The dugong know this and are disappearing.
Soon they will become shapes that only rise
in a ritual to dreamers and magicians
attracted by their luminous nets.

For his ring and watch on the night stand.

"Porcelain is personal," he smiles.
There is intimacy in the way he holds the vase
cupped between his hands.
"For instance, this container has a mouth, neck,
shoulders, belly, foot. It is a pleasure to touch."
The women's eyes become heavy-lidded.
Like sensitives they feel caresses on the slopes
of their own bodies. He says what they already know.
"The clay and its constituents are called the body.
Kaolin and feldspar in proper amounts are not enough,
the mix needs small impurities to make it fluid."
They are sisters knowing the same near river
and far, high peaks. Their glittering skin
has been fashioned with hands until it flows.
"This vase is typical of the classic wares
of the Song period. Notice its snow white color,
its *blare de chine,* how translucent it is.
It has been fired inside the dragon."
As if coming from a distance across water,
the clean tones chime and the Governor of Old Beijing
plays his porcelain bowls. They are more resonant
than the finest jade bells.
"The potter must learn the shape and balance
true for his clay. Strength and elegance, calm,
generosity and power, gaiety, they are all
there within the powdered rock and water."

He has not yet realized how the room sways,
that it is filled with cargo;
amphoras of milk and jars of honey, jugs of wine,
stemmed blood cups, basins for entrails, crazed urns
for ash, cylinders of gas and platters of light.
The room is heavy with the ballast of broken pieces.
"When picking up a piece of fine porcelain,
it is nice to remove the purse from your arm,
or any bracelets that might scratch."

LANCE HENSON

(1944–   )

Solitary

on a cold night
i forget the story of my birth

i forget the long fingers of sleep
the magic of names

to go alone

i begin by asking the winds
forgiveness

Day Song

perhaps on a sunday
like today
under the sound of a lone bell

perhaps in the brightest snow of the year
or in autumn
while the leaves are in their last clothes

someone will lie down
feeling in his blood a singing wind
that in all his days
he has witnessed
only once

when dust stopped on the shivering road
and looked into the mirror

Nam Shim

nam shim
ni hi i ssta vi ho mi vi
i ma o vi no ss si i di ni
voo ho do gi
vi i ni min ni
ni vi hist ta zi

Grandfather

grandfather
my heart looks toward you
red sage of sunset
evening star
the night hawk sings
your name

"Grandfather" is Lance Henson's translation of "Nam
Shim."

At Chadwick's Bar and Grill

a sky the color of a wren's breath
hangs over red clouds
hint of rain
and home is dirt underfoot

tu fu and li po have
forgiven nothing
not waking drunk under any moon
or the incessant calling
of a loon
so waiting is the roses own
signature
the spider catches the fly
at morning
whether i am there
or not

coyote fragments

1

he is rust
    in moonlight

2

when the roadman paused
    we heard our brother's voice

3

one track
        in snow

4

eight without ears
hang upside down from fence posts
near hammon oklahoma

5

the moonlight splashes
    in their eyes

near twelve mile point

for my grandparents

at times the heart looks toward open fields
and sees itself returning

orange pall of sun
the low hymn of trees

in the garden
a north wind blows over dry stalks of corn
birds gather there
scratching over the echoing footsteps

your names
have become the dark feather

to whom the stars sing

splitting wood near morris, oklahoma on robbie and lesa mcmurtry's farm

a gray heron flies past
mixes its wings with the stark
winter limbs of trees

splitting wood this morning with my brother's axe
i trace the seam through a red elm
it splits clean with one strike
the sound crosses the water of a small pond
and dissipates in a circle around me
later stacking the wood
the smell of resin strong in the air
i raise a small piece of oak to my mouth
chewing the sweet dry heart
i face east
in the mist of this new day
and ask for something from the wind
something bright and clean
to carry forward
and leave behind

north

north of my grandfather's house
shadows of first winter storm walk
the fields toward the north canadian

without a word
the pregnant dog i have tried
to be rid of for weeks
has gone

in the house my daughter
has disappeared into dream

her small trembling hands
flower into a cold wind that smells
of the moon

Ni Hoi Nim Mi Ni Hon Ido Mi Moo

for charles white antelope

ni hoi nim mi ni hon   ido mi moo
ni hoi nim mi ni hon   e inif
ni hoi das i woi nu
na wodstan ni hi vist
na dutz   na ho utz

Charles White Antelope is a Native American church
elder in Chapter #1, Calumet, Oklahoma.

I am Singing the Cold Rain

for charles white antelope

i am singing the cold rain
i am singing the winter dawn
i am turning in the gray morning
of my life
toward home

"I am Singing the Cold Rain" is Lance Henson's trans-
lation of "Ni Hoi Nim Mi Ni Hon Ido Mi Moo."

BARNEY BUSH

(1945–   )

Autumn Warrior

I.

Crouched on one knee   one
hand on the wet limestone
edge   he appeared ready to
leap   but it was wind
rain biting into his face
nights cold dark rain
dampening fall that has
begun to settle   His
childhood friends were
walking ghosts   calling
his name in the woods behind
him   descendents of
blood   stone axes rounded
grooves
Gusts of wind shaped like
luminous waves from the
great river   whistled
through his hair   his ears
whistled
like short bursts from
flute   into memory that
weaves wet nights into a
billion years   His
eyes are the web.

II.

He is the smell of wet
leaves   the smell like an
animal's musk   that he
has left on cornerstones of
america
But here   forest is his
mother's teats   his
grandmother's teats   his
wife's teats   nourishing

him and those to come
Sunlight melting into
scarlet limbs is his
grandfather's breath   all
that breathe it are brother
and sister
Among relatives   female
goes first through the door
Among enemies   male spirit
enters first
It is the way of this life.

III.

Bare feet that left the
ledge before daylight
avert thorns   sharp
edges like a wildcat's
paws
He is the seeker of
night hollows   where
there are waterfalls and
owls hunt   where
brothers and sisters are
called by their names
It is autumn
Shadows stretch across
the mountains   Skies
darken   thunder
Wild geese sound like
children playing
He feels warm sweat of
horseback on his inner
thighs   and shadows
catch him   blend his
shivering lean form into
cold rain.

Directions in Our Blood

for two suns
Phil and Colin

I

West Kansas full moon
cool breeze   leads us

through heat that killed
60 people in St Louis
this same moon that made
light for families on
horseback   travois and
hardtimes journeying into
this buffalo country
Crickets   cicadas   dance
inside my road weary
head   we watch the
night   and grassy plains
i tell my two sons who
want to sit on every hill
that every shadow is a
buffalo spirit   They
watch from the truck bed
and watch me too   marking
with my eyes   roads on
which their mothers and i
have hitchhiked   And
there is a road filled
with summer moons   where
a hitchhikers nostrils
bleed from stings of
winter stars   years ago
even now   the road smells
the same
When i am moving   when
we are moving   there is
an urgency like escaping a
world surrounded by wagon
trains   sometimes like
escaping with their horses
Morning   Nights prairie
filled with buffalo and
covered with grass   has
been plowed under   replaced
with urban sprawl
with miles of electric and
telephone wires   My sons
shut their eyes to sleep
through it   to wake up
from this dream   i pull
over to wake up too

II

One week in Boulder at
Charlies   (the original
Navajo taco himself)
in his two pueblo sized
rooms   that are crammed
with files   proposals and
government resolutions that
date back to the first
Long Walk starring Kit Carson
a cast of Navajo patriots
some sheep and silver bridles
In Boulder my two boys burn
out on white girls   video
games   movies and roller
skates   burning down to
the excitement of freedom
from vermont mentality
burning on the taste of
roads in their blood
They say   Lets go   and
i say   Load up the truck
We cross mountains to
Lindas hogan   to her
mansion of wild herbs and
grasses   her daughters
luminous eyes that shine
like two polished apache
tears   Linda takes
me out   now get this   to
the loudest cowboy bars in
colorado   where she dances
with every cowboy but me
Hell   i just shoot pool
with her rejects   consoling
some   Yes i think she is
always like this   and
i like pool better than
dancing anyway   Thats what
he said
My boys are loaded up again
Got me ready just in time
to drive past the sundown
and they wrestle all the

way over Wolf Creek Pass
all the way to Ignacio   right
into the front door of my
cousins house

III

Being with relatives is
always a long story   where
time is long hours
long afternoons doing
beadwork   stringing chokers
sewing moccasins   some for
gas money to get to powwows on
If you are indian   you will
understand about my relatives
Hanko is really my brother
but i call him my cousin because
he belongs to a different
tribe   and his cheekbones
are a little higher too   his
rear ones
At breakfast   one of the
meals between morning and noon
Hanko asks my boy Colin if
he has ever been with a woman
Colin says   Well uh   sort
of like   well
Hanko says to my other boy
Phil   have you ever been with
a woman   Phil says yes
Hanko says   Now sere Colin   all
you have to say is yes or no
Colin says no
Hanko says   OK   I just wanted
to know
Ball games are played at night
on every res in n america
Big white lights stare down
into brown faces   scattered
about the diamond   reminding
me of BIA training films
My boys skirt the perimeter
fighting off mosquitoes and
looking for women

The rest of us sit in back
of pickup trucks   watching
sometimes yelling   but mostly
watching   sometimes laughing
sometimes recalling old memories
The same cars drive round and
round   same eyes checking us
out   We check back   sometimes
wave   but mostly we
watch

IV.

Between Pagosa Springs and
Chama NM   a wedge from
another world   Out past
Red Ryders Rodeo Grounds is
the road through the yellow
veil   a world that Whitemen
have left partially intact
a road almost too sacred to
mention
My boys ride in the back
sitting high   their faces
prowing through this artery
                liquid mesas
                summer aspen
sweet smell of pine air
Hitchhiker   waist deep in
roadside grass   a short
haired whiteman who makes up
songs for indians
He sings one for us   We
tell him that   Brave Buck
is not really a good name
for a indian song   He is
willing to learn   We explain
and he can laugh   So can we
At Echo Canyon   one of
the old days stopovers for us
Ft Lewis students   we stop
again   midnight   cougar
tracks   We put out tobacco for
                Every
all the relatives   star
is watching   Once   i heard

the name of Jesus spoken
and it is here that i realize
instructions given to whitemen
on how to live on this earth
have never been taken   and
it is here that i hear how the
doors to their heaven have
been shut against them   and
it is here that i finally
understand why the whiteman
behaves savagely   and there
is more but another time
My son Phil is eager to see
his mother   We hear

V.

On the straight away east
out of a New Mexico sundown
my two sons   full of
adrenelin and sopapillas
rock the truckbed   until
I am swerving all over the
road
They get up front   with
me   wrestle open skies and
massive clouds retreating
behind the rainbow
My boys wrestle into oncoming
headlights and signs that say
Oaklahoma City   349 miles
Through rainstorms passing on
to northwest mountains   we
blaze into the cool shadows
of   struck
driving nights
bearing down on the plains
into the Texas Panhandle and
on to Oklahoma
The long road of old 66 is
americas last rough edge of

the automobile age
Alongside is highway 40
smoothing out americas land
scape   smoothing out the
kinks in manifest destiny
but yet we ride   through
herds of buffalo that by day
are stands of mesquite and
juniper
Our headlights search out
bug infested humid air   the
road to my brothers
No lights in the house but
our headlights bounce off
greasy looking faces   slick
hair and aluminum cans
They said they had been waiting
that someone was coming
We are here   silence   We
touch each others faces and
remember the smells   Children
come from sleep   Chris   Jon
Phil   Colin   We cannot see
bloodshot eyes   cannot see
all the beauty   even with
dawn about to break

VI.

My pickup is a lathered
roan   kicking red dust
from Calumet OK onto the
Will Rogers Turnpike
blazing into eastern hills
blazing through the
history of native nations
with political turmoil   and
defense   somehow linked to
savagery   written in
white texts   whose
realities are undeveloped
but whose destruction nears
perfection   We carry
their symbols in our
ceremonies   i say i

am your kin   your blood
but my source is further
east   from these Oklahoma
hollers   Every trail i
take is one of tears   and
the return is no less
severe than the exodus
On 60 East out of Spring
field MO   heading for the
homeland   nights aroma
already cooling into dreams
Midnight riders are the
truck stop cowboys slicing
Ozark air past me   and
my kids in the travois bed
We ride night like invisible
spectres   at the edge of
frontier settlements
i sing   pull in at quiet
one light gas stops
White traveler who sees our
blood   nods a mystic
gesture   sympathetic but
longing reverence for our
crimson past   i teach my
boys to nod back   to keep
the song that is being sung
inside   keep it going a
little longer   to let them
know that no one sees the
other side without a song.

The Memory Sire

He is the oldest grandfather
whose spirit wind   pelts
circular snow gusts   against
my window
He makes it known that we
are related   that he
has visited all my grandparents
since the first breath   he
who whirlwinds his icy
tongue into ancestral sleep

leaving slivers of icicle hair
scattered about my room
I know who he is   that
snowsnakes his gelid fingers
between cracks in my floor
Progenitor of the West Door
he races about the house
drifting with crystaline ooze
looking for those who would
try an escape
More logs   more stoking into
red embers   that thaw
stories   to remind us   to
make us strong everytime he
covers the ground   for
he hovers biting the ears of
dogs   and lashes out at
every edge to steal away ones
whose memories have weakened.

Her Voice

I hear her voice   like
tornado-warning chimes
It is limestone bluff still
alive
Limestone clinks at
water's edge
Each clink   a tone from
creation's ghostly voice
Mortal voice   inaudible
murmur that keeps the
wind
that plasters spring moisture
onto the walls of cliffs
It is the smell of mud and river
and holes that bring forth
gusts from inside the earth
She doesn't cry
Her mind's footsteps still
carry her across the gift
She still hums the songs
covers her eyes at gravesites
stares across behind folded

arms   into the precision of
past events
The ceremony   her voice
when the giveaway was the
beginning of life.

Taking a Captive/1984

A light drizzle falling   off
and on for days
Kentucky hills   yellow leaves
matted to damp black   your
pensive eyes in smokey hollows
My son   you are born by
mistake in another world where
your vision lingers too
long
too long to teach those who
seek wisdom from the future
Three generations back   in
my village   you would be
painted   have a name
Waylahskese
You would carry flute of
polished cedar   inlaid with
finest abalone shell   bound
with soft white buckskin
On humid evenings I would hear
your cavernous melodies
rolling off limestone bluffs
above Spaylaway Theepi
You would grow into manhood
bringing fresh meat to the
door of your grandmothers'
weegiwa   carry your
opahwahka in the oracle of
your heart
Stalking figures yet roam
shadows of colonial america
yet drawing breath   continuous
memory absorbed into blood
Your ivoried tiger form spoors
its way to my heart   not as
a killer but as   one of grace
Here in my center   M'qua seeks

power to bring you home   sniffs
the air for winter
Too soon   shemegana pepoou
Your real name awaits
Come into your dreams   my young
captive   Hear the hawk shriek
as he soars outside your window
Come into the lodge of winter
dreams   hibernate with the
bear.

Spaylaway Theepi—Ohio River
Weegiwa—house
Opahwahka—medicine
M'qua—black bear
Shemegana pepoou—foreign cold, threat of winter

Voyeur's Dream

Over northeast mountains
blue-bellied clouds weld
into opalescence
Early morning wind came from
my sleep   southwest
vision where herbs
hang from vigas   drying
And paint dries on canvas
stretched by moon's
reflection in
last night's creek
Bare feet quietly pace
the east window to the
west   streaking
brown eyes with new color
new light   glaring from
the brush tip   trapped
inside the voyeur's green
mirrors   feigning
sleep   longing for
bare feet torso   and
brown eyes   to inch its
way back here   beneath
this warm starquilt.

GAIL TREMBLAY

(1945–   )

Night Gives Old Woman the Word

Dark whispers
behind the echo
of the wind. Mind
is trapped by patterns
in the sound.
Night works a spell—
Moon spills her naked light.
Reflected fire illuminates
the ground. The pull
of night words makes Earth-Woman
give off heat. Soil glistens
dampened by her sweat.
Corn seed feels the planet's turn,
unrolls her root,
prepares to send a shoot
above the dirt. Moon
attracting water in the veins
makes corn leaves uncurl
and probe nocturnal air.
The leaves stretch out
to catch the coming dew.
Clan mother, watching,
hears the planets move.
Old, clan mother listens
to the words—all nature
speaks as slowly seasons
turn—marked by the waxing,
waning Moon; messages

become imprinted on old bones.
Earth works in dark
as well as light. Life
moves through the sky. We plant;
we harvest, and, at last,
we feast. Clan mother listens
and is filled with thanks.
Night murmurs and plants
grow in the fields.
Old Woman hears dark
speak the ancient word.

Medicine Bearer

The Medicine Bearer comes like a red
apparition; he knows the plants and the time
of the moon for gathering magic rooted
to a murmuring Earth that makes it possible
to be. He bruises branches with his teeth
and tells by taste what young shoots
and roots will make the proper tea
to heal a heavy heart. He gathers things
to himself which sparkle and whisper
in the wind of another's breath. Even
in the dark, light glints and his presence
is revealed by power lumbering bearlike
over ground. At noon, he arrives and tells
the one who cried four days the words
to say when preparing to make medicine
to help the people needing to grow strong.
Love shapes the lessons he teaches
as he dances on this spinning planet;
his footsoles keeping rhythm to a pulse
beating steady like the song of a great drum.

Indian Singing in 20th Century America

We wake; we wake the day,
the light rising in us like sun—
our breath a prayer brushing
against the feathers in our hands.
We stumble out into streets;
patterns of wires invented by strangers
are strung between eye and sky,
and we dance in two worlds,
inevitable as seasons in one,
exotic curiosities in the other
which rushes headlong down highways,
watches us from car windows, explains
us to its children in words
that no one could ever make
sense of. The images obscures
the vision, and we wonder
whether anyone will ever hear
our own names for the things
we do. Light dances in the body,
surrounds all living things—
even the stones sing
although their songs are infinitely
slower than the ones we learn
from trees. No human voice lasts
long enough to make such music sound.
Earth breath eddies between factories
and office buildings, caresses the surface
of our skin; we go to jobs, the boss
always watching the clock to see
that we're on time. He tries to shut
out magic and hopes we'll make
mistakes or disappear. We work
fast and steady and remember

each breath alters the composition
of the air. Change moves relentless,
the pattern unfolding despite their planning—
we're always there—singing round dance
songs, remembering what supports
our life—impossible to ignore.

Reflections on a Visit to the Burke Museum, University of Washington, Seattle

The things live there, held still in glass cases,
set on pedestals, displayed—the masks,
clothing, boxes, baskets, feast bowls, all
made beautiful so the legends could be told
in ceremonial splendor, so raven, killer whale,
bear, and wolf would dance in the circle
of the people to the songs the families possessed.
On those days, masks inlayed with shell of abalone
reflected firelight more subtly than oil
on water makes rainbows in the sun.
Some masks, made to split apart, transformed
characters inside the rhythm of the dance,
a ritual bursting forth that in a moment
altered everything that was. The dancers
dressed in woven aprons and in shawls; cedar
bark ruffs encircled ankles, necks, and wrists
and flapped in wind created by motion contained
inside the vibration of the drums. Song and story
filled the room and beat as steady as the heart
of the people who knew the magic that made
life sacred as it emerged from changer's mind,
who still perform at feasts how things came to be
and know performance is a gift. Even without the people
to move in them, magic resides in these objects.
The vision of the makers informs the eye.

Around the edges of the room are bones
of long dead creatures who bear exotic names:
Allosaurus, Nannippus, Tylosaurus, Tomistoma-
Machikanese, beasts from before the time of man
that no hunter ever killed. These creatures
who have evolved and ceased to have these ancient
forms are mere frames for a past so long dead
we think in awe, in fear, how we could never
fit in such a world. Extinct, they make space
for other bones, for mammoths young enough
to be hunted by ancestors of the makers
of masks and bowls some twelve thousand years
before the carvers held their tools. But bones speak
of death, of things that cannot come to earth again.
Why should they rest next to the works of men
whose grandsons still explain how we did this
in the old days. The carvers and lovers
of this vision still reside among the people
even though the Europeans who took the land
worked laws to make the old ways die.
Those who made the myth Indians would vanish
as surely as the creatures in the corners
and stairwell of this room, put Native works
of art together with these long-gone bones—
the vision of the makers informs the eye.

To Grandmother on Her Going:

(a description of how things looked from Earth)

Old woman, time and your own
bad habits ravaged you at the end.

Your body grew pregnant with death
and that fire that all your life
possessed you, withdrew, hovered above
tethered by a lightning cord
that kept you breathing
but nothing more. Your soul
waited out its long gestation
for rebirth into space.

A great gambler in your prime,
in the last months you ceased
even to deal out poker hands
and play penny ante
with imaginary friends.
You lay bound and blind,
lips and fingers turning blue,
while relatives spoke without thinking
to that place above you
where you had moved your wit.

On the final day, the nurses
chose to get you up.
You sat strapped
in a wingbacked chair,
the wreck of a dowager empress
in a parody of a Chinese portrait,
your hands and feet so frail
they already spoke of the bare bone
underneath. Then being done with Earth,
you cut the cord and gave up breath.

LINDA HOGAN

(1947–   )

To Light

At the spring
we hear the great seas traveling
underground
giving themselves up
with tongues of water
that sing the earth open.

They have journeyed through the graveyards
of our loved ones,
turning in their graves
to carry the stories of life to air.

Even the trees with their rings
have kept track
of the crimes that live within
and against us.

We remember it all.
We remember, though we are just skeletons
whose organs and flesh
hold us in.
We have stories
as old as the great seas
breaking through the chest
flying out the mouth,
noisy tongues that once were silenced,
all the oceans we contain
coming to light.

Man in the Moon

He's the man who climbs his barn
to look down on the fields,
the man leading his horse from the barn
that finally fell down.

When I'm quiet he speaks:
we're like the spider
we weave new beds around us
when old ones are swept away.

When I see too much
I follow his advice
and close my worn-out eye.

Yesterday he was poor
but tomorrow he says his house
will fill up with silver
the white flesh will fatten on his frame.

Old man, window in a sky
full of holes
I am like you
putting on a new white shirt
to drive away on the fine roads.

Celebration: Birth of a Colt

When we reach the field
she is still eating
the heads of yellow flowers
and pollen has turned her whiskers
gold. Lady,
her stomach bulges out,
the ribs have grown wide.

We wait, our bare feet dangling
in the horse trough,
warm water
where goldfish brush
our smooth ankles.
We wait
while the liquid breaks
down Lady's dark legs
and that slick wet colt
like a black tadpole
darts out
beginning at once
to sprout legs.
She licks it to its feet,
the membrane still there,
red,
transparent
the sun coming up shines through,
the sky turns bright with morning
and the land
with pollen blowing off the corn,
land that will always own us,
everywhere it is red.

Eclipse II

The earth shows her face to the moon.
Murderers are exposed
in light's false astronomy of longing.
Lovers bare the silver oceans of themselves.

History, growing red in our shadow,
is written on that blood round pupil.

Take my hand.
You can see the moon rising
with our lives on it
and we are surrounded
by murder in the west
and rumors of war in the south.
The east's old history repeats itself
and there are reports of guns in the north.

Take my hand.
This river beside us is singing.
It is saying, *Yes*
to our touching of hands,
this uprising of arms
around one another,
the hearts beating on this hemisphere
and that.
Yes, the moonlight of ourselves.
What roaring along the river.
What fire, the moon traveling.
What singing.
And there are more rivers than this.

The Rainy Season

The women are walking to town
beneath black umbrellas
and the roofs are leaking.
Oh, let them be,
let the buckled wood give way this once
and the mildew rot the plaster,
the way it happens with age
when a single thought of loneliness
is enough to bring collapse.

See, here they come,
the witches are downstairs
undermining the foundations.
The skeletal clothes hanger
has unwound from its life at last,
hidden in a dark coat
thrown over its shoulders.
Nothing is concealed,
not silver moths
falling out the empty sleeves
or the old cat with shining fur
covering his bony spine,
that string of knots
for keeping track of this mouse
and that.

Even the mice have their days of woe.
In the field and in the world
there are unknown sorrows.
Every day collapses
despite the women
walking to town with black umbrellas
holding up the sky.

Seeing through the Sun

How dishonest the sun,
making ruined cities
look like dust.

In that country of light
there is no supper
though the sun's marketplace
reveals the legs inside young women's skirts,

burning round oranges,
wheat loaves,
and the men's uniforms with shining buttons.

We are polite in the sun
and we ask for nothing
because it has hit the walls with such force.

But when the sun falls
and we are all one color
and still in danger
we tell each other
how this child was broken open by a man,
this person left with only fingerprints.

Sometimes one of us
tries to stand up to the light.
Her skin burns red as a liar
in fear's heat.
So in the light we say only,
Never mind, I was just passing through
the universe. It's nothing.

But there are times we tell the truth;
Sun, we see through you
the flashing of rifles and scythes.

Let's stand up. The enemy
is ready for questions.
There is light coming in beneath the door.
Stop it with a rag.
There is light entering a keyhole.
Cover it with your hand
and speak, tell me everything.

Gamble

Those men with dollars on the mind
are pushed around by Monday
and tricked by Crow,
tricked by the broken look of Crow's thin legs.
That hungry Crow.
But its wings, oh!
Oh! and its laughter
and theft of radishes
from those big men's fingers
like a handgame
where dark women
deceive white men, singing
You're crazy,
bad luck,
those words sounding like love songs
until the men pay up
with big grins on their faces.
Those women, oh!
in blue shoes
arm in arm
with their laughter.
They have even bilked the moon;
that's why I love them so
and why tonight is rich and dark.

Workday

I go to work
though there are those who were missing today
from their homes.
I ride the bus
and I do not think of children without food
or how my sisters are chained to prison beds.

I go to the university
and out for lunch
and listen to the higher-ups
tell me all they have read
about Indians
and how to analyze this poem.
They know us
better than we know ourselves.

I ride the bus home
and sit behind the driver.
We talk about the weather
and not enough exercise.
I don't mention Victor Jara's mutilated hands
or men next door
in exile
or my own family's grief over the lost child.

When I get off the bus
I look back at the light in the windows
and the heads bent
and how the women are all alone
in each seat
framed in the windows
and the men are coming home,
then I see them walking on the Avenue,
the beautiful feet,
the perfect legs
even with their spider veins,
the broken knees
with pins in them,
the thighs with their cravings,
the pelvis
and small back
with its soft down,
the shoulders which bend forward
and forward and forward
to protect the heart from pain.

The New Apartment, Minneapolis

The floorboards creak.
The moon is on the wrong side of the building,

and burns remain
on the floor.

The house wants to fall down
the universe when earth turns.

It still holds the coughs of old men
and their canes tapping on the floor.

I think of Indian people here before me
and how last spring white merchants hung an elder

on a meathook and beat him;
he was one of The People.

I remember this war
and all the wars

and relocation like putting the moon in prison
with no food and that moon was a crescent

but be warned, the moon grows full again
and the roofs of this town are all red

and we are looking through the walls of houses
at people suspended in air.

Some are baking, with flour on their hands,
or sleeping on floor three, or getting drunk.

I see the businessmen who hit their wives
and the men who are tender fathers.

There are women crying or making jokes.
Children are laughing under beds.

Girls in navy blue robes talk on the phone all night
and some Pawnee is singing 49s, drumming the table.

Inside the walls
world changes are planned, bosses overthrown.

If we had no coffee,
cigarettes or liquor,

says the woman in room 12,
they'd have a revolution on their hands.

Beyond walls are lakes and plains,
canyons and the universe;

the stars are the key
turning in the lock of night.

Turn the deadbolt and I am home.
I have walked to the dark earth,

opened a door to nights where there are no apartments,
just drumming and singing;

The Duck Song, The Snake Song,
The Drunk Song.

No one here remembers the city
or has ever lost the will to go on.

Hello aunt, hello brothers, hello trees
and deer walking quietly on the soft red earth.

The Truth Is

In my left pocket a Chickasaw hand
rests on the bone of the pelvis.
In my right pocket
a white hand. Don't worry. It's mine
and not some thief's.
It belongs to a woman who sleeps in a twin bed
even though she falls in love too easily,
and walks along with hands
in her own empty pockets
even though she has put them in others
for love not money.

About the hands, I'd like to say
I am a tree, grafted branches
bearing two kinds of fruit,
apricots maybe and pit cherries.
It's not that way. The truth is
we are crowded together
and knock against each other at night.
We want amnesty.

Linda, girl, I keep telling you
this is nonsense
about who loved who
and who killed who.

Here I am, taped together
like some old civilian conservation corps
passed by from the great depression
and my pockets are empty.
It's just as well since they are masks
for the soul, and since coins and keys
both have the sharp teeth of property.

Girl, I say,
it is dangerous to be a woman of two countries.
You've got your hands in the dark
of two empty pockets. Even though
you walk and whistle like you aren't afraid
you know which pocket the enemy lives in
and you remember how to fight
so you better keep right on walking.
And you remember who killed who.
For this you want amnesty
and there's that knocking on the door
in the middle of the night.

Relax, there are other things to think about.
Shoes for instance.
Now those are the true masks of the soul.
The left shoe
and the right one with its white foot.

WILLIAM OANDASAN

(1947–   )

Grandmothers Land

around the house stood an
orchard of plum, apple and pear
a black walnut tree, one white pine,
groves of white oak and willow clumps
the home of Jessie was largely redwood

blood, flesh and bone sprouted
inside her womb of redwood
for five generations
the trees now stand unpruned and wild

after taking to the four directions
the seeds of Jessie have returned

afternoon sunlight on the field
breezes moving grass and leaves
memories with family names wait
within the earth, the mountains,
the valley, the field, the trees

Words of Tayko-mol

1.

from heart through mind into image:
the pulse of the four directions
the voice of our blood
the spirit of breath and words

2.

from fresh currents of night air
above manzanitas near the cemetery
the words of ancient lips
turn in our blood again

Tayko-mol–Creator of the Yuki people and the Yukian
world

Acoma

For many distant travelers
The way to Acoma is merely
Interstate-40,
A fourlane sear
Of asphalt
Stitched in between wire
fences and telephone lines,
Running like a scar
Across the flesh
Of an ancient landscape;
They almost never know
The old way south by north
Where you can fly today
From a uranium stripmine
To the sacred Sky City
Standing on top
White Rock Mesa.
Corn and rituals predate
the Christian mission there
Like a breathing shrine,
And the way to Acoma for many
Is a place for curious pottery,
Or a refreshment stop.
But for those who still

Travel the four directions,
the way to Acoma
Is always the way.

Acoma is one of the eastern Keresan-speaking Pueblos
located in west-central New Mexico approximately 60
miles south-by-west of Albuquerque.

Song of Ancient Ways

song give birth to
the story and dance
as the dance steps
the story speaks

the woman with white hair
only whispered   *Tatu*
but through my ears
30,000 years echo

with brilliant feathers and strength
three Filipino gaming cocks
appear from across the water
in yard pullets cluck excitedly

swimming up the Eel
a spirit sings   *acorn-*
pound-the-old-way-draws-
the-milk-of-Earth

free as the bear
and tall as redwoods
throb my blood roots
when spirits ride high

long ago black bears
sang around our lodge fires
tonight they dance
alive through our dreams

in the chipped and tattered
weavings of a willow basket
the voice of an ancient age
dreaming of breath

the icy mountain water
that pierces the deep thirst
drums my fire
drums my medicine pouch

from fresh currents of night air
above manzanitas near the cemetery
the song of ancient ways
turns in our blood again

ROBERTA HILL WHITEMAN

(1947–   )

Climbing Gannett

While you clambered up ahead,
jabbing a staff into chunks of snow,
I rested on a rock shelf, wedded
to my breath, to ridges and plateaus,
careening blue and bluer,
to aspens below, flickering
in a downhill draft.

Lengthening its hollows,
the teal blue peak above us
made you laugh. Never did you feel
as close as then,
straddling the distant slope,
balancing in cold wind.
As you climbed beyond my help,

a rim of the crevasse broke to foam.
I heard your wild echo.
"It's no storm." When the mountain
hurled boulders across the sky,
your face blazed in the close grey air,
then the slide pulled you
with a roar, whirring loud

and long, like the wingbeats
of a hundred hawks. Although I held on,
my life leapt at your glance.
I held on for weeks, for weeks I walked
the crumbling fields. In the homeland
of ravens, I stroked the shadow
of each gangling pine, and measured

the distance of your grave.
Across the vista, other peaks darkened.
You were swept away so suddenly.
Surely you'll tap,
perhaps below that copper ridge,
or in that far ravine.
I dream on the icy plain.

Nameless and alone, I sang
in the yellow light of a lily,
and woke to welcome you,
bound by a miniature range.
Outside our window, a warbler claims
another dawn. Do you think
the light drove away that colder wind?

For Heather, Entering Kindergarten

She tests the curb with a chubby boot,
lolls around the door,
then offers a smile before she walks
down halls that smell of crayon.

When the bell rings, each chart clings
to another from the day before.
Too willing to be wrong, she knows our clock
doesn't tock the same as theirs, and I'm afraid

she'll learn the true length of forlorn,
the quotient of the quick
who claim that snowflakes never speak,
that myths are simply lies.

Aware of each minute and its death,
I scrubbed my Catholic
desk with nubs of tissue and piqued
the sister's early prayers.

Some, bullied into disbelief,
want clues to the terrible cutting
taking place as we race to reason.
I want to gather shreds of bark

and press them in my forehead.
I want to stand near curbs and sing:
The stars can hear. In what season
will you send a message?

Sixth graders scorn my truth. Heather walks away,
sways in delightful idleness while somewhere
mountain flowers in a sudden gust of wind
openly send word to Algol and Procyon.

Woman Seed Player

for Oscar Howe

You balanced her within a cyclone
and I believe the young wind
that frequents the graveyard
tugs her sleeve. Her hand never wavers,
though the stakes are always high.

When running shadow turns rattler,
her concern is how the mountain rises
beyond its line of sorrow. Then,
shooting her seeds, she bids
the swallow fly over rolling hills.

I have been obsessed with permanence.
Struggling in that open space under every word,
I've heard exuberant waves drift
denying limitations. Last April
when we trudged upstairs

to where we found you sketching,
you said no one had ever gone full circle,
from passion through pattern and back again
toward pebbles moist with moonlight.
How easily the rain cross-stitches

a flower on the screen, quickly
pulls the threads, varying the line.
Many times this year, I've watched that player
play. She doesn't force the day
to fit her expectations.

Now she pulls me through.
The leaf light dust and her stable hand
allow my will its corner of quiet.
Watch dust embracing the nervous wheat;
every throw's a different combination.

Dust whirs brighter in the door jamb,
one last uproar before the rain.
Her bundle contains and yet foregoes
the dark dust already fallen for tomorrow
from long since gentle stars.

The title and subject come from a picture by Oscar
Howe.

Variations for Two Voices

I.

Where do we live?
 Underneath sunset.
How long have we been here?
 Since your grandfather's death
 when war came without effort
 and hearts didn't own
 a tear or a victory.
 We stand in a stranger's field
 beyond pardon.
What do we do?
 We hide. We bargain.
 We answer each question
 with a difficult anger,
 map the future for heartache
 and rattle old bones.
When is it time?
 Time is that beggar
 living in the basement.
 He dictates to us
 when to move, how to dream.
 Run and he'll be there
 waiting at crossroads,
 with pitch for your ribcage
 and pins for your eyes.
Who'll come to save us?
 No one. Nothing.
 Yet when the wind stirs
 I hear voices call us
 inside the snow drift.
 I've heard it those nights
 when snow writhes before Spring.
 Don't ever listen.
 Don't ever listen.
 Don't listen. What
 it can bring!

II.

Where do we live?
    Inside this morning.
How long have we been here?
    Only the lakes remember
    our arrival. Go there at dawn
    when reeds ride the slow wash.
    An answer will come
    from the small world of crayfish.
What do we do?
    Balance our shadows
    like oaks in bright sunlight,
    stretch and tumble
    as much as we're able,
    eat up the light
    and struggle with blindness.
When is it time?
    Time is a thrush
    that preens in the wood
    and sings on a slender branch
    in your ribcage. Listen.
    What comes on invisible wings,
    darting above the blue roots
    of flowers? Fly   Dragon
    fly. Now the bird sings.
Who'll come to save us?
    For some, it's the rattling
    cloud, the air before evening.
    Come, take my hand,
    for all that it's worth.
    Our hearts learn
    much too soon
    how to speak like mountain
    stones.

The White Land

When Orion straddled his apex of sky,
over the white land we lingered loving.
The River Eridanus flickered, foretelling
tropical waves and birds arrayed
in feathers of sunset, but we didn't waste
that prickling dark.

Not a dog barked our arrival before dawn.
Only in sleep did I drift vagabond
and suffer the patterns that constantly state
time has no time. Fate is a warlord.
That morning I listened to your long breath
for decades.

That morning you said bears
fell over the white land. Leaving their lair
in thick polar fur, they roused our joy
by leaving no footprint. Fat ones fell headlong,
but most of them danced, then without quarrel,
balanced on branches.

I couldn't breathe in the roar of that plane,
flying me back to a wooded horizon.
Regular rhythms bridge my uneven sleep.
What if the wind in the white land keeps you?
The dishwater's luminous; a truck
grinds down the street.

Reaching Yellow River

in memory of Mato Henlogeca's grandson

"It isn't a game for girls,"
he said, grabbing a fifth
with his right hand,
the wind with his left.

"For six days
I raced Jack Daniels.
He cheated, told jokes.
Some weren't even funny.

That's how come he won.
It took a long time
to reach this Yellow River.
I'm not yet thirty,

or it is thirty-one?
Figured all my years
carried the same hard thaw.
Out here, houselights hid

deep inside the trees.
For awhile I believed this road
cut across to Spring Creek
and I was trucking home.

I could kid you now,
say I ran it clean,
gasping on one lung,
loaded by a knapsack

of distrust and hesitation.
I never got the tone
in all the talk of cure.
I sang Honor Songs, crawled

the railroad bridge to Canada.
Dizzy from the ties,
I hung between both worlds.
Clans of blackbirds circled

the nearby maple trees.
The dark heart of me said
no days more than these.
As sundown kindled the sumacs,

stunned by the river's smile,
I had no need for heat,
no need to feel ashamed.
Inside me then the sound

of burning leaves. Tell them
I tumbled through a gap on the horizon.
No, say I stumbled through a hummock
and fell in a pit of stars.

When rain weakened my stride,
I heard them singing
in a burl of white ash,
took a few more days to rave

at them in this wood.
Then their appaloosas nickered
in the dawn and they came
riding down a close ravine.

Though the bottle was empty,
I still hung on. Foxtails beat
the grimace from my brow
until I took off my pain

like a pair of old boots.
I became a hollow horn filled
with rain, reflecting everything.
The wind in my hand

burned cold as hoarfrost
when my grandfather nudged me
and called out
my Lakota name."

Patterns

If I could track you down to have you taste
the strawberry shaded by beggar's green,
the winter wheat, remote as sunlight
through low moving clouds, we'd face
the squash blossom, fixed in its quiet temple,
and breathe in rhythm to our own beginnings.

Instead I step without your echo
over the cucumbers' tapestry of tendril
and wooly stem. The corn, my blind children,
mingle with wind and I walk naked
into their midst to let them brush my hips
with searching fingers, their cuffs alive with rain.

When I ask if they are happy,
a few by the fence whisper "Yes." It comes
through the rows, yes again
and again yes. My feet take root
in rings of corn light; the green earth
shouts more green against the weighted sky,

and under poppies of ash, patterns emerge:
lilacs collecting dark beneath the sheen of elms,
cedar buds tinting air with memories of frost,
a tanager's cry deep inside the windbreak,
my life's moire of years. When my jailers,
these brief words, fumble with their bony keys,

I listen to the arguments of flies, to the long
drawn-out call of doves, for lessons in endurance.
Moths, twilight in their wings, dance above the oatleaf,
and I know you stand above the same muted sea,
brooding over smoke that breaks
around hollyhock's uneven pinnacles.

For a moment, we are together,
where salt-stunted trees glory in the sun, where verbena
and jasmine light the wind with clean tomorrows.
I felt us there, felt myself and not-myself there.
We lived those promises ridiculed in solemn days.
We lived with a hunger only solitude can afford.

From the Sun Itself

While something hummed along the river,
I sat on a wooded hill in Spring,
playing my flute to fluttering green.
At my feet, a bellwort and a fern.

A white pine churned above me.
From the sun itself, the bellwort's flame.
An oak branch snapped, then crashed behind me,
as he came through the canopy.

A huge hawk folded, fell, then opening
his mantle, swooped under oaks with no qualm.
With the mastery of ashes, he twisted, lifted
and turned, breezing easily on broad wings.

I clung to a high note, more for my health
than his. No stranger to the scheming wind,
he hit the rim of the hill, flicked
his red tail and broke into blue.

The mottled light underneath his wings
scattered into beeches below.
Heady with flight, I stood silent, for
he knew what the human heart renounces.

He circled east and flew to the sun itself.
So drawn to him by my longing,
I didn't hear the deepening drone.
As bellwort, fern and pine bough grew greener,

the chopper's keen blade lagged for a moment,
after a dawn raid on the gypsy moths.
The pilot may never know he was swinging
the fierce edge of our twilight.

Waiting for Robinson

You nurtured grief until that leap
toward one translucent wave,
wanting a greener world,
a world you couldn't reach,
except in those brief moments
when lights on distant hills
glimmered through the eucalyptus leaves.

Chrome on the back fenders of your coupe
folded into wings. Tar melted
in the cracks near the front tire.

With a tremor in your shoulder,
you let luminol spin you
down Bridge Street in steady traffic.
You passed a vestibule
where under a jardiniere, two drunks argued,
who got the tattered blanket, who
the cardboard bed. Robinson,
you gathered up their grief
and stumbled on.

There were no survivors, no shutters
you could close. Dead or insane,
insane or dead. Remembering
how rain told the truth, you tried
to tear the roof away, to stand
under the sun, human and whole,
beyond the fears that seized you.

That July I was eight.
The neighbor lady hid behind venetian
blinds. Warm evenings, I'd wait
until an eye peered from the even shade.
Across the table made of dust,
you taunt me now. Aloof chimera,
how I wanted you to find a green world
spinning in other earth dark eyes.

One hand waves from a train.
Another from outgoing tide.
Gulls cry, search for the hand no one
could reach, as it held a card
complete with birth star, braided rug,
blue crystal and an easy chair.

Don't believe these melancholy lines.
The summer I turned twenty-eight,
I heard you hitched to Salton Sea,
away from rain and eucalyptus.
The glow from your cigarette
danced at dusk in the desert air.
You found it serene, dry there, though
not as green as you once hoped.

One More Sign

in memory of Norbert Seabrook Hill

Last night I dreamed you drank coffee
in my kitchen. After telling me of Teapot Dome,
how you roamed by boxcar
through the thirties, you blew four times
in your left fist, nodding at the hiss
of snow outside the screen. One more sign
an island will rise in the Caribbean.

Peering through our earthly dark, you laugh
when I say we won't find you again.
When I explain you cannot be here,
you hitch your belt in back, balancing
that rubber ball above a wound from World War II.
You grip the cup as you once did a drill,
then rise and quickly drink it down.

My uncle, I reach for an embrace,
but brimming through that space, cedar smoke
and the language of rain, lost in its
soliloquy. We didn't listen closely enough
to those rim world people singing in the pines.
We didn't thrill at the wind,
racing through a rhombus of stars.

You knew how secret influences—
leaf, stone, web—converge upon a life
and keep it fed with wonder.
Let others suspect you of false dreams,
an old man speaking to the cosmos
with a pendulum of keys. We whirled
unaware you were the balance wheel.

A week before you left, I thought
you the man crossing Barstow.
On the other side of the street, he
became a stranger, digging in his pocket
for change to buy a paper. Then I feared
your spirit traveled while you catnapped
in a room. Television glow. Closer zoom.

That day you danced away
air around Oneida held such moxie
it lingers on the ridges yet,
incandescent blue. The beating drum.
The beating heart. The galaxy's great arm
sparkled closer with each step
until the heart you often hit

to start again refused. I wait for you
to visit me in dreams. Some moments,
it seems I only need to call
to ask how ball players will arrive
from their court beneath the waves.
Even now, I listen in the dawn
to voices, calm, subterranean.

WENDY ROSE

(1948–   )

Alaskan Fragments
June 1981–Summer Solstice

1. *(from the air)*

Islands are green
and blackest black,
the water around them
cobalt; clouds melt
into glaciers
that melt into mountains
and canyons fill
silently
with white flesh
waiting.

2. *(from the air)*

Islands more islands:
great hands push
water between them
blackening fjords against
the never-setting sun
and placing deep
into tongues
the teeth of copper
and caves. Fish
become black

on black and spread
already their mouths
as if eager
for the bone hook,
the spear's thrust
and the smoking rack.

3. *(Fairbanks)*

At some point
during the round day
the blue breath
of the mountain range
jaggedly south
burns toward July
rehearsing for a dance
that will last sixty days—
resting from arctic fevers
and tentative rumbles
and rivers that break
into thousands of arrows,
ice that turns clear
then explodes into mist, valleys
that become a fog of insects
floated over the beaver ponds like nets
and the frantic clicking
of round aspen leaves
like fragile coins
in the afternoon rain,
the evening breeze.

4. *(Fairbanks—2:00 a.m.)*

Brought to the window
by a brilliant flash
not a snowbank stolen home
in June but the Tanana

shining with midnight's
red sun, early summer's great moon
that dances on the river
turning to platinum
the whole
of the Fairbanks
basin.
This is a Drum Dance
turning toward town
from a dozen Yukon villages,
a thousand
native throats.

5. *(Fairbanks—during the worst forest fire in ten years)*

Smoke settles all afternoon
and toward evening touches
the aspens; the red fog drops
like a great roan horse
its old flanks bending brittle
and groaning down among
the dimming streetlights,
the vapor trails receding
in the once-blue-white sky,
the Chena like a snake
curled about its eggs.
But inside these tightest of bonds
we continue to sweat changes,
heat ourselves into water and dream
of the future ice
on which the spirits
will dance and quarrel.
Southeast
low mountains of the Alaskan Range
grip the sun
to blur summer smoke
along broken highways

and the silver pipeline
covered with graffiti and blood.
Old women are leaving
the villages now; men
bring out their hatchets and shovels,
preparing the way back
to winter
and to home.

6. *(from the air–flying south)*

A long look back:
the sun is sloughing
its salmon skin
along the northernmost
horizon, a line so thin
that it steps through the dark
like a seal slips
through water.
And what remains:
a dissolving touch
or echo of whispers
begun long ago
but kept into summer
remaining to melt
                    smaller and
                    smaller into
                    the sea.

Throat Song: The Whirling Earth

*"Eskimo throat singers imitate the sounds
the women hear . . . listening to the sound of
wind going through the cracks of an ig-
loo . . . the sound of the sea shore, a river of
geese, the sound of the northern lights while
the lights are coming closer . . . in the old
days the people used to think the world was
flat, but when they learned the world was
turning, they made a throat-singing song
about it."*
  Inuktitut Magazine, *December 1980*

I always knew
          you were singing!

As my fingers have pulled your clay,
as your mountains have pulled the clay of me,

as my knees have deeply printed your mud,
as your winds have drawn me down and dried the mud of
     me,

around me always the drone and scrape of stone,
small movements atom by atom I heard like tiny drums . . .

I heard flutes and reeds that whine in the wind,
the bongo scratch of beetles in redwood bark,

the constant rattle that made
of this land a great gourd!

Oh I always knew

you were singing!

Loo-wit

The way they do
this old woman
no longer cares
what we think
but spits
her black tobacco
any which way
stretching
full length
from her bumpy bed.
Finally up
she sprinkles
ash on the snow,
cold buttes
promise nothing
but the walk
of winter.
Centuries of cedar
have bound her
to earth,
huckleberry ropes
lay prickly
on her neck.
Around her
machinery growls,
snarls and ploughs
great patches
of her skin.
She crouches
in the north,
her trembling
the source
of dawn.

Loo-wit–Woman of Fire (Cowlitz name for Mount St. Helens)

Light appears
with the shudder
of her slopes,
the movement
of her arm.
Blackberries unravel,
stones dislodge;
it's not as if
they were not warned.

She was sleeping
but she heard the boot scrape,
the creaking floor, felt
the pull of the blanket
from her thin shoulder.
With one free hand she finds her weapons
and raises them high; clearing the twigs from her throat
she sings, she sings, shaking the sky
like a blanket about her
Loo-wit sings and sings and sings!

Comparison of Hands
One Day Late Summer
El Sobrante

My hand
held between
leaf and bud
is white
clay unshaped,
the earth
parched,
the empty
ravine;
horizontal cracks

trace the bone
and fat of me
reluctantly
it doesn't matter
as I dodge
the droughts,
configuration of colors
mixed up and unsettled,
oil
upon the puddle.

Solid on mine
and strong,
your hand
contains summer
thunder,
the moist dark belly
in which seeds
sprout,
the beginning
of laughter,
a little boy's voice,
the promise
perhaps
of tomorrow.
The wash deepens
east into night,
sculpted by blood
and tumbling
there comes
end over end
everyone's names.

And myself jealous
of the bones
you hold
so well,
their proper shapes,

precision
of length;
those old songs
whirling from your throat
easy and hot
for the dancers
and the sweat.
You and your memories
of berries
picked ripe,
late summer
days like this
with tongue turning black
and teeth blue,
a loosely made basket
bouncing from your hip.
Your people stretched you
till one day you woke up
and you just knew
who you were.

I would mention
my memories now
but who would want to hear
of afternoons alone
and cold nights
on Eagle Hill,
of being a wild horse
among oats, bamboo,
eucalyptus and bay,
sunset-colored women
with braided bridles
in their hands.

Or would you want to know
that I who sing
so much of kin
grew alone and cold
in places so quiet

the dragonflies
thunder.
Would you want to hear
the sound of being tough,
or the hollow high winds
in my mother's heart.
Would you want to count
the handfuls of pills
or touch the fingers
that tighten
on my thigh
even now

for what is a ghost
after all
but dry
years or apples
buckeye or sage
dry memories, dry berries, dry earth, dry corn,
clocks, eyes, womanplace, words,

not enough crows
to quarrel
for the seeds . . .

If I am too brown or too white for you

remember I am a garnet woman
whirling into precision
as a crystal arithmetic
or a cluster and so

why the dream
in my mouth,
the flutter of blackbirds
at my wrists?

In the morning
there you are
at the edge of the river
on one knee

and you are selecting me
from among polished stones
more definitely red or white
between which tiny serpents swim

and you see
that my body is blood
frozen into giving birth
over and over, a single motion,

and you touch the matrix
shattered in winter
and begin to piece together
the shape of me

wanting the curl in your palm
to be perfect
and the image less clouded,
less mixed

but you always see
just in time
working me around
the last hour of the day

there is a small light
in the smoke, a tiny sun
in the blood, so deep
it is there and not there,

so pure
it is singing.

Truganinny

> *"Truganinny, the last of the Tasmanians,*
> *had seen the stuffed and mounted body of*
> *her husband and it was her dying wish that*
> *she be buried in the outback or at sea for*
> *she did not wish her body to be subjected to*
> *the same indignities. Upon her death she*
> *was nevertheless stuffed and mounted and*
> *put on display for over eighty years."*
>   Paul Coe, Australian Aborigine
>   Activist, 1972

You will need
to come closer
for little is left
of this tongue
and what I am saying
is important.

I am the last one.

I whose nipples wept
white mist
and saw so many
daughters dead
their mouths empty and
round
their breathing stopped
their eyes gone gray.

Take my hand   Please
black into black   take my body
as yellow clay   to the source of night,
is a slow melt   to the great black desert
to grass gold

of earth

and I am melting
back to the Dream.

Do not leave me
for I would speak,
I would sing
one more song.

They will take me.
Already they come
even as I breathe
they are waiting
for me to finish
my dying.
We old ones
take such
a long time.

where Dreaming was born.
Put me under the bulk
of a mountain or in
the distant sea;

put me where
they will not
find me.

The Day They Cleaned Up the Border
El Salvador, February, 1981

> *"[Government soldiers] killed my children. I
> saw it. Then I saw the head of a baby float-
> ing in the water."*
>   Surviving village woman as quoted in
>   the news

How comforting
the clarity
of water,
flute music

in a rush
or startling
hush,
crackle of grass
like seeds
in a gourd
and the soothing
whisper
of the reeds.
I prayed the whole night
to be taken to my past,
for the pounding of rifles
comes again and again
morning by morning
till my two babies lay,
names stolen away,
in their beds
and in the yard
where they played.
So many gone
and I pray to be taken,
for the lizards to notice
and begin eating
at my feet,
work their way up
till even my heart
is nibbled away.
I have come so many mornings
to the stream, so many times prayed
in the glistening mist
and now
drink oceans to drown myself
from the mountains
of memory.   But look—
that little melon rind
or round gourd, brown and white

in the water
where I could pluck it out
and use it dry, slipping past me
in the ripples and turning
till its tiny mouth,
still suckling,
points
at me.

Robert

> *"I am death, the destroyer of worlds . . . the*
> *physicists have known sin and this is a*
> *knowledge they cannot lose."*
>   J. Robert Oppenheimer

the lines of your arteries
begin to glow   making maps
finger follows afraid &
firm   pale like the alamagordo sky
the white lizards in the sand

are you humming or is it
a wayward insect or the tremble
of your deepest bones. los alamos
trinity   alamagordo   (frail robert)
jornada del muerto   you crouch
in the bunker   hands to your eyes
your light gray business suit
loosened tie   speaking to
transparent friends or to no one
in particular

"It's amazing how
the tools, the technology
trap one"

       & you are amazed at the welts
       so wide on your wrists, those chains
       enormous from your belt.
       not even your wife was awake
       morning pivot of your life
       the radio groaned   you twisted
       the knob feeling for
       an end to feeling   but the voice
       said anyway how your kids went screaming
       from the crotch of the plane
       mouth-first onto play yard & roof top
       & garden & temple, onto hair & flesh
       onto steel & clay   leaving you
       leaving you   leaving you
       your own fingerprints   in the ashes
       your vomit your tears

Leaving Port Authority for the St. Regis Rezz

I saw a mesa
between two buildings,
a row of tall
thin houses on top
bare like the desert I know,
the roofs occurring
in clumps like greasewood. Oh Wendy, he said,
looking at his fingernails,
that's Weehawken.

Well
one way or another
we'll get some
where soon
for I have seen crows
dancing on the snow,
a hawk on Henry Street,
smoke plumes on the lips
of streetkids,
mesas
along the Hudson.
I am getting ready.

Six Nations Museum
Onchiota, New York–January

for Ray, John, Salli and Maurice

Is this your special light,
salmon blushing west to sky
and these your tall white pines,
your tangled twigs, the brush
of your fingers through everything

                      tobacco to north
                      tobacco to east

and this the meaning
of the Eastern Gate,
the faces and feet
crowding between
the silence of willow,
bare waving hands
of redbud, stark
bones of birch

                      tobacco to south
                      tobacco to west

and the moon that waited
within my belly
for the smoking song
to blossom and fade, the wild turkeys
to appear then gently came
wide open as the wise
women are

                              tobacco to sky
                              tobacco to earth

          tobacco
          to all
          my relations

STEVE CROW

(1949–   )

Revival

Snow is a mind
falling, a continuous breath
of climbs, loops, spirals,
dips into the earth
like white fireflies
wanting to land, finding
a wind between houses,
diving like moths
into their own light
so that one wonders
if snow is a wing's
long memory across winter.

Water Song

Water travels a long shot
into our house. When
we find a leaf or
the wing of a dragonfly
in the water we pour it out.
To return means something else
must die and be rejected.
Or if the water is pure,
we taste nothing strong
and nothing decays.

El Alamein

*"Wounds in the desert
heal slowly."*
    NBC News

1.

A machine gunner aims
over the desert,
his tubular eye following
whatever shadow of sun.
I read into his moon-cratered
face that he cannot be lonely.
He knows the speed of light
and the distance between deserts.
He is young and still dreams
of dancing with women
in Alexandria and Berlin.

2.

I should know him better.
He is my brother I carry
on my back from war,
through desert darkness
into a chapel.
He sees only the sand eaten
walls, the water stains
on the face of Madonna.
The Bible I carry is empty

and does not mention how
I can raise him from the dead.
How he could say he loves me
from the desert.

During W.W.II combat missions, American aviators
often carried pocket-size Bibles specially made with a
metal cover to protect flyers' chests from puncture by
bullets or shrapnel. Even aviators who were not Chris-
tian adherents carried the Bibles for good luck.

From *Songs*

XIV

They say a man dies
without magic.
They say the womb
never lies, a woman's
spirit is the warmth
a fire makes in the dark.
I am only one moment,
but together we are
alike and alive
when we listen, talk,
make love far into the night
dancing toward sunset
on the soft summer sand.

Louisiana

I can't say our garden is a delight
because the patch in our backyard
is the shape of Louisiana by accident.
Weeds the shape of brown pelicans
by reincarnation, and a small swamp,
unsafe to be around after dark.

Each time I drain the garden
a swamp water bubbles to the surface
with gar minnows and water moccasins
the size of earthworms. When I set
the weeds afire they begin mouthing
the air, wingless, pulling at their
roots to take seed elsewhere.

And tonight, magic in the wind,
rain the color of ashes.
I expect Lafitte to come poling
his pirogue across the yard,
whistling for his pirates
to follow him out of the cypress
with my head on a flambeau.
I never trusted Louisiana.
I should have stayed there.

Jean Lafitte, the famous French pirate of Barataria Bay,
was actually a pretty neat guy who, so the legend goes,
with the unexcelled combat skills of his own men and
the help of equally skilled southern Indian warriors,
literally saved Louisiana and the Gulf Coast from Brit-
ish dominance during the Battle of New Orleans when
Andrew Jackson and his American troops would have
lost the fight alone.

EARLE THOMPSON

(1950–   )

Song

Woman sits on her porch
knitting and begins singing
a Shakerhouse song:
      Hoy-hoy-ee . . .
      Hoy-ee-hoy . . .
Young Pah-temas rests
on the steps watching
a bough drifting inland
while the current tries taking
it to sea.
Cedar bough resists,
and in the boy's eyes
it becomes a dugout canoe—long,
with dark-haired men
naked to the waist paddling,
singing an old Lummi song.

Pah-temas and grandmother
watch seahawk dive from fine mist,
swoop upon a glint transformed
into fish
      Sudden splashing breaks
stillness of morning.

No Deposit

Sometimes
you feel
like
a
bottle
sitting
by itself;
no
return,
just
empty;
ready
to
be
thrown away.

The Juniper Moon Pulls at My Bones

I have tried to shift the stars
for her to rest upon
so she doesn't have to dwell
on the beach
or in the junipers,
because the ochre particles
will become a nest of bones
in the moonlight of fragile leaves.

Mythology

My grandfather placed wood
in the pot-bellied stove
and sat; he spoke:

"One time your uncle and me
seen some stick-indians
driving in the mountains
they moved alongside
the car and watched us
look at them
they had long black hair
down their backs and were naked
they ran past us."

Grandfather shifted
his weight in the chair.
He explained,
"Stick-indians are powerful people
they come out during the fall.
They will trick little children
who don't listen
into the woods
and can imitate anything
so you should learn
about them."

Grandfather poured himself
some coffee and continued:
"At night you should put tobacco
out for them
and whatever food you got
just give them some
'cause stick-indians
can be vengeful
for people making fun of them.
They can walk through walls
and will stick a salmon up your ass
for laughing at them
this will not happen if you understand
and respect them."

My cousin giggled. I listened and remember
Grandfather slowly sipped his coffee
and smiled at us.
The fire smoldered like a volcano
and crackled.
We finally went to bed. I dreamt
of the mountains and now
I understand my childhood.

Love Song

She is a reed swaying in blue;
Chokecherries are the color of her
skin and her feet moisten the earth.
She sings and prays for the ochre moon
like the first woman.

RAY A. YOUNG BEAR

(1950–   )

The Language of Weather

The summer rain isn't here yet,
but I hear and see the approaching
shadow of its initial messenger:
Thunder.
The earth's bright horizon
sends a final sunbeam directly
toward me, skimming across the tops
of clouds and hilly woodland.
All in one moment, in spite
of my austerity, everything
is aligned: part land, part cloud,
part sky, part sun and part self.
I am the only one to witness
this renascence.
Before darkness replaces the light
in my eyes, I meditate briefly
on the absence of religious
importunity; no acknowledgement
whatsoever for the Factors
which make my existence possible.
My parents, who are hurrying
to overturn the reddish-brown dirt
around the potato plants, begin to talk
above the rumbling din.
"Their mouths are opening.
See that everyone in the household
releases parts of ourselves
to our Grandfathers."

While raindrops begin to cool
my face and arms, lightning
breaks a faraway cottonwood
in half; small clouds of red
garden dust are kicked into
the frantic air by grasshoppers
in retreat.
I think of the time I stood
on this same spot years ago,
but it was under moonlight,
And I was watching this beautiful
electrical force dance above
another valley.
In the daylight distance,
a stray spirit whose guise
is a Whirlwind, spins and attempts
to communicate from its ethereal
loneliness.

The Significance of a Water Animal

Since then I was
the North.
Since then I was
the Northwind.
Since then I was nobody.
Since then I was alone.

The color of my black eyes
inside the color of King-
fisher's hunting eye
weakens me, but sunlight
glancing off the rocks
and vegetation strengthens me.
As my hands and fingertips
extend and meet,
they frame the serene
beauty of bubbles and grain—
once a summer rainpool.

A certain voice of *Reassurance*
tells me a story of a water animal
diving to make land available.
Next, from the Creator's
own heart and flesh
Ukimau was made:
the progeny of divine
leaders. And then
from the Red Earth
came the rest of us.

"To believe otherwise,"
as my grandmother tells me,
"or to simply be ignorant,
Belief and what we were given
to take care of,
is on the verge
of ending . . . "

The First Dimension of Skunk

It is the middle of October
and frosted leaves

continue to introduce
their descent as season
and self-commentary.
On the ground yellow-jacket
bees burrow themselves
into the windfall apples.
On the house the empty body shells
of locusts begin to rattle with
the plastic window covering
torn loose the night previous
in the first sudden gusts of wind.
South of the highway bridge
two extinct otters are seen
by Selene's father while
setting traps.
"Mates swimming;
streamlined and playing
games along the Iowa River."
In the midst of change
all it takes is one anachronism,
one otter whistle.

For us, it began with the healthy-
looking salamander who stopped our car.
So last night we stood in the cold
moonlight waiting for the black
coyote. No animal darted
from tree to tree, encircling us.
Here was a time in an orange grove
next to the San Gabriel mountains
when I was surrounded by nervous
coyotes who were aware
of the differences
between thunder
and an earth tremor.

Selene motioned for me to stand
still, and the moonlit foothills
of Claremont disappeared.
An owl began to laugh.
I remained quiet and obliged
her gesture not to mimic its laugh,
for fear we might accidentally trigger
the supernatural deity it possesses
to break this barrier—
and once again find ourselves
observing a ball of fire
rise from an abandoned garden
which separates into four fireflies
who appear like four distant jets
coming into formation
momentarily
before changing into one intense
strobe light,
pulsating inside an appletree,
impervious to hollow-point bullets,
admissions of poverty and carlights.
We stood without response
and other thoughts came.
From the overwhelming sound
of vehicles and farm machinery,
together with the putrid odor
of a bee slaughterhouse,
such anticipation
seemed inappropriate.
Whoever constructed
the two railroad tracks
and highways through Indian land
must have planned and known
that we would be reminded daily
of what is certainty.
In my dream the metal
bridge plays an essential part

and subsequent end of what
was intended to occur.
I would speak to the heavy
glass jar, telling it
the paper bullet
was useless underwater.

Three days ago, in the teeth
of Curly and Girl, a skunk
was held firmly and shook
until lifeless.
The first evening
we hear its final death call.
At the same hour the second night
we hear it again. The third night-
sound is more brave and deliberate;
it waits to blend with the horn
of an oncoming Northwestern train,
forcing us to step backward,
taking random shots at objects
crashing through the brush.
We have a theory that Destiny
was intercepted, that the Executioner
ran elsewhere for appeasement.
We also think the skunk's
companion returned on these nights
to mourn a loved one,
but all had to be deleted,
leaving us more confused.
Yesterday, we examined the dead
skunk and were surprised to find it
three times less the size I first
saw it with Mr. D.
My parents offered an explanation.
"A parrot or a pelican on their
migratory route."
With our surroundings

at someone else's disposal,
all we have are the embers
and sparks from our woodstove
and chimney: the fragrance
to thwart the supernatural.

From the Spotted Night

In the blizzard
while chopping wood
the mystical whistler
beckons my attention.
Once there were longhouses
here. A village.
In the abrupt spring floods
swimmers retrieved our belief.
Their spirit remains.
From the spotted night
distant jets transform
into fireflies who float
towards me like incandescent
snowflakes.
The leather shirt
which is suspended
on a wire hanger
above the bed's headboard
is humanless; yet when one
stands outside the house,
the strenuous sounds
of dressers and boxes
being moved can be heard.
We believe someone wears
the shirt and rearranges
the heavy furniture,
although nothing
is actually changed.

Unlike the Plains Indian shirts
which repelled lead bullets,
ricocheting from them
in fiery sparks,
this shirt is the means;
this shirt *is* the bullet.

Nothing Could Take Away the Bear-King's Image

At first I thought I would feel
guilty in not missing you,
that despite its unfortunate
occurrence,
I would see you again
(exactly the way you were
before a hunter's arrow
glanced off some willows—
lodging near the pulsating song
of the Red Earth heart)
either here,
or towards that memorable direction
near the oily air of Los Angeles
where once a Zuni Indian companion
peered into a telescope aimed
at the Orion constellation:
"These three faint stars
are known for their parallel
formation rather than by four
of the bright stars which
frame them."
While we were sitting
on a manicured knoll
positioned above a Greek theatre,

we heard the distant skirling
sound of Scottish bagpipes
coming through the eucalyptus trees.
We went to them, and there,
the astronomer-physicist
invited us to share his interest
in the night skies he was playing for.
He told a story of this Greek hunter
composed of stars;
The "Three-Stars-In-A-Row"
were his belt.
"I think that's me, Grandfather,"
responded my Zuni companion,
"but I will believe you more
if you sell us your scotch whiskey—
and consider the magnitude of my belief
if I told you the bubbles of my Creator's
saliva made the stars, Grandson."
"Grandfather? Grandson? In the same
sentence? I am not related to you
in any way!" demurred the scholarly man.
The two Hispanics, Sergio & Camacho,
who were with us reaffirmed the Zuni's
request by bumping the academician
with their expanded chests.
"Grandfather, Grandson,"
they repeated.
Later, with erratic wind-notes
and chinking necklace shells,
my companion tripped and fell on
the professor's bagpipes
as he was completing
his third revolution
around the observatory.
He rolled down the sandy incline
breaking the instrument
into several pieces.
Suddenly, the professor's eyes
possessed a wild gleam:

a distant fire we hadn't seen before;
a nebula of sorts.
He knelt next to the dead instrument
and began to weep.
"My dear chanter! My drone!"
Like gentlemen, Sergio & Camacho
offered to pay for the irreplacable
parts, but it was too late.
We left (no, we fled from)
the observatory.

Back at the Greek theatre,
we found solace by the singing
of round and grass dance songs
with three white friends:
one jeweler, one ROTC student,
and one KSPC disc jockey,
until we were greeted
by Sioux voices from the dark.
There was immediate silence,
and then the Sioux National Anthem:
"The United States flag will stand forever.
As long as it stands the people will live
and grow; therefore, I am doing this
say the Indian soldier boys."
The radio announcer advised us
the voice was amplified,
possibly by a handheld system.
Pretty soon, we were surrounded
by figures wearing bronze helmets.
The jeweler whispered to us.
"They look like Mudheads with metallic paint."
The military student observed and commented
on their evenly-spaced formation.
Several descended the stone steps
and their boot heels echoed
onto the stage.
When they got close
with their glistening visors,

nightsticks and badges,
we were bewildered.
The police officer explained
that he was a boy scout leader
and learning Siouan was essential.
"Would you boys consider singing
for our troop in Pomona?"
he queried before stating
the purpose of his visit.
"What disturbance?" we asked
in regard to bagpipes and walked back
to our individual dormitory rooms.
We called each other on the phone,
laughing at times, exchanging crazy
warhoops in a warm California night;
that ancient but comical time and place
where we hypothesized the draft
which lifted Marilyn Monroe's dress
came from the San Andreas Fault.
When it shifted, Orozco's murals
in Frary Hall actually moved,
responding to the land wave
and the force of the Pacific Ocean.

We are endless like the Midwestern
breeze in winter which makes the brittle
oak leaves whisper in unison of this
ethereal confidence.
Nothing could take away
the Bear-King's own image
who is human and walks.
There remains a bottle of champagne
beside the charred concrete block;
the half-smoked cigarette
of corn husk and Prince Albert tobacco
which was propped next
to the green bottle
has disappeared
into the snowdrift.

The Bow Priest hasn't been summoned.
In the tribal gymnasium, exercise
equipment is marked by the greasy
handprints of a phantom infant.
The caretaker's two bows
and their arrows lie unpropelled.
The crooked snakelike arm doesn't
have the strength to draw back
the taut string, which would
have triggered an old time
message to the brain.
On top of a moonlit hill
stands a boy whose lithe body
has been painted black
with numerous light-blue spots.
He signals us to follow him,
and he lights small fires
along the way.
Inside the earth-mound,
a small man in a bright-red headband
places an arrow in the bowstring
of his left hand which is bent
like a bow.
He explains the meaning
of the arrow's crest.
"From birds the bison dreams about.
This shaft of wood tipped with sharpened flint,
together with the wolfskin draped over the hunter
crouching low against the salty earth . . . "

Wadasa Nakamoon, Vietnam Memorial

Last night when the yellow moon
of November broke through the last line
of turbulent Midwestern clouds,
a lone frog, the same one
who probably announced
the premature spring floods,
attempted to sing.
Veterans' Day, and it was
sore-throat weather.
In reality the invisible musician
reminded me of my own doubt.
The knowledge that my grandfathers
were singers as well as composers—
one of whom felt the simple utterance
of a vowel made for the start
of a melody—did not produce
the necessary memory or feeling
to make a Wadasa Nakamoon,
Veterans' Song.
All I could think of
was the absence of my name
on a distant black rock.
Without this monument
I felt I would not be here.
For a moment, I questioned
why I had to immerse myself
in country, controversy and guilt,
but I wanted to honor them.
Surely, the song they presently
listened to along with my grandfathers
was the ethereal kind which did not stop.

The king cobra as political assassin

May 30, 1981

About two miles east of here
near the Iowa River bottom
there is a swampy thicket and inlet
where deer, fox and eagles
seem to congregate every autumn
without fail.
When I am hunting there
I always think:
if I were an eagle
bored by the agricultural
monotony of Midwestern landscape,
I would stop, too.
This morning I dreamt
of a little-used road going
from an overlooking hill down
into their divine sanctuary.
I tried to drive through
thinking it was a short cut
towards the tribal homeland,
but stopped after the automobile
tires sank into the moist earth.
I walked down the ravine and met
two adolescents and inquired
if the rest of the road was intact
or passable. A bit wary of me
they indicated that they didn't
know. A faceless companion
rolled down the car window
and spoke in Indian.
"Forget them! They shouldn't
be here, anyway."

I walked on. Further down
I met a minister and began
to chat with him about
the tranquil scenery,
how far the road extended
into the land founded
by the Boy-Chief in 1856.
(I avoided the personal
question of whether the dense
timber reminded him of South America.)
He turned and pointed with his black arm
to a deteriorating church mission
in a distant valley.
"Yes," I said. "Mamwiwaneka's wish—
when he purchased this land—
was a simple one."
Soon, a hippie with an exotic snake
wrapped decoratively around
his bare arms and shoulders joined
our polite and trivial
conversation about directions.
As we were talking the hippie
released his hyperactive pet.
For a moment we watched it slither
over some willows.
We did not think too much
of the snake until it slid
toward a nearby stream,
stopping and raising its beady-eyed
head intermittently, aware of prey.
Following it, we discovered what held
its attention: a much larger snake
was lying still and cooling itself
in the water. I told the hippie,
"You better call your pet."
With a calm face he said,
"I'm not worried; watch
the dance of hunting motions."
And we did.

The larger water snake recoiled
into its defensive stance
as the smaller slid into
the water. Before they each came within
striking distance, the hunter-snake
struck. They splashed violently
for a few moments.
Decapitated, the water snake's
muscled body became lax
in the sunlit current.
I thought about this scene today
and the events which led to it
many times over, analyzing its
discordant symbolism.
I finally concluded this dream
had nothing to do with would-be
assassins, cinema-child prostitutes,
political decisionmakers or anything
tangible. In *Journal of a Woodland Indian*
I wrote:
"It was a prophetic yearning
for real estate and investments;
something else, entirely . . . "

Emily Dickinson, Bismarck and the Roadrunner's Inquiry

I never thought for a moment
that it was simply an act of fondness
which prompted me to compose
and send these letters.
Surely into each I held
the same affection as when
we were together on a canoe
over Lake Agassiz in Manitoba,
paddling toward a moonlit fog
before we lost each other.

From this separation came
the Kingfisher, whose blue and white
colored bands on chest and neck
represent the lake-water and the fog.
But this insignia also stands
for permafrost and aridity:
two climate conditions
I could not live in.

It's necessary to keep your apparition
a secret: your bare shoulders,
your ruffled blouse, and the smooth
sounds of the violin you play
are the things which account
for this encomium for the Algonquin-
speaking goddess of beauty.

Like the caterpillar's toxin
that discourages predators,
I am accustomed to food
which protects me,
camouflages me.
I would be out of place
in the tundra or desert,
hunting moose for its meat and hide,
tracking roadrunners for their feathers.

But our dialects are nearly the same!
Our Creation stories begin on a neat
floor of undigested bones,
overlooking the monolithic glaciers.
This is what we are supposed to have
seen before our interglacial internment.
That time before the Missouri River
knew where to go.

My memory starts under the earth
where the Star-Descendant taught me
to place hot coals on my forearm.
"In the afterlife, the scar tissue
will emit the glow of a firefly,
enabling one to expedite the rebirth
process. This light guides one's way
from Darkness."

The day I heard from you,
I accidently fell down the steps
of a steamboat and lost consciousness,
which was befitting because
there was little rationale
for the play (I had just watched
onboard) of a man who kept
trying to roll a stone uphill,
a stone which wanted to roll downhill.
I found myself whispering
"No business politicizing myth"
the moment I woke up.
Gradually, in the form of blood
words began to spill from
my injuries: Eagle feathers
1–2–3 & 4 on Pipestone.

I now keep vigil for silhouettes
of boats disappearing over
the arête horizon.
I keep seeing our correspondence
arrange itself chronologically,
only to set itself ablaze,
and the smoke turns to radiant
but stationary cloud-islands,
suspended on strings above

Mt. St. Helens, Mt. Hood
and Mt. Shasta: Three Sisters
waiting Joseph's signal.
They tell me of your dissatisfaction
in my society where traffic signs
overshadow the philosophy
of being Insignificant.
It is no different
than living under a bridge in Texas
beside the Rio Grande.
Please accept advice from the Blind
pigmentless Salamander
who considers his past an inurement.
"Perplexity should be expected,
especially when such a voyage
is imminent."

I want to keep you as the year
I first saw your tainted photograph,
preserved in an oval wooden frame
with thick convex glass,
opposite the introvert
you were supposed to be,
walking in from the rain,
a swan minus the rheumatism.

All of a sudden it is difficult
to draw and paint your face
with graphic clarity,
when the initial response is to alter
your age.
Automatically, the bright colors
of Chagall replace the intent.
When the Whirlwind returned
as a constellation,
we asked for cultural acquittance,
but when the reply appeared as herons

skimming along the updraft
of the Reservation's ridge,
we asked again.
It was never appropriate.
We were disillusioned,
and our request became immune
to illness, misfortune and plain hate,
or so we thought.

Contempt must have predetermined
our destiny.
To no avail I have attempted to
reconstruct the drifting halves
to side with me.
All that time and great waste.
Positive moon, negative sun.

Way before she began to blossom
into a flower capable of destroying
or healing, and even during the times
she precariously engaged herself
to different visions,
I was already dependent upon her.
Whenever we were fortunate
to appear within each other's prisms,
studying and imploring our emissaries
beyond the stations
of our permanence,
I had no words to offer.

Mesmerized, she can only regret
and conform to the consequences
of an inebriate's rage
while I recede from her
a listless river
who would be glad
to cleanse and touch
the scar the third mutant-flower
made as it now burns and flourishes
in her arms.

I would go ahead and do this
without hint or indication
you would accept me,
                    Dear Emily.

The Personification of a Name

Our geodesic dome-shaped lodge
redirects the drifting snow.

Above us, through the momentary
skylight, an immature eagle
stops in its turbulent flight
to gaze into our woodland
sanctuary.

Easily outstared, we rest our eyes
on the bright floor. He reminds us
further of his presence through
the shadow movement of his wings:

Portrait of a hunter
during first blizzard.

Black Eagle Child.

Race of the Kingfishers

1.

Nobody on earth has a book of matches.
The German-silver tobacco box
and the optical burning lens
which has been built into its lid
is useless on gray blustery days.
For the moment, however, the mirrorlike
antique represents a star on the walnut
coffee table next to the iron striker,
flint and black antelope tine.
"This arrangement," notes
the elderly man named Bumblebee
"is the tribal celestial system."
He illustrates this concept further
through the quick sculpturing
of minature Sturgeon and Kingfisher
effigies in the frosted dirt.
I urge myself to pronounce
and memorize this sequence
correctly. *Should I ever see*
the real night Sky:
The Child-Twin is trapped
between two of the brightest
stars in the Orion constellation,
and the child's earthly counterpart
is an air bubble, moving in accordance
to the pressure of our combined weight
beneath the clear river ice.

Stars have been hiding though,
and the eight snowdrift formations
cover the landscape without order.
Startled by a rushing noise, we strain
our heads upward. For no reason, I think
of distant Polynesians who cannot navigate

in darkness over the ocean. In the sky,
we observe Midwestern seagulls,
propelling themselves against
the onslaught of brilliant snowflakes:
A blizzard which once deflected laser
beams from their target. But bullhead-
fish feeds are firm imprints in seagull
mind. A visual prayer now a year old,
Unaffected by the sounds of floods
and ice jams, a lone frog—
the invisible musician—begins to emit
low mournful croaks, which represent a song
of tribute to men-relatives whose names
are carved on a monument of black
polished rock. We understand part
of the song goes to those other men
who became an Indochina memory
after their return home.
Although they are gone, they
frequent our surreal dreams:
Two bloody mary drinks, a silk
navigator's scarf and golden
shoulder braids with specks
of red sand. On a concrete bridge
where giant frothy waves respond
to an unseen ocean, we honor them
in the same breath as the Trung sisters.
This hour when the river carries
the wreath northward—the other way.

2.

Above us, through the canvas lodge
opening, the sun's mirage appears,
causing small insects to release
their numb bodies from the ceiling
into flight. We question which myth

tells of this Incongruity. Through the thin wall, a voice
  informs us we've
lost controllable fire—the very factor
which can heal as well as destroy.
"When we find this element," answers
the elderly Bumblebee, "we hope to
discern by the remaining grains of flint,
rust and bone when the last thunderstorm
occurred." In a gesture made by thoughtless
men, we invite the person with the voice
to sit with us in further conversation.
But when a child entity enters our abode,
wearing a perforated parka, we shield
our eyes from starlight coming through
clothes of poverty.
Each social order of the locust
and vulture worlds we briefly inhabit
in the course of our evolution
finds contempt in our belief.
From each existence we learn
when the wooden stake in our backs
can no longer be twisted to make
our mature features anew, or when
our artificial intestines cease
to pulsate with the land, we disappear.

Motivated by the view of mountains
being encircled by clouds, eagles
and pine saplings, we attempt to make
ourselves credible to the Salamander
who lived with the first creatures
so long ago.

If Paracelsus only knew . . .

3.

Outside in the wintry wind,
elegantly dressed women dance around us,
holding silver saxophones, which they pretend
to smoke. Before building up enough courage
to step outside and ask for a precious match
from the observers, I think of Sherlock Holmes
and his double-brimmed hat, wondering whether
he could have solved the mystery
of the missing Night-Sky. Upon my return,
Bumblebee hands me a crumpled cigarette.
After a short pause for a light, he takes
a drag and begins to talk in his smoke.
"Imported beer makes me philosophical . . . "
In a demanding gesture, accompanied
by a raspy voice, he inquires
if I have more pheasant or Manitan beer.
My wife Selene is offended, but she shrugs
it off. (Her eyes tell me she knows
something we don't.)

Pointing to the women dancers,
our metamorphic guest narrates
the importance of their movements:
"Later, in their Kingfisher costumes,
they will manipulate with strings and pulleys
the bird's hunting motions while reciting
complex prose. Their sole purpose
is to serve the Aurora Borealis,
which they believe will signal
our universal demise." During a break
before the race, several dance attendants
walked up to the Kingfishers and laid out
blankets over the snow beside them,
displaying mementos from previous
Flag Wars. "Simply by inhaling their air
with imaginary straws," whispers our guest,

"we derive good luck, but the whole endeavor
seems meaningless in a winter plagued
by darkness."

4.

Rappeling on their life strings,
caterpillars slowly stream down
from the intersecting lodge poles.
Without the presence of a healthy
cooking flame, they descend onto
the cool ashes. As fiery sparks begin
to materialize on an overturned skillet,
the caterpillars stop.
I resolve that wounded men
are being retrieved or dug out
somewhere in the Persian terrain.

Acknowledging the need for conflict,
and citing the story where the Heron
flies over Montana, following
the Missouri River,
familiarizing itself
with the land of Afterlife,
I rise from my chair and walk
towards the octagon drum.
Suddenly, before I have a chance
to tighten the glossy drumhide
with the antelope tine,
I find myself standing in blue
tropical water. Like an infant,
I try to maintain my balance,
but a huge fish swirls by,
sending a wave through
my tremulous body.

5.

Before our elderly guest left,
content the *Race of the Kingfishers*
coincided with his goal, he knelt
on the floor again and doubled
his right hand into a fist as if
he was about to send forth a marble.
Instead, he drew diagrams of the earth's
interior with lines of bone-white sand.

As the blizzard changed into harmless clumps
of wet snow, the dim candlelight became
more steady and bright. My last thought
had to do with a painting which I had stored
long ago. In dynamic poster colors,
an individual with ironed Levis
and cowboy boots sits in a jetseat
with his brown crooked hand
clutching a plastic cocktail glass;
and the window beside him shows
the distant snowcapped mountains
with a city below them protruding
from mud. (I knew then that our beginning
was to be our end.) I unwrapped the painting,
wiped the grime from the acetate cover
and read its title: *Indian Subject Asleep
On Flight 544 From Albuquerque After Lecture
On Indigenous Literature: A Corroboration
On Prophecy.*

6.

The next day when I met him
on the community's lone dirt road,
he explained his temperament was a result
of his marital separation. I responded
that it made no difference to my esteem,

that Selene knew all the facts.
Afterwards, he showed me his
Czechoslovakian-cutbead buckle:
A moon of half-green and half-red beads
divided by a single horizontal line
of pearl beads. "It looks pretty good,"
I said. "A simple idea," he replied,
"but they are colors of sanctity."
I continued my walk feeling glad
alcohol had not ruined my day.
"By the way," he said sternly
after we had walked a few paces
from each other like chivalrous foes,
"you have a bug in your ear!"
in my heart I thought:
Why would anyone want me
under surveillance?
But my left ear had been humming.
When I turned around, three conspicuous men
with recording apparatus and earphones
tried to act as if they couldn't hear me.
In their pretense to mingle into
the circus crowd, they stumbled
when I spoke to them . . .

JOY HARJO

(1951–   )

I Give You Back

I release you, my beautiful and terrible
fear. I release you. You were my beloved
and hated twin, but now, I don't know you
as myself. I release you with all the
pain I would know at the death of
my daughters.

You are not my blood anymore.

I give you back to the white soldiers
who burned down my home, beheaded my children,
raped and sodomized my brothers and sisters.
I give you back to those who stole the
food from our plates when we were starving.

I release you, fear, because you hold
these scenes in front of me and I was born
with eyes that can never close.

I release you, fear, so you can no longer
keep me naked and frozen in the winter,
or smothered under blankets in the summer.

I release you
I release you
I release you
I release you

I am not afraid to be angry.
I am not afraid to rejoice.
I am not afraid to be black.
I am not afraid to be white.
I am not afraid to be hungry.
I am not afraid to be full.
I am not afraid to be hated.
I am not afraid to be loved.
to be loved, to be loved, fear.

Oh, you have choked me, but I gave you the leash.
You have gutted me but I gave you the knife.
You have devoured me, but I laid myself across the fire.
You held my mother down and raped her,
                        but I gave you the heated thing.

I take myself back, fear.
You are not my shadow any longer.
I won't hold you in my hands.
You can't live in my eyes, my ears, my voice
my belly, or in my heart my heart
my heart   my heart

But come here, fear
I am alive and you are so afraid
                        of dying.

She Had Some Horses

She had some horses.

She had horses who were bodies of sand.
She had horses who were maps drawn of blood.
She had horses who were skins of ocean water.
She had horses who were the blue air of sky.

She had horses who were fur and teeth.
She had horses who were clay and would break.
She had horses who were splintered red cliff.

She had some horses.

She had horses with long, pointed breasts.
She had horses with full, brown thighs.
She had horses who laughed too much.
She had horses who threw rocks at glass houses.
She had horses who licked razor blades.

She had some horses.

She had horses who danced in their mothers' arms.
She had horses who thought they were the sun and their
bodies shone and burned like stars.
She had horses who waltzed nightly on the moon.
She had horses who were much too shy, and kept quiet
in stalls of their own making.

She had some horses.

She had horses who liked Creek Stomp Dance songs.
She had horses who cried in their beer.
She had horses who spit at male queens who made
them afraid of themselves.
She had horses who said they weren't afraid.
She had horses who lied.
She had horses who told the truth, who were stripped
bare of their tongues.

She had some horses.

She had horses who called themselves, "horse."
She had horses who called themselves, "spirit," and kept
their voices secret and to themselves.
She had horses who had no names.
She had horses who had books of names.

She had some horses.

She had horses who whispered in the dark, who were afraid
to speak.
She had horses who screamed out of fear of the silence, who
carried knives to protect themselves from ghosts.
She had horses who waited for destruction.
She had horses who waited for resurrection.

She had some horses.

She had horses who got down on their knees for any savior.
She had horses who thought their high price had saved
   them.
She had horses who tried to save her, who climbed in her
bed at night and prayed as they raped her.

She had some horses.

She had some horses she loved.
She had some horses she hated.

These were the same horses.

New Orleans

This is the south. I look for evidence
of other Creeks, for remnants of voices,
or for tobacco brown bones to come wandering

down Conti Street, Royale, or Decatur.
Near the French Market I see a blue horse
caught frozen in stone in the middle of
a square. Brought in by the Spanish on
an endless ocean voyage he became mad
and crazy. They caught him in blue
rock, said
        don't talk.

I know it wasn't just a horse
              that went crazy.

Nearby is a shop with ivory and knives.
There are red rocks. The man behind the
counter has no idea that he is inside
magic stones. He should find out before
they destroy him. These things
have memory,
          you know.

I have a memory.
          It swims deep in blood,
a delta in the skin. It swims out of Oklahoma.
deep the Mississippi River. It carries my
feet to these places: the French Quarter,
stale rooms, the sun behind thick and moist
clouds, and I hear boats hauling themselves up
and down the river.

My spirit comes here to drink
My spirit comes here to drink.
Blood is the undercurrent.

There are voices buried in the Mississippi
mud. There are ancestors and future children
buried beneath the currents stirred up by
pleasure boats going up and down.
There are stories here made of memory.

I remember DeSoto. He is buried somewhere in
this river, his bones sunk like the golden
treasure he traveled half the earth to find,
came looking for gold cities, for shining streets
of beaten gold to dance on with silk ladies.

He should have stayed home.

                (Creeks knew of him for miles
                   before he came into town.
                     Dreamed of silver blades
                    and crosses.)
And knew he was one of the ones who yearned
for something his heart wasn't big enough
to handle.
         (And DeSoto thought it was gold.)

The Creeks lived in earth towns,
                   not gold,
     spun children, not gold.
That's not what DeSoto thought he wanted to see.
The Creeks knew it, and drowned him in
    the Mississippi River
        so he wouldn't have to drown himself.

Maybe his body is what I am looking for
as evidence. To know in another way
that my memory is alive.
But he must have got away, somehow,
because I have seen New Orleans,
the lace and silk buildings,
trolley cars on beaten silver paths,
graves that rise up out of soft earth in the rain,
shops that sell black mammy dolls
holding white babies.

And I know I have seen DeSoto,
                having a drink on Bourbon Street,
                mad and crazy
                dancing with a woman as gold
                as the river bottom.

The Woman Hanging from the Thirteenth Floor Window

She is the woman hanging from the 13th floor
window. Her hands are pressed white against the
concrete molding of the tenement building. She
hangs from the 13th floor window in east Chicago,
with a swirl of birds over her head. They could
be a halo, or a storm of glass waiting to crush her.

She thinks she will be set free.

The woman hanging from the 13th floor window
on the east side of Chicago is not alone.
She is a woman of children, of the baby, Carlos,
and of Margaret, and of Jimmy who is the oldest.
She is her mother's daughter and her father's son.
She is several pieces between the two husbands
she has had. She is all the women of the apartment
building who stand watching her, watching themselves.

When she was young she ate wild rice on scraped down
plates in warm wood rooms. It was in the farther
north and she was the baby then. They rocked her.

She sees Lake Michigan lapping at the shores of
herself. It is a dizzy hole of water and the rich
live in tall glass houses at the edge of it. In some
places Lake Michigan speaks softly, here, it just sputters
and butts itself against the asphalt. She sees
other buildings just like hers. She sees other
women hanging from many-floored windows
counting their lives in the palms of their hands
and in the palms of their children's hands.

She is the woman hanging from the 13th floor window
on the Indian side of town. Her belly is soft from
her children's births, her worn levis swing down below
her waist, and then her feet, and then her heart.
She is dangling.

The woman hanging from the 13th floor hears voices.
They come to her in the night when the lights have gone
dim. Sometimes they are little cats mewing and scratching
at the door, sometimes they are her grandmother's voice,
and sometimes they are gigantic men of light whispering
to her to get up, to get up, to get up. That's when she wants
to have another child to hold onto in the night, to be able
to fall back into dreams.

And the woman hanging from the 13th floor window
hears other voices. Some of them scream out from below
for her to jump, they would push her over. Others cry softly
from the sidewalks, pull their children up like flowers and
    gather
them into their arms. They would help her, like themselves.

But she is the woman hanging from the 13th floor window,
and she knows she is hanging by her own fingers, her
own skin, her own thread of indecision.

She thinks of Carlos, of Margaret, of Jimmy.
She thinks of her father, and of her mother.
She thinks of all the women she has been, of all
the men. She thinks of the color of her skin, and
of Chicago streets, and of waterfalls and pines.
She thinks of moonlight nights, and of cool spring storms.
Her mind chatters like neon and northside bars.
She thinks of the 4 a.m. lonelinesses that have folded
her up like death, discordant, without logical and
beautiful conclusion. Her teeth break off at the edges.
She would speak.

The woman hangs from the 13th floor window crying for
the lost beauty of her own life. She sees the
sun falling west over the grey plane of Chicago.
She thinks she remembers listening to her own life
break loose, as she falls from the 13th floor
window on the east side of Chicago, or as she
climbs back up to claim herself again.

For Alva Benson, and for Those Who Have Learned to Speak

And the ground spoke when she was born.
Her mother heard it. In Navajo she answered
as she squatted down against the earth
to give birth. It was now when it happened,
now giving birth to itself again and again
between the legs of women.

Or maybe it was the Indian Hospital
in Gallup. The ground still spoke beneath
mortar and concrete. She strained against the
metal stirrups, and they tied her hands down
because she still spoke with them when they
muffled her screams. But her body went on
talking and the child was born into their
hands, and the child learned to speak
both voices.

She grew up talking in Navajo, in English
and watched the earth around her shift and change
with the people in the towns and in the cities
learning not to hear the ground as it spun around
beneath them. She learned to speak for the ground,
the voice coming through her like roots that
have long hungered for water. Her own daughter
was born, like she had been, in either place
or all places, so she could leave, leap
into the sound she had always heard,
a voice like water, like the gods weaving
against sundown in a scarlet light.

The child now hears names in her sleep.
They change into other names, and into others.
It is the ground murmuring, and Mt. St. Helens
erupts as the harmonic motion of a child turning
inside her mother's belly waiting to be born
to begin another time.

As we go on, keep giving birth and watch
ourselves die, over and over.
And the ground spinning beneath us
goes on talking.

Anchorage

for Audre Lorde

This city is made of stone, of blood, and fish.
There are Chugatch Mountains to the east
and whale and seal to the west.
It hasn't always been this way, because glaciers
who are ice ghosts create oceans, carve earth
and shape this city here, by the sound.
They swim backwards in time.

Once a storm of boiling earth cracked open
the streets, threw open the town.
It's quiet now, but underneath the concrete
is the cooking earth,
                              and above that, air
which is another ocean, where spirits we can't see
are dancing   joking   getting full
on roasted caribou, and the praying
goes on, extends out.

Nora and I go walking down 4th Avenue
and know it is all happening.
On a park bench we see someone's Athabascan
grandmother, folded up, smelling like 200 years
of blood and piss, her eyes closed against some
unimagined darkness, where she is buried in an ache
in which nothing makes
                              sense.

We keep on breathing, walking, but softer now,
the clouds whirling in the air above us.
What can we say that would make us understand
better than we do already?
Except to speak of her home and claim her
as our own history, and know that our dreams
don't end here, two blocks away from the ocean
where our hearts still batter away at the muddy shore.

And I think of the 6th Avenue jail, of mostly Native
and Black men, where Henry told about being shot at
eight times outside a liquor store in L.A., but when
the car sped away he was surprised he was alive,
no bullet holes, man, and eight cartridges strewn
on the sidewalk
                    all around him.

Everyone laughed at the impossibility of it,
but also the truth. Because who would believe
the fantastic and terrible story of all of our survival
those who were never meant
                              to survive?

Transformations

This poem is a letter to tell you that I
have smelled the hatred you have tried
to find me with; you would like to destroy me.
Bone splintered in the eye of one you choose
to name your enemy won't make it better for you
to see. It could take a thousand years if you name it
that way, but then, to see after that time never
could anything be so clear. Memory has many forms.
When I think of early winter I think of a blackbird
laughing in the frozen air; guards a piece of light.
I saw the whole world caught in that sound. The sun
stopped for a moment because of tough belief. I don't
know what that has to do with what I am trying to tell
you, except that I know you can turn a poem into something
else. This poem could be a bear treading the far northern
tundra, smelling the air for sweet alive meat. Or a piece
of seaweed stumbling in the sea. Or a blackbird, laughing.

What I mean is that hatred can be turned into something
else, if you have the right words, the right meanings
buried in that tender place in your heart where
the most precious animals live. Down the street
an ambulance has come to rescue an old man who is slowly
losing his life. Not many can see that he is already
becoming the backyard tree he has tended
for years, before he moves on. He is not sad, but
compassionate for the fears moving around him.
That's what I mean to tell you. On the other side
of the place you live stands a dark woman.
She has been trying to talk to you for years.
You have called the same name in the middle of a
    nightmare,
from the center of miracles. She is beautiful.
This is your hatred back. She loves you.

Resurrection

Esteli
        this mountain town means something
                        like the glass of Gloody stars.
Your Spanish tongue will not be silent.
                            In my volcano heart
soldiers pace, watch over what they fear.
            One pretty one leans against his girlfriend.
They make promises, touch, plan to meet somewhere else
                                    in this
                                    war.

Not far down the fevered street
                a trace of calypso
                        laughter from a cantina.

We are all in a balloon that's about to split.
                              Candles make oblique circles
in the barrio church, line the walls
                     with prayers.
                              An aboriginal woman
as old as Momotombo fingers obsidian
                              recalls dreams, waits for the light
to begin to break. I don't imagine anything.
                              Lizards chase themselves all night
over the tin roof of the motel.
                              I rock in a barrage of fever
feel the breathing-sweat of the whole town stop, pause
                                        and begin again.
I have no damned words
                     to make violence fit neatly
                                        like wrapped
                                        packages
of meat, to contain us safely.
                              The songs here speak tenderly of honor and love
sweet melody is the undercurrent of gunfire
                                        yet
the wounded and the dead call out in words that sting
                                        like bitter limes.
Ask the women who have given away the clothes of their dead
     children,
Ask the frozen soul of a man who was found buried
                              in the hole left by his missing
                              penis.
They are talking, yet,
                     the night could change.
We all watch for fire
                     for all the fallen dead to return
and teach us a language so terrible
                              it could resurrect us all.

Esteli is a mountain town in Nicaragua, not far from
the Honduran border.

Eagle Poem

To pray you open your whole self
To sky, to earth, to sun, to moon
To one whole voice that is you.
And know there is more
That you can't see, can't hear
Can't know except in moments
Steadily growing, and in languages
That aren't always sound but other
Circles of motion.
Like eagle that Sunday morning
Over Salt River. Circled in blue sky
In wind, swept our hearts clean
With sacred wings.
We see you, see ourselves and know
That we must take the utmost care
And kindness in all things.
Breathe in, knowing we are made of
All this, and breathe, knowing
We are truly blessed because we
Were born, and die soon, within a
True circle of motion,
Like eagle rounding out the morning
Inside us.
We pray that it will be done
In beauty.
In beauty.

Bleed Through

I don't believe in promises, but there you are,
balancing on a tightrope of sound.
                                        You sneak into the world
inside a labyrinth of flame
                          break the walls beneath my ribs.
I yearn to sing; a certain note can spiral stars,
                    or knock the balance of the world askew.
Inside your horn lives a secret woman
              who says she knows the power of the womb,
can transform massacres into gold, her own heartache
                                        into a ruby stone.
Her anger is yours and when her teeth bite through
                                  a string of glass
you awaken
              and it is not another dream, but your arms
                    around a woman
              who was once a dagger between your legs.
There are always ways to fall asleep,
                              but to be alive is to forsake
                                    the fear of blood.
And dreams aren't excuses anymore. You are not behind
                              a smoking mirror,
but inside a ceremony of boulders that has survived
                              your many deaths.
It is not by accident you watch the sun
                              become your heart
              sink into your belly, then reappear in a town
                              that magnetically
                                    attracts you.
What attracts cannot naturally be separated.
              A black hole reversed is a white hot star,
                              unravels this night
inside a song that is the same wailing cry as blue.

There are no words, only sounds
                that lead us into the darkest nights,
where stars burn into ice
                where the dead arise again
                       to walk in shoes of fire.

DANIEL DAVID MOSES

(1952–   )

Report on Her Remains

   The Micmac woman's body has been disinterred and her severed hands are being transported by air for identification in Washington. In a refrigerated drawer in South Dakota a thirty eight caliber bullet floats, an icy glimmer within her skull. A similar glimmer comes off her fingernails. In the box passing above the Mississippi her hands are rustling, the nails growing, the fingers unfolding, refolding, pale wings migrating toward the Atlantic.

Her body sleeps the sleep of the abandoned. Its marrow refuses to condense. Her blood searches for the pine ridge under which the shallow grave is. It finds only turquoise left over from the last wind and leather so softly cured it welcomes starlight through. The leather's stained with sweat and semen, but even these relics fade.

Her hands remember only the last jet of breath, the warm gun butt, and the dream of power. They try to dream it again, the dream of black soil flooding and drowning the prairie, of the sky clearing with light like the shine of warm blood, of the woman perching on the palm of a flying stone. But that dream imploded when the woman died. Through their own glimmer her hands dream the remnants, dream of men with no faces swimming a storm of hot powder; their heads oiled and hands sharp as shovels, they dig up and burn the Dead to ash in the steely air.

Through the sinking light her body feels a sound. Her
hands have escaped the box and her bones the wrappings of
skin. They swing on their tendons, chiming.

Some Grand River Blues

Look. The land ends up
in stubble every
October. The sky
today may feel as

empty. But just be
like the river — bend
and reflect it. Those
blues already show

through the skin inside
your elbow — and flow
back to the heart. Why
let a few passing

Canada geese up
set you? Just remind
yourself how the land
also renews. Don't

despair just because
they're already too
high to hear. Your heart
started beating with

their wings the moment
you got sight of them
—but that's no reason
to fear it will still

when they disappear.
Look away now. Let
loose. See? The river's
bending like a bruise.

The Corn

I'd already lost my hair. Now my sun
fed children have been taken somewhere. Next

I'll lose these comfortable shoes of mud
to the cold—and be unconcerned. After

all, I no longer need a firm foothold.
There's no flood of light anymore—to stand

in and turn toward. Trickling away, the low
sun's only laying shadows out. They don't

move or fulfill one or feed some. Nor do
they do a thing for one's colour. One's left

with only crystals of frost growing—no
childish ears to get brightly wet behind,

no hands to wave as you stand whispering
about the land. Those children were taken

as I said and my hands grew as heavy
as ice, caressing only emptiness.

They dropped off and soon I'd guess the rest of
me will be ready to follow. Down through

the icebound soil to underground fields where
stars are planted in hills. At least that's what

I've seen, staring through the frost. Light will not
be lost but will grow and bud green again.

Party Favour

When you bared your china
coloured shoulder, telling

the whole room how a steel
pin had been popped in, how

thin a feel the air had
then, the naked scar blushed

deep enough to kiss. It
seemed the only part of

you in the smoky mix
of your party to keep

up modesty, a mouth
shaped spot holding shut while

the rest of your flesh spoke
out, dancing loudly and

alone in the middle
of the room. Only at

the end of the night were
you quiet, did that spot

seem to speak through the kiss
on the cheek and embrace

each of the last few to
take leave of you received.

Descending to the slick
street where flooded gutters

and darkness chilled my feet
and music and an orange

glow seeped out of your bay
window—I thought it had

a magic lantern sort
of look—I felt how close

in those inebriate
hours comradery

came to love. As close as
healing did to your wound.

ANITA ENDREZZE

(1952–   )

Birdwatching at Fan Lake

Our blue boat drifts
on the flat-shelled water.

In my lap: the red Book of Birds,
genesis of egg and feather

in the leavened air, begetting
the moist nests of osprey

and the mallard that floats
like bread on the water.

Around the lake are dark crowns
of granite and tall reeds with eyes

that burn gold in afternoon sun.
We eat salt crackers, green apples,

round cheese. On the shore,
a woman bends for a bright towel,

a white horse chews on wood.
The creek sings: *dribblestone*

pebblelarvae. The red faces
of salamanders are wise

under the green bracken.
Waxwings sing to a chokecherry sun,

their throats shrill glass whistles.
We check our lists, compare.

Mine has notes like: the birds fly
into the white corridor of the sky.

Or: does the ruffed grouse's drumming
enter into the memories of trees?

Lately, we've talked less, been less
sure of each other. Love, why

travel this far to find rarity
and remain silent

in the curved wing of our boat?
Your hand on the oar is enough

for me to think of love's migration
from the intemperate heart to halcyon soul.

You point to a kingfisher,
whose eggs are laid on fish bones.

The fish are fin to the fisher's crest.
On a rocky beach, a kildeer keens,

orange-vested children pull up canoes,
camp smoke nests on the leafy water.

You take my hand and call it *wing*.
Sunlight is reborn in the heart

of the wild iris. Its purple shadows
sway over the root-dark fish.

Look: the long-necked herons
in the green-billed water

are pewter. Their wet-ash wings wear
medallions of patience. We drift on,

buoyed by the tiny currents between us,
the light long-legged, the wind

full of hearts that beat quick
and strong.

Sunset at Twin Lake

Colville Indian Reservation

The heron stalks
the webbed water,
its feathers made of mirrors.

We hear the white breath
of water lilies as they float
in the cooling air.

The heron is a bringer
of reed music:
legs, beak, feathers—
all are godly instruments
in the evening wind.

Even the mountains
have a distant message
although we are more concerned
with things closer:
our hands still seeking
the last light
as we cast our lines
and the trout jumping
into the net
of the low-rising moon.

Song-Maker

There is a drunk on Main Avenue, slumped
in front of the Union Gospel Mission.
He is dreaming of pintos the color of wine
and ice, and drums that speak the names
of wind. His hair hides his face,
but I think I know him.

Didn't he make songs people still sing
in their sleep?
Didn't coyotes beg him for new songs
to give to the moon?
Didn't he dance all night once and laugh
when the women suddenly turned
shy at dawn?
Didn't he make a song just for me,
one blessed by its being sung only once?

If he would lift his face
I could see his eyes, see
if he's singing now
a soul dissolving song.
But he's all hunched over
and everyone walks around him.
He must still have strong magic
to be so invisible.

I remember him saying:
Even grass has a song,
'though only wind hears it.

Reviewing Past Lives while Leaf-Burning

the air is a smoke-tree, the wind
is the song of branches burning
into a brief sleep. I breathe the atoms
of yellow leaf and crumbled sun
until I am back scraping lichen
from my nest of rocks, my old eyes milky
as quartz. I know the names of seven winds
and seven colors and the herbs that heal
and I see the flocks of crystal birds
mending the sky where it cracks each morn,
but I am old. Tribeless. My skin breaks
its oath to me, leaving me unfulfilled.
I see palms of smoke in the air
and badgers tunneling under my song
until I become a young boy
riding the red mare in my father's herd,
following the fog off the coast.

Close by, the sacred island is a black hip
in the sea. There the priestesses
like boys with dark eyes.
I only remember the smoke that whispered
like a woman and her fluttering tongue
that she called fire and my father's face
far away crying in the mare's mane
until I became a woman, beautiful in my veils,
beckoning my dark hand to the fisherman
who never returns and my lungs turn to smoke
my bones to luminous shells, my voice as nowhere
as the wind. Then I am blond, kneeling
in the fields only men till, scratching out
the grave of my girl-child whose father
would not take her to our hearth
and my breasts are smothering in ash,
the milk dripping into the earth where fog
rises with its sucking mouths and I keen
believing only in the horned hands of death.
Yet, I am born again to smell the bitter
cordite of guns as the bullets burn the air
into little flags of resistance.
It is the last bullet that narrows
my name to earth and sky
takes my faith on its lips to praise.
Nearby, smoke hovers over the barracks,
singing sarahabrahamrebecca.
Until, at last, I am here: burning
leaves and my life as a woman
is full of everyday happiness:
the grasses are seeding the air
with green blessings, my husband
fills my room with red roses,
and my son is my only jewel,
until I am loved and loved and loved
and still, it's not enough.

The Girl Who Loved the Sky

Outside the second grade room,
the jacaranda tree blossomed
into purple lanterns, the papery petals
drifted, darkening the windows.
Inside, the room smelled like glue.
The desks were made of yellowed wood,
the tops littered with eraser rubbings,
rulers, and big fat pencils.
Colored chalk meant special days.
The walls were covered with precise
bright tulips and charts with shiny stars
by certain names. There, I learned
how to make butter by shaking a jar
until the pale cream clotted
into one sweet mass. There, I learned
that numbers were fractious beasts
with dens like dim zeros. And there,
I met a blind girl who thought the sky
tasted like cold metal when it rained
and whose eyes were always covered
with the bruised petals of her lids.

She loved the formless sky, defined
only by sounds, or the cool umbrellas
of clouds. On hot, still days
we listened to the sky falling
like chalk dust. We heard the noon
whistle of the pig-mash factory,
smelled the sourness of home-bound men.
I had no father; she had no eyes;
we were best friends. The other girls
drew shaky hop-scotch squares
on the dusty asphalt, talked about
pajama parties, weekend cook-outs,
and parents who bought sleek-finned cars.

Alone, we sat in the canvas swings,
our shoes digging into the sand, then pushing,
until we flew high over their heads,
our hands streaked with red rust
from the chains that kept us safe.

I was born blind, she said, an act of nature.
Sure, I thought, like birds born
without wings, trees without roots.
I didn't understand. The day she moved
I saw the world clearly; the sky
backed away from me like a departing father.
I sat under the jacaranda, catching
the petals in my palm, enclosing them
until my fist was another lantern
hiding a small and bitter flame.

Return of the Wolves

All through the valley, the people are whispering:
the wolves are returning, returning
to the narrow edge of our fields, our dreams.
They are returning the cold to us.
They are wearing the crowns of ambush,
offering the rank and beautiful snow-shapes
of dead sheep, an old man too deep in his cups,
the trapper's gnawed hands, the hunter's tongue.
They are returning the whispers of our lovers,
whose promises are less enduring than the wolves.

Their teeth are carving the sky into delicate antlers,
carving dark totems full of moose dreams: meadows
where light grows with the marshgrass and water
is a dark wolf under the hoof.
Their teeth are carving our children's names
on every trail, carving night into a different bone—
one that seems to be part of my body's long memory.

Their fur is gathering shadows, gathering
the thick-teethed white-boned howl of their tribe,
gathering the broken-deer smell of wind
into their longhouse of pine and denned earth,
gathering me also, from my farmhouse
with its golden light and empty rooms, to the cedar
(that also howls its woody name to the cave of stars),
where I am silent as a bow unstrung
and my scars are not from loving wolves.

Hansel, Gretel and Ruby Redlips

The moon's a path
into the forest.
Gretel is thin
as rain.

Hansel
is resourceful:
his pockets
are heavy
with white
pebbles.
They look
like little skulls
in the moonlight.
He marks the way
shadows trap eyes.

Then the clouds
drift out
of the hollows
of trees
and cover
the moon.
Only the witch
can see
that darkness
is a piece of flint.

She is called Ruby Redlips,
the Bewitcher,
the stepmother's rival.
Her beauty is the mask
of hunger.

Her hunger is a frame
of bones.
So she has a pretty house,
when all others are splinters
and harsh words.
And if she knows
a few spells
to make her body softer,
who could it hurt
to use that wisdom?
Not Gretel
who needs to learn
a few tricks of her own,
and not Hansel
who is just young enough
to see Ruby
with refreshing innocence.
A resourceful boy
is a resourceful man

and with his blue eyes . . . !
Gretel only needs rouge
and a wink or two
but Ruby needs
the magic mirror
of a young man's love.

If you've heard
a different version
of this tale,
then maybe
you've talked to the wrong person:
like the stepmother
who was stuck
with the woodcutter
who got drunk
every Friday night
in fits of remorse
for the loss
of his golden-haired children
and the kisses
of Ruby Redlips.

Meditating on Star Light
While Traveling Highway 2

> *"Why does [the star's] accumulated light*
> *not keep the heavens bright?"*
>   Alan Lightman in *Science 84*

We are visitors into
the dry interior.
This is the fossil country
with names like major points
of interest: Wasteway,
Reservoir, Hartline.

Near Creston, we spot
two short-eared owls flying
over the constellations of sage.

The light that drifts
so slowly down
upon the Buttes
is a question
of years. We all travel
at a finite speed: the light,
the gift of muscle and bone.

What we owe to the light
—from stars blind
in their empty sockets—
is not lost in the retinas
of our souls.
Handspans of papyrus
to laser: all the stars' light
is a visible sphere
at the base of the brain.
Here is the song of the infinite.

Nightly, coyote songs ascend
into the sky
where calcified stars still shine
their shell-like light upon us.
We absorb it, becoming more
like dawn.

November Harvest

Barns huddle over the horns
of cattle, whose dreams
are four-chambered,
the white hearts of winter.

In the shadows of thorns,
the farmers are without
substance.
Under the roots,
the warm slow sleepers
are not dreaming of us.
Their breaths pass into
the myths of animals.

All November fields are dark
passages into the earth.
What the owl flies into
we call night.
The moon is a windfall, a pear
weathering to the core.
The scarecrow is quiet;
a small wind lifts
his eyeless sack of a head.

When the Harvest God comes,
he wears a suit black
as parson's cloth.
His tongue is a brown leaf,
his sermon a mouthful of wheat.
What we leave in the fields
is his: misshapen pumpkins,
spotted apples, rotted beans.
Where the soft decay touches
the soil, mouths form,
then heads thick as clay,
bodies like corn shocks,
hands, fingers, legs, toes
like odd-sized gourds.

In the furrows of our beds,
we hear their clumping walk
and dream of weak breaths,
lungfuls of seeds.
They circle our houses,
tapping the windows,
their pale tongues
sprouting out to us
in our mutual darkness.

The Language of Fossils

Vantage, Washington

This desert is a plateau of light:
small diggers live in the soft stone
tongues of ancient beasts.

Calcified waves still-flow under
the sulfur-bellied marmots
and badgers claw at the salty star
fish that tremble into dust.

These stone logs are only weathering
time, friend, waiting
for the Cascades to become ash
and the ocean's green winds
to transform the sky
into acres of ferns.

What will we become?
Cool shadows in the red
mineral belly of the earth?

Fossils speak the language of *Ginkgo*:
vowels like flat stones
with the carbonized wings
of leaf and beetle
and consonants like a bone
caught in the earth's throat.

Diceratherium:
rhino pillowed in lava
layers of basalt bone
calcite dolomite pyrite
stratas of chalky diatoms
agate   flint   chert

What language is my passing
shadow? My name is lost
off the Columbia's cliffs:
immersed in silica and water
it will become an opal
with a woman's soul.

An arrowhead whispers *flight!*

All the dark birds,
but one,
rush from the river
leaving only the stillness
of their language.

NIA FRANCISCO

(1952–   )

Kayenta Times   Yet Dreaming On

Quietly   step onto   a land
        that is my soul

Streaks of soft blues   coral shades
          land   meadows   valleys
    sky
   as far as you can see
  mountains   mountains way way over there

Mountains edged onto a stretched-out
  horizon   ahead of you
as you   might be driving or walking

Cardinal directions
   my strongest senses
my directions are four seasons
none like that you might know

Stillness of hail storms
   hang white onto the eastern side
     eastern mountains
clouds are whirling like curls
  of mohair pelts
sunlight angled @ 45° angle
  angled just so
descending secrets of shadows
  into depths

of my never to be known mesas

Sleep
baby   sleep baby child
fluency of dreams overcoming you
        a peaceful haze
wrapping an antelope-hide-soft body
  the cooling   breeze becoming a gentle touch

Quietly walk   listen   see
a rocky ridge shaped
in a Naabeeho man sitting by a highway
as if napping   waiting for a pickup truck
    to give him a hitch to Kayenta, Arizona

To a Man Who is Rob Southland

Raindrops fall
on the gray roof of our framed house
the sun never shines
        just rainy days   ending in a sigh
                        now and then

i thought of winter
sage brushes covered with snow
   heavy weight of snow creating dens
      for cotton tails   or coyotes
winter
is the old age of Nahasdzaan/Earth

Naabeeho man   Rob Southland
my tribal brother yet my "old man"
and i,   your sister   not a missionary
      Earth our mother
the divine ones require of all lovers
to be of different clans   and we are

i'll stay awhile   you say

in the evening of the coming storm
  as forecasted on the radio
we sat   shivering in the cold
  your wife gone and not wanting you

i put out my hands   warming them
by the flames of a fire that belongs
        to your heart   and in your soul

you tried   Rob Southland
to warm your hands
by the fire that belongs to my inner self
      i looked at you   tears say too much

slowly and carefully you picked cedar splinters
    placed them on the   dying coal
    hope in your eyes and the glee of
    an expectant father

Soon the spring sprouts   push through the wet soil
like Changing woman   re-juvenated herself
    after her Old Age
    and   Mr. Southland you have a son

Roots of Blue Bells

        Female spider
swept her legends into her palms
    then   gently blew on it
        like powder
she blew   dampness
     of her breath
    felt in the southern wind

      Powdered roots
of blue bells   water crest leaves
        blossoms
and rose mary shrubs
only the she-bear knows the mixtures
for she   sunbaked them
high on the mountain top in Crystal

      She-spider
blew the powder
onto the deep   deep wounds
  and holocaust of USA
  and global pains
then
she sat
on life-giving mountains
  while she spun
webs   and webs
 of unspoken legends
into looms of Milky Way

She spun
the blackness of Universe
as clothing for the twins
      Night
who is the twin of day
      Day
who is the twin of night

Modern on the Surface

Vibrant   naive Naabeeho women
whiteman's   magazine beauty
their short eyelashes curled
like a black woman's lashes
    eyelids like a turkey's head
shaded   baby blue   reddish amber
and their black eyes outlined
cat-like
dressed to win something

Naabeeho folks
    in their old days of
Spanish wars and Gallup whores
in the long winter night of Navajo country

they mimicked   holy people   their forefathers
in playfulness   they tossed a hit-stick
        for a winter Shoe Game
            a nighttime game

Holy Ones   said
if a shoe game is played
    in the day light
players painted beneath
their eyes like a raccoon
blackened   dark   so not to go blind

Holy Ones   said
in the warmer days of spring
    players must   they must
bring in a chunk of ice   centered
re-creating Winter   in the hooghan

Players sing songs of all animals
feasted on simmering deer/corn stew
all night long   ending at dawn
with the White Dawn song

       Inside myself,   i reasoned it out
beyond my reach   my voice   my mind

Screwdrivers   Tequila Sunrises   & ice
sipping slowly   wagering
   what i can not return to
   icy thoughts centered in me

ROBERT H. DAVIS

(1954–   )

Raven Tells Stories

Raven, gather us to that dark breast.
Call up another filthy legend.
Keep us distracted from all this blackness,
sheltered and cloaked by your wing. Answer us
our terror of this place we pretend to belong,
the groping spirits we're hopeless against,
from where this bleakness keeps arising.
We ask you only to lull us with lies,
expecting the moon attached with day.
Because we're your parasites
nested in feather, we hope you'll
offer any false expectation
we'll never be left to this; that when
your mouth opens to tell this
we will not notice
your tongue black,
your mouth full of shadow.

Raven is Two-Faced

Raven eyes blink
day/night   day/night . . .

The world has its top
and its underside and
Raventracks lead every direction.
You can tell he's been busy.
Shifty. That he's got this game
of intrigue down because
definitely everything,
He's made certain,
is the opposite of something else.

There's no way out
of his two-sided setup;
you can turn
this poem inside
out, trying to interpret
its other meaning.

At the Door of the Native Studies Director

In this place years ago
they educated old language out of you,
put you in line, in uniform, on your own two feet.
They pointed you in the right direction but
still you squint to that other place,
that country hidden within a country.
You chase bear, deer. You hunt seal. You fish.
This is what you know. This is how you move,
leaving only a trace of yourself.
Each time you come back
you have no way to tell about this.

Years later you meet the qualifications—native scholar.
They give you a job, a corner office.
Now you're instructed to remember old language,
faded legend, anything that's left.
They keep looking in on you, sideways.
You don't fit here. You no longer fit there.
You got sick. They still talk of it, the cheap wine
on your breath as you utter in restless sleep
what I sketch at your bedside.
Tonight father, I wrap you in a different blanket,
the dances come easier. I carve them for you.
This way you move through me.

I come to tell now, the moving men
are emptying your office.
Everyone thought I would take your place
but as I turn in your dark chair I recall the night
you tossed in dream on breath-waves
that break the pebbly shores of canoes,
where the fog people move
in old Tlingit village among your clanhouse
and an emerging totem, a woman I remember
as Grandmother. She gestures, talks words
that become familiar. Your sleep speech
grows gutteral and I feel something pull
that when you wake I want to ask you about.

Black Buoy

I dreamed it rose,
giant against the islands'
graves.

I dreamed we approached
alone, hands outstretched.

We felt its hollowness.
We were impressed.
We were intimidated.

The sea was there.
It was ancient.

I wondered,
would we even
drift back
to our village growing small?

—— 🔲 ——

LOUISE ERDRICH

(1955–   )

The Butcher's Wife

1

Once, my braids swung heavy as ropes.
Men feared them like the gallows.
Night fell
When I combed them out.
No one could see me in the dark.

Then I stood still
Too long and the braids took root.
I wept, so helpless.
The braids tapped deep and flourished.

A man came by with an ox on his shoulders.
He yoked it to my apron
And pulled me from the ground.
From that time on I wound the braids around my head
So that my arms would be free to tend him.

2

He could lift a grown man by the belt with his teeth.
In a contest, he'd press a whole hog, a side of beef.
He loved his highballs, his herring, and the attentions of
    women.
He died pounding his chest with no last word for anyone.

The gin vessels in his face broke and darkened. I traced
    them
Far from that room into Bremen on the Sea.
The narrow streets twisted down to the piers.
And far off, in the black, rocking water, the lights of
    trawlers
Beckoned, like the heart's uncertain signals,
Faint, and final.

Indian Boarding School: The Runaways

Home's the place we head for in our sleep.
Boxcars stumbling north in dreams
don't wait for us. We catch them on the run.
The rails, old lacerations that we love,
shoot parallel across the face and break
just under Turtle Mountains. Riding scars
you can't get lost. Home is the place they cross.

The lame guard strikes a match and makes the dark
less tolerant. We watch through cracks in boards
as the land starts rolling, rolling till it hurts
to be here, cold in regulation clothes.
We know the sheriff's waiting at midrun
to take us back. His car is dumb and warm.
The highway doesn't rock, it only hums
like a wing of long insults. The worn-down welts
of ancient punishments lead back and forth.

All runaways wear dresses, long green ones,
the color you would think shame was. We scrub
the sidewalks down because it's shameful work.
Our brushes cut the stone in watered arcs
and in the soak frail outlines shiver clear
a moment, things us kids pressed on the dark
face before it hardened, pale, remembering
delicate old injuries, the spines of names and leaves.

Jacklight

> *The same Chippewa word is used both for
> flirting and hunting game, while another
> Chippewa word connotes both using force in
> intercourse and also killing a bear with
> one's bare hands.*
> > R. W. Dunning, *Social and Economic
> > Change Among the Northern Ojibwa*
> > (1959)

We have come to the edge of the woods,
out of brown grass where we slept, unseen,
out of knotted twigs, out of leaves creaked shut,
out of hiding.

At first the light wavered, glancing over us.
Then it clenched to a fist of light that pointed,
searched out, divided us.
Each took the beams like direct blows the heart answers.
Each of us moved forward alone.

We have come to the edge of the woods,
drawn out of ourselves by this night sun,
this battery of polarized acids,
that outshines the moon.

We smell them behind it
but they are faceless, invisible.
We smell the raw steel of their gun barrels,
mink oil on leather, their tongues of sour barley.
We smell their mothers buried chin-deep in wet dirt.
We smell their fathers with scoured knuckles,
teeth cracked from hot marrow.
We smell their sisters of crushed dogwood, bruised apples,
of fractured cups and concussions of burnt hooks.

We smell their breath steaming lightly behind the jacklight.
We smell the itch underneath the caked guts on their
    clothes.
We smell their minds like silver hammers

cocked back, held in readiness
for the first of us to step into the open.

We have come to the edge of the woods,
out of brown grass where we slept, unseen,
out of leaves creaked shut, out of our hiding.
We have come here too long.

It is their turn now,
their turn to follow us. Listen,
they put down their equipment.
It is useless in the tall brush.
And now they take the first steps, not knowing
how deep the woods are and lightless.
How deep the woods are.

Family Reunion

Ray's third new car in half as many years.
Full cooler in the trunk, Ray sogging the beer
as I solemnly chauffeur us through the bush
and up the backroads, hardly cowpaths and hub-deep in
   mud.
All day the sky lowers, clears, lowers again.
Somewhere in the bush near Saint John
there are uncles, a family, one mysterious brother
who stayed on the land when Ray left for the cities.
One week Ray is crocked. We've been through this before.
Even, as a little girl, hands in my dress,
Ah punka, you's my Debby, come and ki me.

Then the road ends in a yard full of dogs.
Them's Indian dogs, Ray says, lookit how they know me.
And they do seem to know him, like I do. His odor—
rank beef of fierce turtle pulled dripping from Metagoshe,
and the inflammable mansmell: hair tonic, ashes, alcohol.
Ray dances an old woman up in his arms.
Fiddles reel on the phonograph and I sink apart
in a corner, start knocking the Blue Ribbons down.
Four generations of people live here.
No one remembers Raymond Twobears.

So what. The walls shiver, the old house caulked with mud
sails back into the middle of Metagoshe.
A three-foot-long snapper is hooked on a troutline,
so mean that we do not dare wrestle him in
but tow him to shore, heavy as an old engine.
Then somehow Ray pries the beak open and shoves
down a cherry bomb. Lights the string tongue.

Headless and clenched in its armor, the snapper
is lugged home in the trunk for tomorrow's soup.
Ray rolls it beneath a bush in the backyard and goes in
to sleep his own head off. Tomorrow I find
that the animal has dragged itself off.
I follow torn tracks up a slight hill and over
into a small stream that deepens and widens into a marsh.

Ray finds his way back through the room into his arms.
When the phonograph stops, he slumps hard in his hands
and the boys and their old man fold him into the car
where he curls around his bad heart, hearing how it knocks
and rattles at the bars of his ribs to break out.

Somehow we find our way back. Uncle Ray
sings an old song to the body that pulls him
toward home. The gray fins that his hands have become
screw their bones in the dashboard. His face
has the odd, calm patience of a child who has always
let bad wounds alone, or a creature that has lived
for a long time underwater. And the angels come
lowering their slings and litters.

The Lady in the Pink Mustang

The sun goes down for hours, taking more of her along
than the night leaves her with.
A body moving in the dust
must shed its heavy parts in order to go on.

Perhaps you have heard of her, the Lady in the Pink
    Mustang,
whose bare lap is floodlit from under the dash,
who cruises beneath the high snouts of semis, reading
the blink of their lights. *Yes. Move Over. Now.*
or *How Much.* Her price shrinks into the dark.

She can't keep much trash in a Mustang,
and that's what she likes. Travel light. Don't keep
what does not have immediate uses. The road thinks ahead.
It thinks for her, a streamer from Bismarck to Fargo
bending through Minnesota to accommodate the land.

She won't carry things she can't use anymore.
Just a suit, sets of underwear, what you would expect
in a Pink Mustang. Things she could leave anywhere.

There is a point in the distance where the road meets itself,
where coming and going must kiss into one.
She is always at that place, seen from behind,
motionless, torn forward, living in a zone
all her own. It is like she has burned right through time,
the brand, the mark, owning the woman who bears it.

She owns them, not one will admit what they cannot
come close to must own them. She takes them along,
traveling light. It is what she must face every time
she is touched. The body disposable as cups.

To live, instead of turn, on a dime.
One light point that is so down in value.
Painting her nipples silver for a show, she is thinking
You out there. What do you know.

Come out of the dark where you're safe. Kissing these
bits of change, stamped out, ground to a luster,
is to kiss yourself away piece by piece
until we're even. Until the last
coin is rubbed for luck and spent.
I don't sell for nothing less.

Captivity

> *"He [my captor] gave me a bisquit, which I*
> *put in my pocket, and not daring to eat it,*
> *buried it under a log, fearing he had put*
> *something in it to make me love him."*
>> from the narrative of the captivity of
>> Mrs. Mary Rowlandson, who was
>> taken prisoner by the Wampanoag
>> when Lancaster, Massachusetts, was
>> destroyed, in the year 1676

The stream was swift, and so cold
I thought I would be sliced in two.
But he dragged me from the flood
by the ends of my hair.
I had grown to recognize his face.
I could distinguish it from the others.
There were times I feared I understood
his language, which was not human,
and I knelt to pray for strength.

We were pursued! By God's agents
or pitch devils I did not know.
Only that we must march.
Their guns were loaded with swan shot.
I could not suckle and my child's wail
put them in danger.
He had a woman
with teeth black and glittering.
She fed the child milk of acorns.
The forest closed, the light deepened.

I told myself that I would starve
before I took food from his hands
but I did not starve.
One night
he killed a deer with a young one in her
and gave me to eat of the fawn.
It was so tender,
the bones like the stems of flowers,
that I followed where he took me.
The night was thick. He cut the cord
that bound me to the tree.

After that the birds mocked.
Shadows gaped and roared
and the trees flung down
their sharpened lashes.
He did not notice God's wrath.
God blasted fire from half-buried stumps.
I hid my face in my dress, fearing He would burn us all
but this, too, passed.

Rescued, I see no truth in things.
My husband drives a thick wedge
through the earth, still it shuts
to him year after year.
My child is fed of the first wheat.
I lay myself to sleep
On a Holland-laced pillowbear.
I lay to sleep.
And in the dark I see myself
as I was outside their circle.

They knelt on deerskins, some with sticks,
and he led his company in the noise
until I could no longer bear
the thought of how I was.
I stripped a branch
and struck the earth,
in time, begging it to open
to admit me
as he was
and feed me honey from the rock.

A Love Medicine

for Lise

Still it is raining lightly
in Wahpeton. The pickup trucks
sizzle beneath the blue neon
bug traps of the dairy bar.

Theresa goes out in green halter and chains
that glitter at her throat.
This dragonfly, my sister,
she belongs more than I
to this night of rising water.

The Red River swells to take the bridge.
She laughs and leaves her man in his Dodge.
He shoves off to search her out.
He wears a long rut in the fog.

And later, at the crest of the flood,
when the pilings are jarred from their sockets
and pitch into the current,
she steps against the fistwork of a man.
She goes down in wet grass
and his boot plants its grin among the arches of her face.

Now she feels her way home in the dark.
The white-violet bulbs of the streetlamps
are seething with insects,
and the trees lean down aching and empty.
The river slaps at the dike works, insistent.

I find her curled up in the roots of a cottonwood.
I find her stretched out in the park, where all night
the animals are turning in their cages.
I find her in a burnt-over ditch, in a field
that is gagging on rain,
sheets of rain sweep up down
to the river held tight against the bridge.

We see that now the moon is leavened and the water,
as deep as it will go,
stops rising. Where we wait for the night to take us
the rain ceases. *Sister, there is nothing
I would not do.*

I Was Sleeping Where the Black Oaks Move

We watched from the house
as the river grew, helpless
and terrible in its unfamiliar body.
Wrestling everything into it,
the water wrapped around trees
until their life-hold was broken.
They went down, one by one,
and the river dragged off their covering.

Nests of the herons, roots washed to bones,
snags of soaked bark on the shoreline:
a whole forest pulled through the teeth
of the spillway. Trees surfacing
singly, where the river poured off
into arteries for fields below the reservation.

When at last it was over, the long removal,
they had all become the same dry wood.
We walked among them, the branches
whitening in the raw sun.
Above us drifted herons,
alone, hoarse-voiced, broken,
settling their beaks among the hollows.

Grandpa said, *These are the ghosts of the tree people,*
moving above us, unable to take their rest.

Sometimes now, we dream our way back to the heron dance.
Their long wings are bending the air
into circles through which they fall.
They rise again in shifting wheels.
How long must we live in the broken figures
their necks make, narrowing the sky.

Night Sky

Lunar eclipse, for Michael

I

Arcturus, the bear driver,
shines on the leash of hunting dogs.
Do you remember how the woman becomes a bear
because her husband has run in sadness
to the forest of stars?

She soaks the bear hide
until it softens to fit her body.
She ties the skinning boards over her heart.
She goes out, digs stumps,
smashes trees to test her power,
then breaks into a dead run
and hits the sky like a truck.

We are watching the moon
when this bear woman pulls herself
arm over arm into the tree of heaven.
We see her shadow clasp the one rusted fruit.
Her thick paw swings. The world dims.
We are alone here on earth
with the ragged breath of our children
coming and going in the old wool blankets.

II

Does she ever find him?
The sky is full of pits and snagged deadfalls.

She sleeps in shelters he's made of jackpine,
eats the little black bones
of birds he's roasted in cookfires.
She even sees him once
bending to drink from his own lips
in the river of starlight.

The truth is she cannot approach him
in the torn face and fur
stinking of shit and leather.
She is a real bear now,
licking bees from her paws, plunging
her snout in anthills,
rolling mad in the sour valleys
of skunk cabbage!

III

He knows she is there,
eyeing him steadily from the hornbeam
as she used to across the table.
He asks for strength
to leave his body at the river,
to leave it cradled in its sad arms
while he wanders in oiled muscles,
bear heft, shag, and acorn fat.
He goes to her, heading
for the open,
the breaking moon.

IV

Simple
to tear free
stripped and shining
to ride through crossed firs

Old Man Potchikoo

The Birth of Potchikoo

You don't have to believe this, I'm not asking you to. But Potchikoo claims that his father is the sun in heaven that shines down on us all.

There was a very pretty Chippewa girl working in a field once. She was digging potatoes for a farmer someplace around Pembina when suddenly the wind blew her dress up around her face and wrapped her apron so tightly around her arms that she couldn't move. She lay helplessly in the dust with her potato sack, this poor girl, and as she lay there she felt the sun shining down very steadily upon her.

Then she felt something else. You know what. I don't have to say it. She cried out for her mother.

This girl's mother came running and untangled her daughter's clothes. When she freed the girl, she saw that there were tears in her daughter's eyes. Bit by bit, the mother coaxed out the story. After the girl told what had happened to her, the mother just shook her head sadly.

"I don't know what we can expect now," she said.

Well nine months passed and he was born looking just like a potato with tough warty skin and a puckered round shape. All the ladies came to visit the girl and left saying things behind their hands.

"That's what she gets for playing loose in the potato fields," they said.

But the girl didn't care what they said after a while because she used to go and stand alone in a secret clearing in the woods and let the sun shine steadily upon her. Sometimes she took her little potato boy. She noticed when the sun shone on him he grew and became a little more human-looking.

One day the girl fell asleep in the sun with her potato boy next to her. The sun beat down so hard on him that he had an enormous spurt of growth. When the girl woke up, her son was fully grown. He said good-bye to his mother then, and went out to see what was going on in the world.

Potchikoo Marries

After he had several adventures, the potato boy took the name Potchikoo and decided to try married life.

I'll just see what it's like for a while, he thought, and then I'll start wandering again.

How very inexperienced he was!

He took the train to Minneapolis to find a wife and as soon as he got off he saw her. She was a beautiful Indian girl standing at the door to a little shop where they sold cigarettes and pipe tobacco. How proud she looked! How peaceful. She was so lovely that she made Potchikoo shy. He could hardly look at her.

Potchikoo walked into the store and bought some cigarettes. He lit one up and stuck it between the beautiful woman's lips. Then he stood next to her, still too shy to look at her, until he smelled smoke. He saw that she had somehow caught fire.

"Oh I'll save you!" cried Potchikoo.

He grabbed his lady love and ran with her to the lake, which was, handily, across the street. He threw her in. At first he was afraid she would drown but soon she floated to the surface and kept floating away from Potchikoo. This made him angry.

"Trying to run away already!" he shouted.

He leaped in to catch her. But he had forgotten that he couldn't swim. So Potchikoo had to hang on to his wooden sweetheart while she drifted slowly all the way across the lake. When they got to the other side of the lake, across from Minneapolis, they were in wilderness. As soon as the wooden girl touched the shore she became alive and jumped up and dragged Potchikoo out of the water.

"I'll teach you to shove a cigarette between my lips like that," she said, beating him with her fists, which were still hard as wood. "Now that you're my husband you'll do things my way!"

That was how Potchikoo met and married Josette. He was married to her all his life. After she had made it clear what she expected of her husband, Josette made a little toboggan of cut saplings and tied him upon it. Then she decided she never wanted to see Minneapolis again. She wanted to live in the hills. That is why she dragged Potchikoo all the way back across Minnesota to the Turtle Mountains, where they spent all the years of their wedded bliss.

How Potchikoo Got Old

As a young man, Potchikoo sometimes embarrassed his wife by breaking wind during Holy Mass. It was for this reason that Josette whittled him a little plug out of ash wood and told him to put it in that place before he entered Saint Ann's church.

Potchikoo did as she asked, and even said a certain charm over the plug so that it would not be forced out, no matter what. Then the two of them entered the church to say their prayers.

That Sunday, Father Belcourt was giving a special sermon on the ascension of the Lord Christ to heaven. It happened in the twinkling of an eye, he said, with no warning, because Christ was more pure than air. How surprised everyone was to see, as Father Belcourt said this, the evil scoundrel Potchikoo rising from his pew!

His hands were folded, and his closed eyes and meek face wore a look of utter piety. He didn't even seem to realize he was rising, he prayed so hard.

Up and up he floated, still in the kneeling position, until he reached the dark blue vault of the church. He seemed to inflate, too, until he looked larger than life to the people. They were on the verge of believing it a miracle when all of a sudden it happened. Bang! Even with the charm the little ash-wood plug could not contain the wind of Potchikoo.

Out it popped, and Potchikoo went buzzing and sputtering around the church the way balloons do when children let go of the ends.

Holy Mass was canceled for a week so the church could be aired out, but to this day a faint scent still lingers and Potchikoo, sadly enough, was shriveled by his sudden collapse and flight through the air. For when Josette picked him up to bring home, she found that he was now wrinkled and dry like an old man.

The Death of Potchikoo

Once there were three stones sitting in a patch of soft slough mud. Each of these stones had the smooth round shape of a woman's breast, but no one had ever noticed this—that is, not until Old Man Potchikoo walked through the woods. He was the type who always noticed this kind of thing. As soon as he saw the three stones, Potchikoo sat down on a small bank of grass to enjoy what he saw.

He was not really much of a connoisseur, the old man. He just knew what he liked when he saw it. The three stones were light brown in color, delicately veined, and so smooth that they almost looked slippery. Old Man Potchikoo began to wonder if they really were slippery, and then he thought of touching them.

They were in the middle of the soft slough mud, so the old man took his boots and socks off. Then he thought of his wife Josette and what she would say if he came home with mud on his clothes. He took off his shirt and pants. He never wore undershorts. Wading toward those stones, he was as naked as them.

He had to kneel in the mud to touch the stones, and when he did this he sank to his thighs. But oh, when he touched the stones, he found that they were bigger than they looked from the shore and so shiny, so slippery. His hands polished them, and polished them some more, and before he knew it that Potchikoo was making love to the slough.

Years passed by. The Potchikoos got older and more frail. One day Josette went into town, and as he always did as soon as she was out of sight, Potchikoo sat down on his front steps to do nothing.

As he sat there, he saw three women walk very slowly out of the woods. They walked across the field and then walked slowly toward him. As they drew near, Potchikoo saw that they were just his kind of women. They were large, their hair was black and very long, and because they wore low-cut blouses, he could see that their breasts were beautiful—light brown, delicately veined, and so smooth they looked slippery.

"We are your daughters," they said, standing before him. "We are from the slough."

A faint memory stirred in Potchikoo as he looked at their breasts, and he smiled.

"Oh my daughters," he said to them. "Yes I remember you. Come sit on your daddy's lap and get acquainted."

The daughters moved slowly toward Potchikoo. As he saw their skin up close, he marveled at how fine it was, smooth as polished stone. The first daughter sank upon his knee and clasped her arms around him. She was so heavy the old man couldn't move. Then the others sank upon him, blocking away the sun with their massive bodies. The old man's head began to swim and yellow stars turned in his skull. He hardly knew it when all three daughters laid their heads dreamily against his chest. They were cold, and so heavy that his ribs snapped apart like little dry twigs.

A. SADONGEI

(1959–   )

Don't Forget

Don't forget
when the sticks are ready for picking
Sing your lucky song
You can see through your mother's eyes
things that happened before you were born
It was on your journey back downriver
the sky was waiting
holding rain
pick your way slowly
over the wet river rocks
When coyote talks to you
do you listen?
Don't forget
when it's time to pick sticks
sing your lucky song
you can see through your mother's eyes
things that happened before you were born
They call it the center of the world
spirits long dead
live on in trees and rocks
Remember to make things right
don't forget
when the sticks are ready for picking
sing your lucky song
You can see
through your mother's eyes
things that happened before you were born

Poems come to me in the night

Poems come to me in the night
pressed compacted air
it is you against me
do you want me to tell you how it feels?
your smell is clear
I can see through it like sun on water
you are a list of words
fair skin
a smooth body that dips and curves
blue veins under the white skin
makes me think of
things white like snow
and the crests of ocean waves
you roll like a wave of water
onto me
a slow stretch
rising peaking receding
your thoughts are dreamy
unable to grasp the back of a chair
always surfacing and slipping
back into soft dreams
of green scenery
pastel landscapes

For Carlos Charles Bucillio

I

The noise began in my belly
and was pushed up and out of my throat.
It hurled itself against the furniture
chairs and windows.

This death song had begun high in the hills;
I had to listen to it
traveling home
over the mountains
and down the coastline.
I had nowhere to rest
no one to turn and talk to—
the one I knew was gone.

II

I remember the rabbit I saw
when I drove along the desert floor.
I felt like I was on the bottom of the ocean
inside the salty water.
Carlos used to say that's what the place would have
looked like if the village hadn't given
the lives of two children to stop
the flowing of the water—
their small bodies turned to foam.

III

He's buried near his father
in the small, desert village.
Always a breeze blows among the dwellings,
cooling the hot, dry days
and bending back creosote bushes.
Sometimes, the breeze
gently rocks homemade hammocks
warm with sleeping babies.

IV

Sounds move in and around
in front of each other,
dodge the bushes,

glide up over my shoulder
into my ear.
I remember sitting and waiting for breezes
to stir the corrugated rusty tin of the barn
that smelled of hay and sounded like mice.

Wind blew like water

Wind blew like water
my voice went flying up over the trees
they got caught
snagged on the roof of your house.
Love is truly uninspiring
if it drags the life out of you
if you wear it like a necklace of river stones
that look pretty only when they're wet.
Love gets in the way of moist touches
of skin on skin
dewy drops cling to arms and legs
and the soft round spot
that is your mouth.
They don't know which way your heart lies
how you dream at night
what time of day belongs to you when you think
those golden thoughts
full of sounds you've saved
since you were a young boy.
I've left you twice in two different dreams
left you
left you
I come circling back
like a vulture in the sky
to pick clean your bones.

After Seeing Paintings in a Small Book
by T. C. Cannon (1946–1978)

I don't know
who I'm writing this for.
After reading about T. C.
seeing those paintings
of rainbow tinted
Kiowa/Apaches,
I feel like writing
to someone
about dawn desert winds,
the breathy scream
of an eagle bone whistle
and how those things
make me feel.
I want to talk to T. C.
We could have shared
what we know
about the Washita river
and Carnegie town
when all the gourd dancers
are there in July.
I could have asked him
about the women of the pueblos,
if they are like
the potter I know
who is:
color of sand
rain on skin glistening
cool adobe.

I don't know
who I'm writing this for.
T. C. paintings
often have clouds, white and blue
in the center of the sky.
Look up—
even now
the clouds
are all around.

BIOGRAPHIES

Paula Gunn Allen (1939–   )

Paula Gunn Allen, a Laguna Pueblo/Sioux/Lebanese-American, was born in Cubero, New Mexico. She received a National Endowment for the Arts fellowship for writing in 1978, a post-doctoral fellowship in American Indian Studies at UCLA in 1981 and a Research Grant from the Ford Foundation/National Research Council Fellowship along with appointment as an associate fellow at Stanford Humanities Institute.

Allen's chapbooks include *The Blind Lion, Coyote's Daylight Trip, Star Child,* and *A Cannon Between My Knees.* Her books include *Shadow Country, The Woman Who Owned the Shadows,* and *Studies in American Indian Literature.* In early 1986 a collection of her essays appeared, *The Sacred Hoop: Recovering the Feminine in American Indian Traditions.* She is full professor of ethnic studies (in Native American Studies) at the University of California, Berkeley.

Jim Barnes (1933–   )

Born in eastern Oklahoma, Jim Barnes is of Choctaw-Welsh descent. In the 50s he migrated to Oregon, where he worked for nearly ten years as a lumberjack. He returned to Oklahoma to take a B.A. at Southeastern State University. Later, he earned his M.A. and Ph.D. at the University of Arkansas.

His poems and translations have appeared steadily in literary magazines for the last twenty years. His *Summons and Sign: Poems by Dagmar Nick* won a Translation Prize from The Translation Center in 1980. In 1982 his *American*

Book of the Dead was cited with an honorable mention in the Before Columbus Foundation's American Book Awards. His most recent volume is *A Season of Loss*. He is editor of *The Chariton Review* and a professor of comparative literature at Northeast Missouri State University.

Peter Blue Cloud (1935–   )

Peter Blue Cloud is a Turtle Mohawk from Caughnawaga, Quebec and a former ironworker. He has served as editor of the *Alcatraz Newsletter,* poetry editor of *Akwesasne Notes,* and co-editor of *Coyote's Journal.* He has published six books including *Elderberry Flute Song* and *White Corn Sister.*

Barney Bush (1945–   )

Barney Bush, a Shawnee/Cayuga, was born into a family of hunters and trappers, whose ancestral homelands lay on both sides of the Ohio River. He has traveled North America by foot, thumb, train, raft, and canoe. He gives poetry readings and workshops across the country, often accompanied by a Comanche musician on flute. A graduate of Ft. Lewis College in Durango, Colorado, he later went on to receive a master's degree in English and fine arts at the University of Idaho. He was awarded a grant from the National Endowment for the Arts and has served as writer-in-residence for a number of state universities. His fourth book of poetry, *Inherit the Blood,* was published in 1985.

Gladys Cardiff (1942–   )

Gladys Cardiff is related to the Owl family of the Eastern Cherokees of North Carolina. Born in Montana, she moved to Washington State and attended the University of Washington, where she studied with Theodore Roethke and Nelson and Beth Bentley. She has participated in the Poets-in-the-Schools program.

Her chapbook, *To Frighten a Storm*, won the 1976 Washington State Governor's Award for a first book of poetry. In 1985 she was a winner in the Seattle Arts Commission poetry competition. Her work has appeared in numerous anthologies including *Carriers of the Dream Wheel; The Remembered Earth; Songs from This Earth on Turtle's Back; Rain in the Forest, Light in the Trees; Wounds Beneath the Flesh;* and *That's What She Said.*

George Clutesi (1905–   )

George Clutesi, a Tse-Shaht, is an artist as well as a writer. In his youth he was a pupil of the artist Emily Carr. He has published two books: *Son of Raven, Son of Deer* and *Potlatch*. Through the popularity of *Son of Raven, Son of Deer*—which has been selected as an elementary English text in British Columbia schools—he has become widely known as a spokesperson for the traditional fables and stories of his people.

Elizabeth Cook-Lynn (1930–   )

Elizabeth Cook-Lynn, a member of the Crow Creek Sioux Tribe, was born at Ft. Thompson, South Dakota. She comes from a family of Indian politicians and scholars. (Her father and grandfather served on the Crow Creek Sioux tribal council for many years. Her grandmother, Eliza, was a bi-lingual writer for early Christian-oriented newspapers, and her grandfather, Gabriel Renville, was a native linguist instrumental in developing early Dakotah language dictionaries.)

Her poetry and short stories focus upon the geography of the Northern Plains and the culture of the Lakota-Dakotah of North and South Dakota. She published poems in obscure magazines during her early years of writing, then published two chapbooks of poetry, *Then Badger Said This* and *Seek the House of Relatives*, after the age of forty. Her short stories have appeared in *Prairie Schooner, Pembroke Magazine, South Dakota Review, Sun Tracks, The Ethnic Studies Journal,* and *The Greenfield Review.* Her work has been anthologized in *The Remembered Earth, The Third Woman, Bearing Witness,* and *Earth Power Coming.*

Cook-Lynn is currently associate professor of English and Indian Studies at Eastern Washington University in Cheney and editor of *The Wicazo Sa Review, A Journal of Native American Studies.*

Steve Crow (1949–   )

Steve Crow, of Cherokee and Irish ancestry, was born in Alabama. He began writing poetry in high school then went on to Louisiana State University to major in English and creative writing before entering the M.F.A. program at Bowling Green in 1971. In 1976, he began doctoral work in English at the University of Minnesota. He developed and taught a survey course in contemporary Native American literature at the University of New Mexico.

Nora Dauenhauer (1927–   )

Nora Dauenhauer, a Tlingit Indian, was born in Juneau, Alaska. She has spent most of the last fifteen years collecting, transcribing, and documenting the Tlingit oral tradition. From this work, she and her husband have co-authored two Tlingit language primers for classroom use: *Beginning Tlingit* and *A Tlingit Spelling Book.* Her fiction and poetry have been anthologized in *Earth Power Coming: Short Fiction in Native American Literature* and *That's What She Said: Contemporary Poetry and Fiction by Native American Women.* She has also been published in *The Greenfield Review* and *Northward Journal.* She is currently a translator and principal researcher in language and cultural studies at the Sealaska Heritage Foundation.

Robert H. Davis (1954–   )

Robert H. Davis, a Tlingit Indian, was born of the Woos'cencidi clan. His father was a Tlingit teacher from Kake and his mother, also a teacher, was born in Michigan and is of European ancestry. Davis has spent his entire life vacillating between his Indian and European heritage. This dichotomy influences his poetry, artwork, and carvings in which he explores the evolution of forms and the inherent confusion Native American artists experience in the encounter with European culture.

Jimmie Durham (1940–   )

Jimmie Durham, a Wolf Clan Cherokee, was born in Arkansas. He received a B.F.A. from the Ecole des Beaux Arts in Geneva, Switzerland in 1973. During the 1970s he was a member of the Central Council of the American Indian Movement and was a founder and executive director of the International Indian Treaty Council. His poetry has appeared in *The Minnesota Review, Parnassus, Ikon,* and other publications. A book of collected poems, *Columbus Day,* was published in 1982.

Durham currently lives in New York City, where until recently he was the executive director of the Foundation of the Community of Artists and editor of *Art & Artists* newspaper. He is a sculptor and performance artist as well as a poet.

Anita Endrezze (1952–   )

Anita Endrezze, of Yaqui and European ancestry, was born in Long Beach, California. An artist as well as a poet and short story writer, her watercolor paintings and illustrations have been reproduced in many art books.

Endrezze is the author of two chapbooks, *The North People* and *Burning the Fields,* and a children's novel, *The Mountain and the Guardian Spirit,* published in Denmark in 1986.

Her work has appeared in numerous anthologies including *A Nation Within; Songs from This Earth on Turtle's Back; Rain in the Forest, Light in the Trees: Contemporary Poets of the Northwest; Words in the Blood; A Gathering of Spirit;* and *Carriers of the Dream Wheel.*

Currently she works part-time for the Washington State Arts Commission as Poet-in-Residence. She is the editor of the Spokane chapter of the Audubon Society and the Indian Artists Guild newsletters. She is a member of Atlatl, a Native American arts service organization.

Louise Erdrich (1955–   )

Of German and Chippewa descent, Louis Erdrich is a member of the Turtle Mountain Band of Chippewa; for many years, her grandfather was Tribal Chair of the reservation. Raised in Wahpeton, North Dakota, Erdrich was among the first group of freshman women admitted to Dartmouth College in 1972. At Dartmouth, she was awarded several prizes for her fiction and poetry, including the American Academy of Poets Prize. After graduating in 1976, Erdrich returned to North Dakota where she taught in the Poetry in the Schools Program, sponsored by national and state endowments for the humanities. She received her M.A. in creative writing from Johns Hopkins University in 1979 and in 1982 received a National Endowment for the Arts Fellowship.

Jacklight, a collection of her poetry, was published in January 1984. Erdrich's first novel, *Love Medicine,* was published in October 1984. Foreign editions of the book were published in 1985 by major houses in England, Germany, Italy, Sweden, Norway, Finland, Holland, Spain, France, and Denmark.

Nia Francisco (1952–   )

Nia Francisco was born in the Navajo Tribe; she is of the Red Bottom People and borne for the Salt People. She was raised by her grandparents who she credits for the cultural richness in her writing. In 1976, Francisco received a National Endowment of the Arts Grant for creative writing through the Navajo Community College. She also has received mini-grants from the Arizona Commission of the Arts' Poet on the Road Program. Her poetry has been published in many anthologies of American Indian writers.

Francisco is a family woman. She has a full-time job and has four sons and one daughter. She resides in Crystal, New Mexico.

Joy Harjo (1951–   )

Joy Harjo, of the Creek Tribe, was born in Tulsa, Oklahoma. She has published three books of poetry including her most recent, *She Had Some Horses*. She is an assistant professor at the University of Colorado, Boulder, a member of the Board of Directors for the Native American Public Broadcasting Consortium, and the poetry editor for *High Plains Literary Review*. She also plays tenor saxophone in a big band in Denver.

Lance Henson (1944–   )

Lance Henson, a Cheyenne, was raised near Calumet, Oklahoma. He is the poet-in-residence for more than three hundred schools in Oklahoma and other states. He has lectured throughout the United States on writing and Native American themes.

Henson has published six books of poetry: *Keeper of Arrows, Naming the Dark, Mistah, Buffalo Marrow in Black, In a Dark Mist,* and *A Circling Remembrance*. With his publication of *In a Dark Mist*, Henson became the first Native American to translate a major collection from Cheyenne into English. Two additional volumes, *Selected Works 1970–1983* and *Solitary Songs,* will be published soon.

Linda Hogan (1947–   )

Linda Hogan, a Chickasaw Indian, is the author of several books of poetry and a collection of short fiction. Hogan's poetry, fiction, and essays have been published in numerous magazines and anthologies. Her most recent book, *Seeing Through the Sun,* received an American Book Award from The Before Columbus Foundation.

Hogan has received other awards, including a Colorado Writer's Fellowship in fiction, a Minnesota Arts Board Grant in poetry, and a National Endowment for the Arts Fellowship. She is an associate professor at the University of Minnesota in American Indian and American Studies. She is currently on leave completing a novel and continuing work in wildlife rehabilitation at the Birds of Prey Rehabilitation Foundation. A new book of poems, *Savings,* is due out in 1988.

Maurice Kenny (1929–   )

Born in 1929 between the St. Lawrence and Black Rivers in Northern New York, Maurice Kenny, a Mohawk, currently lives in Brooklyn where he co-edits the poetry journal *Contact/11* with J. G. Gosciak. He is also the publisher of Strawberry Press. He is a member of P.E.N. He has served as panelist and adviser to many organizations such as Coordinating Council of Literary Magazines. For many years he has been associated with both *Akwesasne Notes* and *Studies In American Indian Literature.* Guest poet and speaker at many national art centers and universities, he recently enjoyed a residency at the Writers Room in New York City and presently is poet-in-residence at North Country Community College in the Adirondack Mountains.

Kenny, in addition to his newest collection *Between Two Rivers: Selected Poems,* has authored *Is Summer This Bear* (1985), *Rain & Other Fictions* (1985), *Greyhounding This America* (1987), and *Roman Nose & Other Essays* (1987).

His work appears in many outstanding anthologies, the latest being *The North Country, Words in the Blood, Earth Power Coming, WAH KON TAH, Art Against Apartheid,* and *I Tell You Now: Autobiographical Essays by Native American Writers.* He edited *Wounds Beneath the Flesh.*

Kenny's *Blackrobe: Isaac Jogues* was given the National Public Radio for Broadcasting Award. It is currently being translated into French and Russian. In 1984 he received the American Book Award for *The Mama Poems.* At this time he is completing a new collection of *persona* poems, *Tekonwatonti: Molly Brant, Poems of War.*

N. Scott Momaday (1934–   )

N. Scott Momaday, a member of the Kiowa tribe, was born in Oklahoma. He grew up in the Southwest and considers northern New Mexico his spiritual home. He graduated from the University of New Mexico and holds M.A. and Ph.D. degrees from Stanford University. In 1969 he was awarded a Pulitzer Prize for his novel *House Made of Dawn.* A painter as well as a writer, his paintings have been exhibited in the United States and in Europe. Currently he lives in Arizona with his wife Reina, his daughter Lore, and an airedale named Sabado Tarde.

Daniel David Moses (1952–   )

Daniel David Moses, a Delaware, was born at Ohsweken on the Six Nations lands along the Grand River in Ontario, Canada. He grew up on a farm there and was educated in the Six Nations' schools and at nearby Caledonia High School. He received an honors B.A. from York University in Downsview, Ontario, and a M.F.A. in creative writing from the University of British Columbia in Vancouver which he attended on a fellowship. His first collection of poems, *Delicate Bodies,* was published in 1980. A second collection, *The White Line,* will be published in 1987. He has also written plays, teleplays, short stories and reviews. Moses is President of the Association for Native Development in the Performing and Visual Arts, a director of Native Earth Performing Arts, Inc., and a founding member of the Committee of Re-Establish the Trickster. He is also a member of the League of Canadian Poets and the Writers' Union of Canada.

Duane Niatum (1938–   )

Duane Niatum was born in Seattle, Washington. A Native American of mixed descent, he is a member of the Klallam tribe, whose ancestral lands are on the Washington coast along the Strait of Juan de Fuca. His early life was spent in Washington, Oregon, California, and Alaska, and at age seventeen he enlisted in the Navy and spent two years in Japan. On his return he completed his undergraduate studies in English at the University of Washington. He later received his M.A. from The Johns Hopkins University.

Niatum's poetry, short stories, and essays have been published in such magazines as *The Nation, Prairie Schooner, Northwest Review, The American Poetry Review,* and many other literary journals and anthologies. His previously published collections of poems are *After the Death of an Elder Klallam, Ascending Red Cedar Moon, Digging Out The Roots,* and *Songs for the Harvester of Dreams,* which won the National Book Award from The Before Columbus Foundation in 1982.

In 1973–74 he was the editor of the Native American Authors series at Harper and Row, and in 1975 he served as the editor of *Carriers of the Dream Wheel,* the most widely read and known book on contemporary Native American poetry. He presently lives in Ann Arbor, Michigan where he is working on a Ph.D. thesis on contemporary Northwest Coast art.

William Oandasan (1947–   )

William Oandasan is a member of the Yuki tribe of the Round Valley Reservation in northwest California. An awareness of his tribal history, its transformations at the end of the nineteenth century, and the synthesis of his oral traditions with many of the literary practices of the twentieth century influences his literary work. He is the author of two books of poetry, *A Branch of California Redwood* and *Moving Inland*.

Oandasan has served as senior editor of *American Indian Culture and Research Journal* and has issued his own *A Journal of Contemporary Literature*. He has also taught contemporary American Indian poetry at UCLA. He is currently a member of the Multicultural Arts Panel of the California Arts Council, the executive director of A Writers' Circle of Los Angeles, and a member of the Board of Directors of the Santa Monica Cultural Center in California.

Louis (Little Coon) Oliver (1904–   )

Louis (Little Coon) Oliver, a Creek Indian, was born in Oklahoma. His ancestry can be traced to the Indian clans who lived along the Chattahooche River in Alabama. He is a descendant of the Golden Raccoon Clan. Oliver's poetry is both pastoral and idyllic in keeping with his own reverence for the natural world. He lives in Oklahoma.

Simon J. Ortiz (1941–   )

Simon J. Ortiz, an Acoma, was born and raised in the Acoma Pueblo Community in Albuquerque, New Mexico, and schooled within the Bureau of Indian Affairs on the Acoma Reservation. He attended the University of Iowa where he enrolled in the International Writing Program and received a master's degree in writing. In 1960, he was honored at the White House as a participant in the President's "Salute to Poetry and American Poets." He has authored numerous books: *A Good Journey, Going for the Rain, Fight Back, Howbah Indians,* and *From Sand Creek,* which won a 1982 Pushcart Prize. He has taught Native American literature and creative writing at San Diego State University and the University of New Mexico.

Frank Prewett (1893–1962)

Frank James Prewett, an Iroquois, was born near Mount Forest, Ontario on February 24, 1893 and was educated in Toronto at the University of Toronto where from 1911 to 1916 he studied the arts. He enlisted in the Canadian Artillery before graduating from the university and served as a lieutenant in the Trench Mortars and Amunition Column in the Ypres Salient front of the war where he was wounded. During his convalescence at Craiglockhart Hospital in Scotland, he met Siegfried Sassoon. Sassoon encouraged him and sent his work to Virginia Woolf, who published Prewett's first book *Poems* (1917). This book was followed by publication of *The Rural Scene* and inclusion in Harold Monro's *Georgian Poetry V* (1922).

He received a scholarship to Christchurch, Oxford where he received his B.A. in 1922, his M.A. in 1928, and taught during the early 1920s. He later taught at the University School of Agriculture and Forestry in Oxford where he published a series of studies on the marketing of farm produce and milk. During World War II he served first with a bomb-disposal unit in Birmingham, then with Headquarters Fighter Command as a researcher and eventually as a civilian adviser to the Supreme Command in southeast Asia. He retired to the Cotswolds in 1954 and died suddenly in Scotland on February 16, 1962. A posthumous collection of his work was published and edited by Robert Graves in 1964. A new collected edition of his work will be published in September 1987 by Exile Editions in Toronto, Canada (his first Canadian publication).

Carter Revard (1931–   )

Carter Revard, part Osage on his father's side, was born in Pawhuska, Oklahoma. He grew up in Buck Creek rural community on the Osage reservation with his stepfather Addison Jump and his five Osage brothers and sisters, Ponca aunt and cousins. In 1952 he was given his Osage name and went to Oxford University on a Rhodes Scholarship. He later earned a Ph.D. from Yale and is now professor of English at Washington University in St. Louis, Missouri. He is a board member of the American Indian Center in St. Louis and a Gourd Dancer. He has published poems, stories, essays in *Nimrod, The Greenfield Review, Denver Quarterly, Massachusetts Review,* and in the anthologies *Earth Power Coming, The Remembered Earth, Voices of the Rainbow, Voices of Wahkontah, American Indian Literature,* and *The Clouds Threw This Light.*

Wendy Rose (1948–   )

Wendy Rose was born in 1948 in Oakland, California, and is of Hopi and Me-wuk ancestry. She attended Contra Costa College and the University of California at Berkeley and has taught in American Indian Studies at Berkeley, as well as at California State University Fresno. Currently she is the coordinator of American Indian Studies at Fresno City College. She is the author of ten volumes of poetry and has contributed to more than fifty anthologies. Her most recent book is *The Halfbreed Chronicls and Other Poems,* 1985.

A. Sadongei (1959–   )

A. Sadongei is Kiowa and Tohono O'odham (the latter was formerly known as Papago). She attended Lewis and Clark College in Portland, Oregon, where she received a B.A. in communications. While she was at Lewis and Clark she received the Academy of American Poets College Prize. Her work has been published in *A Gathering of Spirit, New Voices,* and *Fireweed.* Sadongei lives in Phoenix, Arizona and is currently the director of a Native American arts service organization.

Mary TallMountain (1918–   )

Mary TallMountain was born Mary Demonski in the interior of Alaska of Athabaskan-Russian and Scotch-Irish ancestry. Her poetry has appeared in literary journals and has

been greatly influenced by the mountainous terrain of the
Kaiyuh mountain range along the Yukon river in Alaska. She
lives in San Francisco.

Earle Thompson (1950–   )

Earle Thompson grew up on the Yakima Indian Reserva-
tion in Washington. Greatly influenced by the oral tradition
of his people as handed down to him by his grandfather, his
writing reflects his particular interest in creation legends
and the animal people who populate them. The magic of
these legends is recreated in his poetry. Thompson has pub-
lished a chapbook, *The Juniper Moon Pulls at My Bones.* His
poetry has also appeared in *The Greenfield Review, Akwekon
Literary Journal, Native American Journal,* and in the anthol-
ogy *Songs from This Earth on Turtle's-Back.*

Gail Tremblay (1945–   )

Gail Tremblay was born in Buffalo, New York in Decem-
ber in a blizzard that covered the city with six feet of snow.
She is Onondaga (Iroquois) and MicMac, French and Eng-
lish. Her Yankee grandfather used to tease her that she was
the French and Indian War with her alliances mixed up; but
she's always thought that the Great Law of Peace of the
Iroquois people was the only way worth choosing. She still
plants her Sisters—corn, squash, and beans—every time it
starts to get warm. When she's not gardening, she teaches,
works on her art and writes poetry. Her artwork has been
shown internationally, and her poetry has appeared in
Northwest Review, Denver Quarterly, Calyx, and numerous
other journals as well as anthologies like *A Nation Within*
and *Anthology of Magazine Verse and Yearbook of American
Poets.* She has two published collections of poetry, *Night
Gives Woman the Word* and *Talking to the Grandfathers: An-
nex 21, #3.*

Gerald Vizenor (1934–   )

Gerald Vizenor, of the Chippewa tribe, was born in Minnesota. He teaches Native American literature at the University of California, Santa Cruz. He is the author of *The People Named the Chippewa: Narrative Histories* and *Earthdrivers: Narratives on Tribal Descent.* His novel *Griever: An American Monkey King in China* won the Fiction Collective Prize for 1986. *Matsushima: Pine Island,* a collection of original haiku poems, was published in 1985.

Emma Lee Warrior (1941–   )

Emma Lee Warrior, a Peigan Indian, was born in Brocket, Alberta. Raised on the Peigan Reserve, she went on to earn a bachelor's degree in education and a masters degree in English. She is currently employed by the Blackfoot Reserve in Alberta to develop curricula in Blackfoot. She has three children and four grandchildren.

James Welch (1940–   )

James Welch was born in Browning, Montana. He is Blackfeet on his father's side and Gros Ventre on his mother's. He attended schools on the Blackfeet and Fort Belknap reservations and in Minneapolis, Minnesota. He then attended the University of Minnesota for one year and Northern Montana College for two, eventually receiving his B.A. from the University of Montana.

Welch has worked as a laborer, firefighter, and Upward Bound counselor. He is now writing full time. His poetry has been published extensively in literary journals both here and abroad. His first book, a collection of his poems titled *Riding the Earthboy 40,* was published in 1971. His second, a novel called *Winter in the Blood,* was published in 1974. He lives with his wife, Lois, on a farm outside Missoula, Montana.

Roberta Hill Whiteman (1947–   )

Roberta Hill Whiteman is a member of the Oneida Tribe and grew up near Oneida and Green Bay, Wisconsin. She earned a B.A. from the University of Wisconsin and her M.F.A. from the University of Montana. She has participated in several poets-in-the-schools programs throughout the country. Her poetry has appeared in several journals and anthologies including *The American Poetry Review, The Nation, North American Review, A Book of Women Poets from Antiquity to Now, Carriers of the Dream Wheel,* and *Third Woman: Third World Women Writers in America.* In 1984 she published a volume of poetry called *Star Quilt.* Whiteman currently teaches at the University of Wisconsin at Eau Claire.

Ray A. Young Bear 1950–   )

Ray A. Young Bear is a member of the Mesquakie tribe, formerly known as Sauk and Fox. He has been writing since he was sixteen years old. Widely anthologized and published frequently in literary magazines, he is the author of a book of poetry, *Winter of the Salamander.* He is currently living in the Mesquakie settlement of Tama, Iowa.

ACKNOWLEDGMENTS

Paula Gunn Allen—"Taku skanskan" from *Feminary*, 1983. "Dear World" from *Parnassus*, 1986. "Kopis'taya, A Gathering of Spirits" from *The Greenfield Review*, 1984, and *Sinister Wisdom*, 1982.

Gladys Cardiff—"Where Fire Burns" and "Tsa'lagi Council Tree" from *That's What She Said*, edited by Rayna Green, Indiana University Press, 1984. "Making Lists" from *Seattle Arts*, Seattle Arts Commission, 1985. "Candelaria and the Sea Turtle" from *Wounds Beneath The Flesh*, edited by Maurice Kenny, Blue Cloud Quarterly Press, 1983.

Steve Crow—"Louisiana" first appeared in *The Southern Review*, Spring, 1975. Poem "XIV" from "Beautifying Songs" first appeared in *Passages North*, vol. 2, no. 1 (Escabana, Michigan). "Revival" first appeared in *Mississippi Review*, vol. 3, no. 2, 1974.

Nora Dauenhauer—"Voices" first appeared in *Neek* (Sitka). "Kelp" first appeared in *Neek* (Sitka), then in *That's What She Said*, edited by Rayna Green, Indiana University Press. "Skiing on Russian Christmas" first appeared in *Tundra Times*, then in *That's What She Said*. "How to Make Good . . . Salmon" first appeared in *Northward Journal* (Moonbeam, Ontario).

Jimmie Durham—All poems were originally published in *Columbus Day*, by Jimmie Durham, West End Press.

Anita Endrezze—"Reviewing Past Lives While Leaf Burning" first appeared in *Southern Poetry Review*, Fall 1983. "Song-Maker" first appeared in *Songs From This Earth on Turtle's Back*, Greenfield Review Press.

Louise Erdrich—All poems are from *Jacklight*.

Joyce Harjo—"Resurrection," "Transformations," and "Bleed Through," were first published in TYOUNI, Institute for American Arts Press, 1985. These three and "Eagle Poem" also appear on the tape "Furious Light," 1986, Watershed Foundation.

Linda Hogan—"Seeing Through The Sun" was previously published in

Another Chicago Magazine, and *Seeing Through The Sun* (University of Massachusetts Press). "Gamble" first appeared in *North Dakota Quarterly.* "The Truth Is" first appeared in *Seeing Through The Sun.*

Maurice Kenny—"Legacy" and "Wild Strawberry" from *Dancing Back Strong The Nation,* copyright © 1981, published by White Pine Press, Fredonia, NY. "December" and "Reverbertions" from *The Mama Poems,* copyright © 1984, published by White Pine Press, Fredonia, NY. "Wolf Aunt" from *Blackrobe: Isaac Jogues,* © 1987, reprinted by permission of the University Press, Saranac Lake, NY. "Strawberrying" from *Kneading the Blood,* Strawberry Press, copyright © 1981 by Maurice Kenny. "First Rule" and "Sweetgrass" from *North: Poems of Home,* copyright © 1977, The Blue Cloud Quarterly Press. "O Wendy, Arthur" and "They Tell Me I Am Lost" from *The Smell of Slaughter,* copyright © 1982, The Blue Cloud Quarterly Press.

Daniel David Moses—"The Corn" and "Some Grand River Blues," first published in *Whetstone,* Spring, 1985. "Party Favour" first published in *The Malahat Review,* Victoria, B.C.

Duane Niatum—"Pieces" was originally published in *Pieces,* by Duane Niatum, Strawberry Press. "Lines for Roethke Twenty Years After His Death" was first published in *Paris/Atlantic,* Paris, France. "Drawings of the Song Animals," "The Art of Clay," and "First Spring" were first published in *Songs . . . Dreams,* by Duane Niatum. "The Reality of Autumn" was first published by *The Malahat Review.* "Apology" was first published by *The Greenfield Review,* Greenfield Center, NY. "Maggie" was first published in *Poetry Now.* "The Traveler" was first published in *Spindrift Magazine.* "Snowy Owl Near Ocean Shores" was first published in *The Chariton Review,* vol. 11, no. 2, Fall '85, Kirksville, MO.

William Oandasan—"Grandmothers Land" from *Round Valley Songs,* by William Oandasan, West End Press, Minneapolis, MN. "Words of Tayko-mol" was first published in *The Phoenix,* Northeastern Oklahoma State University. "Acoma" appears in *Moving Inland,* A Publications, Venice, CA. "Song of Ancient Ways" appears in *Songs From This Earth on Turtle's Back,* Greenfield Review Press, Greenfield Center, NY.

Frank Prewett—All poems copyright © 1962 by the Estate of Frank Prewett. Grateful acknowledgement and many thanks go to Bruce Meyer, of McMaster University in Ontario, for finding the poems, and research-ing Prewett's history.

Carter Revard—"Driving in Oklahoma" first appeared in *Nimrod,*

1972–73 and then in *Ponca War Dancers*, Point Riders Press, 1980. "In Kansas" first appeared in *Samsidat*, vol. 25, no. 3, 1980. "Looking Before and After" from *Ponca War Dancers*. "And Don't Be Deaf to the Singing Beyond" first appeared in *The Far Point*, 1980. "My Right Hand Don't Leave Me No More" first appeared in *My Right Hand Don't Leave Me No More*, by Carter Revard, Eedin Press, St. Louis, 1970.

A. Sadongei—"Don't Forget . . . " and "Poems Come to Me in the Night . . . " were first published in *Fireweed*, Winter 1986, Toronto, Canada. Copyright © by *Fireweed*.

Mary Tallmountain—"Matmiya" and "There Is No Word for Goodbye" were first published in *There Is No Word for Goodbye*.

Earle Thompson—"No Deposit" was published in *Northwest Arts: Fortnightly Journal of News and Opinions, Argus*, and *Northwest Indian News*. "The Juniper Moon Pulls At My Bones" was previously published in *Northwest Arts*, and *Songs From This Earth On Turtle's Back*, edited by Joseph Bruchac, Greenfield Review Press. "Mythology" was first published in *Songs From This Earth . . .* , *Prison Writing Review* (COSMEP) and *Blue Cloud Quarterly*. "Love Song" has been published in *Bumbershoot Anthology '85*; *Akwekon Literary Journal*, no. 4, edited by Peter Blue Cloud; *Contact II*, edited by Maurice Kenny; and *Northwest Arts*.

Gail E. Tremblay—"To Grandmother on Her Going" and "Night Gives Old Woman The Word" first appeared in *Talking to The Grandfathers: Annex 21 no. 3*. "Night Gives Old Woman The Word" was also published in *Night Gives Old Woman The Word* and *Sandhills and Other Geographies: An Anthology of Nebraska Poets*.

Roberta Hill Whiteman—"Climbing Gannett," "For Heather, Entering Kindergarten," "Variations for Two Voices," "The White Land," "Reaching Yellow River," and "Patterns" were first published in *Star Quilt*, by Roberta Hill Whiteman. "From The Sun Itself" and "Waiting for Robinson" first appeared in *Upriver 3: Wisconsin Poetry and Prose*. "One More Sign" first appeared in *Kalihwi-saks, The Official Publication of the Oneida Tribe of Indians in Wisconsin*, June, 1986.

Ray Young Bear—"Race of the Kingfishers" was originally published in *Tyuonyi*, 1985, Santa Fe. "The King Cobra as Political Assassin" and "Wadasa Nakamoon, Vietnam Memorial" first appeared in *TriQuarterly*, a publication of Northwestern University.

NOTES

Preface

1. Vine Deloria, Jr., *Custer Died For Your Sins: An Indian Manifesto* (New York: Simon and Schuster, 1969), 13.

2. Brian Swann, *Smoothing the Ground: Essays on Native American Oral American Indian Literature* (Berkeley, Los Angeles, and London: University of California Press, 1983), 3.

3. Jarold Ramsey, *Reading the Fire: Essays in the Traditional Indian Literatures of the Far West* (Lincoln and London: University of Nebraska Press), 188.

4. Octavio Paz, *In Praise of Hands: Contemporary Crafts of the World* (Greenwich, CT: New York Graphic Society, 1974), 16.

Introduction

1. Frederick E. Hoxie, "Red Man's Burden," *The Antioch Review* 37 (Summer 1979): 340.

2. I recently received through the mail a brochure for videocassettes available from Film for the Humanities (Princeton, NJ). The series was entitled "The West of the Imagination." Here is part of the copy for the episode "The Trail of Tears": "As explorers and pioneers travelled further and further west, the urge and the technological means to expand led inevitably to the seizure of Indian land and the destruction of Indian culture." And this from "The Warpath": "Indians were the major obstacle to westward expansion. The pioneering American spirit overcame all obstacles. . . . " "Inevitably," "obstacles," "pioneering American spirit"—enough said.

3. D. H. Lawrence, *Studies in Classic American Literature* (New York: Viking, 1971), 7.

4.   William Carlos Williams, *In The American Grain* (New York: New Directions, 1925), 39.

5.   For background on this topic see Larry W. Burt, "Roots of the Native American Urban Experience: Relocation Policy in the 1950s," in *The American Indian Quarterly* 10 (Spring 1986): 85–99. See also a number of works cited in the footnotes to Burt's essay. Useful, on a wider scale, is James S. Olson and Raymond Wilson's *Native Americans in the Twentieth Century* (Urbana, IL: University of Illinois Press, 1984), despite qualifications expressed by Vine Deloria, Jr. in the same issue of *The American Indian Quarterly* cited above (pp.136–37). A national disgrace on a huge scale is now unfolding in Alaska. Native peoples could lose all their land and have their tribal and subsistence way of life destroyed by 1991 if something isn't done soon to undo the Alaska Native Claims Settlement Act of 1971, which is attempting to turn these peoples into corporate businesspeople and shareholders. A powerful book on this is Thomas R. Berger's *Village Journey* (New York: Hill and Wang, 1985).

6.   See A. LaVonne Ruoff, "American Indian Authors, 1774–1899," in *Critical Essays on Native American Literature,* ed. Andrew Wiget (Boston, MA: G. K. Hall, 1985), 191–202. Also see Daniel F. Littlefield and James W. Parins's *A Bibliography of Native American Writers, 1772–1924* (Metuchen, NJ: The Scarecrow Press, 1981) and their *Supplement* (Metuchen, NJ: The Scarecrow Press, 1985).

7.   For a sharp critique of their approach, particularly A. Grove Day's, see William Bevis's essay, "American Indian Verse Translations," *College English* 35 (March 1974): 693–703.

8.   A useful list of publishers today can be found in Kenneth Lincoln's *Native American Renaissance* (Berkeley, CA: University of California Press, 1983), 285–292. Joseph Bruchac provides a "Bibliography and List of Presses" in "American Indians Today," a special issue edited by Elaine Jahner, in *Book Forum* vol. V, no. 3 (1981): 336–342.

9.   Andrew Wiget, *Native American Literature* (Boston: Twayne, 1985). (The quote is from the section "Chronology," no page number given.) Despite the appearance of *Carriers of the Dream Wheel,* however, Native American poetry could still be largely ignored by the white "establishment." In a major compilation of essays entitled *The Harvard Guide to Contemporary American Writing,* edited by

Daniel Hoffman and issued by Harvard University Press in 1979, more space is devoted to reworkings of Native American texts by David Wagoner, Gary Snyder, and Jerome Rothenberg than to the work of Native American writers. The only Native American poets mentioned are in Hoffman's chapter "Poetry: Schools of Dissidents." Momaday, Niatum, Ortiz, and Bruchac are given a princely half page in a 618-page book! One hopes that with books such as Paul Lauter's *Reconstructing American Literature* published by Feminist Press in 1983, and associated attempts to reorder the canon (including Lauter's forthcoming anthology from D. C. Heath), things will be changed, if only a little.

10. On this subject, see Arnold Krupat's "An Approach to Native American Texts," *Critical Inquiry* 9 (December 1982): 323–338, and "Native American Literature and the Canon," *Critical Inquiry* 10 (September 1983): 145–171. *Studies in American Indian Literature,* ed. Paula Gunn Allen (New York: Modern Language Association, 1983) contains useful essays on teaching and course outlines.

11. Vine Deloria, Jr., "Introduction," in *Voices From Wah'Kon-Tah,* ed. Robert Dodge and Joseph B. McCullough (New York: International Publishers, 1975).

12. Wendy Rose, "American Indian Poets and Publishing," *Book Forum* vol. V, no. 3 (1981): 402.

13. Duane Niatum, "On Stereotypes," *Parnassus* vol. 7, no. 1 (Fall/Winter 1978): 160.

14. Ibid.

15. Jim Barnes, "On Native Ground," in *I Tell You Now: Autobiographical Essays By Native American Writers,* ed. Brian Swann and Arnold Krupat (Lincoln, NE: University of Nebraska Press, 1987). Page numbers unavailable at time of writing.

16. Fritz Scholder, "The Native American and Contemporary Art: A Dilemma," *Book Forum,* vol. V, no. 3. (1981): 423.

17. Quoted in the Introduction to *I Tell You Now.*

18. Quoted in the Introduction to *I Tell You Now.*

19.   Linda Hogan, "Who Will Speak," *Shantih* 4 (Summer/Fall 1979):
       28–30. This special Native American issue was edited by Roberta
       Hill [Whiteman] and Brian Swann.

20.   The situation is complex. The issue is discussed in Vine Deloria, Jr.
       and Clifford Lytle's *American Indians, American Justice* (Austin, TX:
       University of Texas Press, 1983) and *The Nations Within* (New
       York: Pantheon Books, 1984), as well as in *Indian Lives,* ed. L. G.
       Moses and Raymond Wilson (Albuquerque: University of New
       Mexico Press, 1980).

21.   James Welch, "The Only Good Indian," *South Dakota Review* 9
       (Summer 1971): 54.

22.   Elizabeth Cook-Lynn, "You May Consider Speaking About Your
       Art," in *I Tell You Now,* ed. Brian Swann and Arnold Krupat (Lin-
       coln, NE: University of Nebraska Press, 1987).

23.   Richard Hugo, "Introduction," *The American Poetry Review* (Novem-
       ber/December 1975).

24.   Ibid., 22.

25.   Ibid.

26.   Ibid.

27.   Ibid.

28.   Ibid.

29.   Ibid.

30.   Ibid.

31.   Ibid.

32.   A similar pattern can be seen in Welch's novel *Winter in the Blood*
       (New York: Harper & Row, 1974). The world is still bleak and
       absurd at the end, but there is some possibility of healing "if only
       a connection could be made between the old people and the young
       ones" and a reconnection established with the animals—in other
       words, if there could be a return to tradition. See Carter Revard,
       "Deer Talk, Coyote Songs, Meadowlark Territory: The Muses Dance

to Our Drum Now" (Paper presented at the Modern Language Association Convention, New York, December 1979). I would like to thank Carter Revard for a careful reading of this introductory essay and for some helpful suggestions.

33. John G. Neihardt, *Black Elk Speaks* (New York: Pocket Books, 1959), 165.

34. David Guss, "Keeping It Oral: A Yekuana Ethnology," *American Ethnologist* 13 (August 1986): 423.

35. Ibid.

36. Ibid.

37. N. Scott Momaday, *House Made of Dawn* (New York: Harper & Row, 1977), 88.

38. The oral tradition is based as much on rumor and gossip (entities located lowest on the literary scale and associated with the "ignorant") as much as anything else. "We make no distinctions between the stories—whether they are history, whether they are fact, whether they are gossip," says Leslie Silko in "Language and Literature from a Pueblo Indian Perspective," in *English Literature: Opening Up the Canon,* ed. Leslie A. Fiedler and Houston A. Baker (Baltimore: Johns Hopkins University Press, 1981), 60. The impulse is to leave nothing out, to be inclusive—to create communal truth, not an absolute. See Silko's essay "Landscape, History, and the Pueblo Imagination," *Antaeus* 57 (Autumn 1986).

39. Momaday, *House Made of Dawn,* 90.

40. Simon Ortiz, *Song, Poetry, and Language—Expression and Perception,* Occasional Papers, vol. III (Music and Dance Series), no. 5 (Tsaile, AZ: Navajo Community Press, 1977), 4. In passing, the "thousand year old man" is close to Valéry's definition of the true poet, *un homme très ancien.*

41. Paula Gunn Allen, *The Sacred Hoop: Recovering the Feminine in American Literature* (Boston: Beacon Press, 1986), 46.

42. Simon Ortiz, "The Language We Know," in *I Tell You Now,* ed. Brian Swann and Arnold Krupat (Lincoln, NE: University of Nebraska Press, 1987).

43.   Ibid.

44.   Ibid.

45.   Ibid.

46.   Ibid.

47.   Ibid.

48.   Duane Niatum, "Autobiographical Sketch of Duane Niatum," in *I Tell You Now,* ed. Brian Swann and Arnold Krupat (Lincoln, NE: University of Nebraska Press, 1987).

49.   "Grandfather" was an honorific title with religious overtones in many native societies. In *Black Elk Speaks,* for instance, the six grandfathers symbolize Wakan Tanka, the "Great Mysterious," the power of the six directions. "Understood as grandfathers, these spirits were represented as kind and loving, full of years and wisdom," writes Raymond J. Demallie, *The Sixth Grandfather* (Lincoln, NE: University of Nebraska Press, 1984), xix.

50.   Niatum, "Autobiographical Sketch," in *I Tell You Now.*

51.   Leonard Bloomfield, *Menomini Texts* (New York: AMS Press, 1974), 536–555.

52.   Frederick Turner, *Beyond Geography: The Western Spirit Against the Wilderness* (New York: Viking Press, 1980), 18.

53.   Ibid., 19.

54.   Ibid.

55.   In *Songs from this Earth on Turtle's Back,* ed. Joseph Bruchac, (Greenfield Center, NY: Greenfield Review Press, 1983), 229.

56.   It would be difficult to demonstrate the effect of a poet's original language on his or her poetry. But, as Joseph Bruchac has noted, "When you speak English / with the memory / of a first tongue / still sweet in your throat / it comes out different." These lines are from "November at Onandaga" in *Entering Onandaga* (Austin, TX: Cold Mountain Press, 1978), 16. Ray Young Bear is one of the few Native American poets who is bilingual in a "first tongue" and

English. The jacket notes to Young Bear's *Winter of the Salamander* (New York: Harper & Row, 1980) tell us that the poet "began thinking his poems in his native tongue then translating them verbatim. Through ten years of writing he has refined his technique so that the poems while no longer word-for-word translations, have become, in essence, an authentic Native American experience, finalized in English."

57.   Ortiz, "The Language We Know," in *I Tell You Now.*

58.   *Songs from This Earth on Turtle's Back,* 158.

59.   Joy Harjo discusses this poem with Paula Gunn Allen in the latter's *The Sacred Hoop,* 166.

60.   Allen, *The Sacred Hoop,* 1.

61.   Simon Ortiz, "Telling," in *A Good Journey* (Berkeley, CA: Turtle Island, 1977), 39. This poem is a good example of the oral tradition at work since it draws on many past stories as well as many in the present. Leslie Silko draws on the poem to make up her own story, "Skeleton Fixer's Story," which first appeared in *Sun Tracks* vol. 4 (1978): 2–3. It is, she says, "a piece of a bigger story they tell around Laguna and Acoma too—from a version told by Simon Ortiz." (In a recent letter to me, Simon Ortiz, after reading a draft of this essay, asks, "Does Leslie draw on the source I give to make her own Skeleton Fixer story? The answer is that both of us draw upon the traditions we know—and it is a good example of the creative continuing work of the oral tradition." I would like to thank Simon Ortiz for a careful reading of this introductory essay and for some helpful suggestions.

62.   Louis Simpson, "American Poetry," in *At the End of the Open Road* (Middletown, CT: Wesleyan University Press, 1963), 25.

63.   Ibid.

64.   Ibid.

65.   Simon Ortiz, "What's Your Indian Name," part of "Four Poems for a Child Son," in *Going For the Rain* (Harper & Row, 1976), 7.

INDEX OF FIRST LINES

INDEX OF TITLES